D1396818

Personality Development in Adulthood

Personality Development in Adulthood

Lawrence S. Wrightsman

SAGE PUBLICATIONS
The Publishers of Professional Social Science
Newbury Park   Beverly Hills   London   New Delhi

For information address:

SAGE Publications, Inc.
2111 West Hillcrest Drive
Newbury Park, California 91320

SAGE Publications Inc.
275 South Beverly Drive
Beverly Hills
California 90212

SAGE Publications Ltd.
28 Banner Street
London EC1Y 8QE
England

SAGE PUBLICATIONS India Pvt. Ltd.
M-32 Market
Greater Kailash I
New Delhi 110 048 India

Printed in the United States of America

Library of Congress Cataloging-in-Publication Data

Wrightsman, Lawrence S.
  Personality development in adulthood.

  Bibliography: p.
  Includes index.
  1. Adulthood. 2. Personality change. 3. Maturation (Psychology) 4. Change (Psychology) 5. Personality.
  I. Title.
  BF724.85.P47W75   1988   155.6   87-35762
  ISBN 0-8039-2776-2
  ISBN 0-8039-3345-2 (pbk.)

FIRST PRINTING 1988

Contents

Dedicated—In Memoriam
to Barbara Strudler Wallston
and Lawrence Kohlberg

Preface

Daniel Levinson, in the preface to *The Seasons of a Man's Life*, states that he began to study the transition into middle age in order to understand what he had been going through himself. I, too, have attempted to employ the vehicles of teaching and writing to facilitate my understanding of those developmental processes faced in adulthood, by each of us.

In teaching a course on adulthood, as I have done for the last five years, I emphasize to students the need to understand and adopt theories of development. We all have raw experience (for some of us, the experience is rawer than for others) but we all can benefit from the organizing and structuring of raw experience that theories can provide. The incorporation of this theoretical focus permits us to more easily compare our experiences with those of others, and theories may also serve, for some of us, as guidelines to possible changes and crises in the future.

This book contrasts three broad theoretical approaches to explaining psychological changes during the period from adolescence to the onset of late adulthood. Each of these approaches has some legitimacy for its claim that it accurately portrays the nature of psychological growth. But no theory can be completely comprehensive, and the overriding orientation of the book is an eclectic one, choosing whichever theoretical constructs that best explain the phenomenon at hand.

Thus, the purpose of this book is not only to present three radically different blueprints for personality development during the adult years but also to identify the implications of each theory for various aspects of adulthood, including vocational change, cognitive development, sex-role conflicts, marriage and sexual behavior, values, and attitudes toward death and dying.

The book's coverage does not seek to be exhaustive. Given the desired length of the book and the huge breadth of topics listed in the prior sentence, that would have been impossible. Rather, specific topics have been included that reflect various aspects of major issues in adulthood.

Several uses for the book seem appropriate. This book may provide a feasible organizing structure for many of the rapidly increasing courses on The Psychology of Adulthood. Within the developmental sequence, courses on adulthood seem to be the last frontier; first we had courses on child psychology, then adolescence, then courses titled the Psychology of Aging and Life Span development courses, but only in the last 10 years has the void begun to be filled with courses that deal in depth with the remaining two-thirds of our years of life.

Second, scholars who wish to have a review of current theoretical and research developments in the psychology of adulthood may find the book a useful source. The book is deliberately written in a nontechnical style, with terms defined whenever they are introduced. It is intended that the book will be accessible to scholars and interested readers from a variety of disciplines who wish an introduction to contemporary frameworks.

As one of the major theories (the dialectical approach) relentlessly emphasizes, human development is never completed. Likewise, no book can be a complete treatment of something as pervasive, complex, and important as the development of adult personality. But the aspiration motivating the writing of this book is, in a small way at least, to facilitate the task of psychological growth we all face.

Acknowledgments

Charles T. Hendrix, Editorial Director of Sage Publications, encouraged me to write this book, and I am pleased that he did. I wish to acknowledge his patience in light of a project whose development took longer than either he or I anticipated or wished. The publication of this book marks the most recent manifestation of an editing and writing relationship between Terry Hendrix and myself that spans more than 20 years, a developmental period of its own!

Administrators and faculty at the University of Kansas also facilitated the development of this book. Michael Storms and Sharon S. Brehm, then Chair and Associate Chair of the Department of Psychology, supported my desire to teach an innovative course for adults in our evening program. I was awarded a travel grant from the University that permitted me to attend a summer institute on Psychology and Autobiography at the Andrus Gerontology Center of the University of Southern California. Conversations with faculty colleagues Franklin Shontz, Susan Kemper, James O'Neil (now at the University of Connecticut), Bill Tuttle (Department of History), and Ray Hiner (Departments of History and Higher Education) have broadened my perspective and helped me clarify viewpoints. My colleague Patricia Schoenrade read and helpfully commented on the draft of Chapter 11. Scholars at other universities, particularly my friend Irwin Altman and the late Klaus Riegel, introduced me to the dialectical approach. Any errors of omission or commission that persist in this book are, of course, my responsibility.

I wish to thank especially Lynn Porter and her backup, Marilyn Sliski, the word processors who cheerfully and professionally typed several drafts of the chapters in this book, and even improved my knowledge of country music in the process.

The staff at Sage Publications has been very solicitous and has nurtured the development of this project to a degree equalling the exceptional level of proficiency they showed on those books of mine previously published by Sage.

To each of these people I offer my appreciation. Writing is inevitably a solitary activity but the production of a book permits a reassuring reentry into the real world of human relationships.

1

CONCEPTIONS OF PERSONALITY DEVELOPMENT IN ADULTHOOD

For many decades the field of psychology treated the topic of personality development in adulthood with benign neglect. Twenty to thirty years ago the assumption held by most psychologists, as well as by society in general, was that once people passed through the traumas of adolescence, completed their formal schooling, entered the world of work, got married, and "settled down," nothing much new happened to them until the inevitability of their death. But now all of us—psychologists and laypersons alike—recognize that things are not that straightforward, that adulthood is not a period of sameness and constancy. As just one type of example, many middle-aged persons claim extensive personality and behavior changes that in some ways resemble a second adolescence. Adulthood—and especially the nature of personality development during this extended period—has become a topic worthy of scholarly study.

The phenomenon of the "mid-life crises" exploded into our consciousness in the middle of the 1970s, concurrently with social scientists reactivating a long dormant interest in adulthood. But just when the publication of *Passages* by Gail Sheehy in 1976 was leading many adults to contemplate their lives from a fresh perspective, social scientists began to disagree about just which theories and which sets of concepts to apply. How do psychologists properly conceptualize the process or processes by which we move through the several decades of adulthood? Do we simply unfold a scenario formed at an earlier age? Do changes reflect a smooth and seamless transition? Or are wrenching disjunctions and disruptive shifts inevitable? May apparent "changes" really reflect a manifestation of consistencies in the underlying structure of one's personality?

Three broad theoretical perspectives provide highly contrasting answers to questions like those above. These are, first, an "early-formation" approach that assumes personality structure is established—and remains essentially unchanged—in the first years of childhood; second, a stage theory of development, as represented in the concepts of Erik Erikson, Daniel Levinson, and Roger Gould; and third, a dialectical analysis, that poses on-going irreconcilable tensions between basic needs.

Chapters in the first half of this book elaborate upon each of these three approaches. Each has its merits. My goal is not so much to conclude which perspective is best, but to describe the approach, while examining the methods used to evaluate each theory and the quality of evidence for each. The second half of this book applies concepts and findings from each of the three perspectives to a multitude of aspects of adulthood, including occupational and career shifts, sex-role development, marriage and other intimate relationships, sexual behavior, changes in values, and attitudes toward death and dying. The book concludes with a chapter on the use of personal documents to understand personality development in adulthood. Until recently, the science of psychology has been unduly restricted in the types of methods it has employed to evaluate differing theories of personality development. In the final chapter, I seek to demonstrate that the use of personal documents as sources of data can improve the knowledge base for each theory, and, not incidentally, provide each of us with greater understanding of ourselves. By "personal documents" I refer to materials such as autobiographies, memoirs, diaries, and collections of letters. Just as the topic of personality development in adults was neglected for many years, so too has the methodology for analyzing personal documents. It is not much of an exaggeration to claim that the "state of the art" regarding the use of personal documents in psychology has not, until recently, advanced beyond that level summarized in Gordon Allport's (1942) monograph review written about 50 years ago.

The major portion of this initial chapter presents an overview of the three divergent theoretical perspectives, including the basic assumptions underlying each. In selecting those theoretical conceptions that provide the structure of our analysis, my focus is on the global nature of personality, as defined in a classic Allportian sense (Allport, 1937). This personality paradigm, as described by Craik (1976), uses the person as the basic unit of analysis, seeks to understand the organization of the individual's behavior, and investigates the relationship of the individual's personality characteristics to his or her behavior and outcomes.

EARLY FORMATION THEORIES

It has been a staple of folklore for a long time that "as the twig is bent the tree is formed," that experiences during childhood structure one's orientation to life as an adult. An extreme reflection of this view proposes that you are what you were, only bigger and more; whatever occurs later is just an elaboration or refinement of an early orientation. Psychological theories have contributed—sometimes intentionally, sometimes not—to this notion. In this section several approaches relevant to an assumption of "early-formation" are introduced.

Personal Construct Theory

Early formation theories are usually associated with a psycho-analytic explanation of personality development, and that approach will be described in the next section. But Sigmund Freud and his followers are not the only ones whose contributions provide support for a view that adult personality is structured at an early age. Cognitive analyses of personality development also may emphasize early developmental processes.

Our behavior is influenced by our perceptions. We react to what we think we see or hear, not just what is actually there. Given the same stimulus—the same painting, the same song—each of us is likely to perceive it as somewhat different. In *personal construct theory*, interpretation thus results from cognitive determinants (in contrast to psychoanalytic theory, that emphasizes motivations).

Interpretation is inevitable, so this theory says, because the world is too complex to be perceived straightforwardly. There is too much going on to process everything; we must notice this and not that; we also have to make decisions rapidly on occasion, forcing us not only to perceive but to interpret.

George Kelly (1955) developed personal construct theory as an effort to systematize these assumptions. As we attempt to super-impose some order on the complex world, we develop constructs, or organizing labels, that help us distinguish between and classify events.

How does a construct develop? First, we notice general features or similarities in stimuli—in people, in events, in sounds, in tastes, in any broad type of stimulus. We note those that are alike; those that are different. A young child may grow up in a family that has both a dog and a cat. At first, the child views these as being alike, that is, in the same construct, "animals," and they are distinguished from other objects that the child is struggling to fit into other constructs. But later the child learns that separate constructs, "dogs" and "cats," are appropriate for distinguishing between and labeling these two objects. As children grow older they develop more specific constructs to deal with the different breeds of dogs, all the while maintaining and using their earlier, broad constructs.

Kelly proposed that our assessment of individual people is based on the particular collection of constructs we have in our repertoire. Although each of us applies order to the mass of individual differences—the variations in looks, age, gender, personality, interests, and so on—by applying constructs, each of us has developed a unique set of constructs. Each of us may view the same behavior by another individual but use radically different constructs to describe it; consider three people watching a brief film of a man in a parking lot who goes back twice to check that his car doors are locked. One viewer may call the person "suspicious," another may call him "overly careful," whereas a third may call him "absentminded."

Central to Kelly's conception of human nature is the proposal that each of us is like a scientist, constantly developing, testing, and revising our constructs as we seek to predict and understand (and sometimes control) the behavior of important people in our lives. Kelly developed an instrument to identify the constructs each of us uses; the Role Construct Repertory Test (or "REP Test") is different from traditional personality inventories because the subjects, rather than the test constructor, generate the test's basic dimensions. As exemplified in Box 1.1, one person may use a great many constructs in describing the essential qualities of those around him; another may "explain" human behavior by using only a few constructs. Kelly (1963, p. 57) noted that a person might classify all people as either "good" or "bad," for example, but this broad construct might subsume a number of qualities (such as "intelligent-versus-stupid") that other people might use as separate constructs. An example of the constructs used by one person is reproduced in Box 1.2.

I stated earlier that "early-formation" theories usually relied on a psychoanalytic conception of development and Kelly's personal construct theory does not. In fact, he adamantly rejected revered psychoanalytic concepts, such as the unconscious, drives, and emotion. So, does Kelly fit as an early-formation theorist? Yes and no. Yes, in the sense that one of his messages is that some

---

BOX 1.1
Rep Test Part A: Role Title List

Instructions

Write the name of the persons indicated in the blanks provided below. Do not repeat names. If any role title appears to call for a duplicate name, substitute the name of another person whom the second role title suggests to you.

(1) Your mother or the person who has played the part of mother in your life.   (1) _____

(2) Your father or the person who has played the part of a father in your life.   (2) _____

(3) Your brother nearest your age. If you have no brother, the person who is most like one.   (3) _____

(4) Your sister nearest your age. If you have no sister, the person who is most like one.   (4) _____

(5) A teacher you liked or the teacher of a subject you liked.   (5) _____

(6) A teacher you disliked or the teacher of a subject you disliked.   (6) _____

(7) Your closest girl (boy) friend immediately before you started going with your wife (husband) or present closest girl (boy) friend (Ex-Flame).   (7) _____

(8) Your wife (husband) or closest present girl (boy) friend.   (8) _____

(9) An employer, supervisor, or officer under whom you served during a period of great stress (Boss).   (9) _____

(10) A person with whom you have been closely associated who, for some unexplainable reason, appears to dislike you (Rejecting Person).   (10) _____

(11) The person whom you have met within the past six months whom you would like to know better (Sought Person).   (11) _____

(12) The person whom you would most like to be of help to, or the one whom you feel most sorry for (Pitied Person).   (12) _____

(13) The most intelligent person whom you know personally.   (13) _____

(14) The most successful person whom you know personally.   (14) _____

(15) The most interesting person whom you know personally.   (15) _____

Rep Test Part B: Construct Sorts

Instructions

The sets of three numbers in the following sorts refer to the numbers 1 to 15, inclusive, in Part A.

In each of the following sorts three numbers are listed. Look at your Part A sheet and consider the three people whom you have listed for these three numbers.

In what important way are two of these three people alike and at the same time, essentially different from the third?

After you have decided what that important way is, write it in the blank opposite the sort marked: Construct.

Next encircle the numbers corresponding to the two people who are alike.

Write down what you believe to be the opposite of the construct in the blank marked: Contrast.

Numbers

Sort	Part A	Construct (Emergent)	Contrast (Implicit)
(1)	9, 11, 14	_____	_____
(2)	10, 12, 13	_____	_____
(3)	2, 5, 12	_____	_____
(4)	1, 4, 8	_____	_____
(5)	7, 8, 12	_____	_____
(6)	3, 13, 6	_____	_____
(7)	1, 2, 9	_____	_____
(8)	3, 4, 10	_____	_____
(9)	6, 8, 10	_____	_____
(10)	5, 11, 14	_____	_____
(11)	1, 7, 8	_____	_____
(12)	2, 7, 8	_____	_____
(13)	3, 6, 9	_____	_____
(14)	4, 5, 10	_____	_____
(15)	11, 13, 14	_____	_____

SOURCE: Kelly, 1955.

simplification is a necessity; he wrote that without the creation of constructs, the world would appear to be an "undifferentiated homogeneity" (1963, p. 9). And once we form constructs, they have a tendency to become so internalized and self-perpetuating that we are not even aware that we are using them to form decisions about behaving toward others. But Kelly would have disclaimed a label that placed him as an early formation theorist, because he believed

---

BOX 1.2
Mildred Beal's Constructs

After a subject has completed the task described in Box 1.1, the psychologist may choose to analyze the responses in a rather subjective or impressionistic way, or, more desirably, apply a systematic analysis of the responses. When the latter is done, a pattern like the following might emerge. "Mildred Beal" is a subject whose responses are reported by Kelly (1955, p. 242).

Sort Number	Similar Figures	Similarity Construct	Dissimilar Figures	Contrasting Construct
(2)	rejecting person (10) pitied person (13)	very unhappy person	intelligent person (13)	contented
(3)	father (2) liked teacher (5)	very quiet and easy going	pitied person (12)	nervous, hypertensive
(4)	mother (1) sister (4)	look alike both hyper-critical of people in general	boyfriend (8)	friendliness
(11)	mother (1) ex-flame (7)	social maladjusted	boyfriend (8)	easygoing, self-confident
(13)	disliked teacher (6) boss (9)	emotionally unpredict-able	brother (3)	even temperament

---

SOURCE: Kelly, 1955, p. 242.

that people can create alternative explanations of their world. In line with this view, his therapeutic procedure, called fixed-role therapy, encouraged people to develop new roles and try out new behaviors for themselves. We will see later that the therapeutic manifestations of other early formation approaches, especially the life script conception, also assume that their own brand of intervention can bring about a dismantling of prematurely formed approaches toward relationships with others.

Psychoanalytic Theory

The specifics of psychoanalytic theory are described in Chapter 2. At this point it is appropriate to discuss why I categorize psychoanalytic theory as an early formation theory. The reason is simple: classic psychoanalytic theory, despite all its modifications, assumes that personality is largely formed during the first five years of life. The structure that is established then influences behavior for the rest of life. If "fixations" (see Chapter 2) occur at these tender ages, they have ramifications on our behavior as adults.

The Life Script Approach

Probably the most extreme variant of a psychoanalytic approach, with respect to the assumption of a premature resolution of personality dynamics, is the life script approach, formulated by Eric Berne, Claude Steiner, and other transactional analysts. A life script presupposes that the young child embraces a consistent orientation to others and to the social environment that is relentlessly "played out" throughout the rest of childhood, adolescence, and adulthood. As such, life script theory rests upon the basic tenet of psychoanalytic theory that the sense of identity is established in childhood and that it produces a consistency in all behavior thereafter (Brim, 1977).

Eric Berne (1961, 1964, 1972), the author of *Games People Play*, defined a life script as a complex set of transactions by nature recurrent but not necessarily recurring, since a complete performance of a script may require a whole lifetime. Yet the life script is assumed to be formed within the first five years of life. For Berne, and other life script theorists, a script results from a repetition compulsion, or the tendency to repeat unhappy childhood events.

Absolutely fundamental to life script theory is this assumption that people develop a characteristic interpersonal strategy in childhood, and that this strategy influences and makes understandable their interactions with others for the rest of their lives. Life scripts reflect Aristotle's principles of drama in the sense that, like the plot of a profound tragedy, they contain a prologue, a climax, and a catastrophe. Berne hypothesized that each of us battles between the nature of our script and the wish to avoid a personal disaster. Just like the tragic pattern inherent in Greek dramas, there is an inevitable outcome. Like the Greek hero, the individual intends to accomplish a particular result with his or her actions, only to achieve the exact opposite. *Oedipus Rex* is a typical example of Greek drama; only long after accomplishing something apparently positive does Oedipus come to the shocking realization of what damage he has done to himself. Today the audience observes this reenactment of a Greek tragedy in horror, because members of the audience have the foresight to anticipate the tragic nature of the ending. But like Greek heroes, each of us encumbered by a life script does not possess the detachment to see its inherently counterproductive nature.

As noted previously, life scripts are developed early. Steiner (1974) proposes that the content of a life script is based on a decision by the child, who, with all the information at his or her disposal at the time, decides that a certain life course is a reasonable solution to an existential predicament; the dilemma results from the behavior of parents and family. Thus, it is a seemingly healthy reaction that actually has unhealthy outcomes.

The main support for the existence of life scripts comes from the case histories and clinical data that are rather informally reported in the books of Eric Berne and Claude Steiner. For example, Steiner (1974, pp. 69-70) provides an example of the creation of a life script involving a 4-year-old girl whose father had a strong influence on her. The father was quite annoyed, because his daughter wanted certain possessions, and he also believed that the best way to build character in the little girl—and hence to avoid spoiling her—was to deny her absolutely everything she wanted and to give her something else in its place. Thus, if he knew that the little girl wanted a teddy bear for Christmas, he would give her an equally lovely toy that she didn't want, believing that this substitution would be good for her character development. Soon the little girl learned that none of her wishes were to come true; circumstances beyond her control made everything she desired automatically unobtainable. Furthermore, she also learned that if she restrained herself from expressing a true wish, the chances were enhanced that such a wish would be granted. Paradoxical as this may sound, it was the life script she developed. She also observed that even as she kept her wishes secret, she still feared that she would unwittingly reveal what she wanted by crying when she was disappointed. As a result, in order to keep her father from concluding what her true wishes were, she concluded that crying was undesirable. This little girl grew into adulthood, carrying within her these injunctions from her father against asking for anything and showing any feelings when disappointed. Steiner concludes that the life script served as a relentless influence that guided every one of her significant decisions for years and years.

Do many of us organize our responses to others in an unconscious effort to perpetuate a life script? Although few of us would overtly use such a term to describe ourselves, autobiographies do provide some examples. Some, as in Box 1.3, reflect an explicit link between the person's own characteristic style as an adult and a significant experience that person had as child, usually involving an interaction with a parent.

Others reflect that the person, as an adult, maintains an orientation developed very early in life. Candace Bergen (1984), the movie actress and photographer, whose father was ventriloquist Edgar Bergen, chooses to describe as the first event in her autobiography an event when she was 6 years old. Her main concern then was "pleasing her father." The theme recurs throughout the book. "I am nervous about performing well for my father" (1984, p. 12). When in her twenties, she begins to live with a man who differs radically from her father's conservative political values, she is unable to reveal this to her father. "Not only did I not tell my father; I implied otherwise, inviting my parents to dinners at (my house), where I rarely went now, to indicate that in spite of my relationship I had not strayed but had stayed close to home" (1984, p. 257). Even at her father's funeral, when she is 32, she notes that she is nervous, "wanting more than anything to please" her father (p. 13).

To summarize the life script conception, development is seen as

---

BOX 1.3
A Dramatic Life Script

The actor Sidney Poitier (1980), in his autobiography, writes:

I was drawn to dangerous things. Ever since I can remember I have enjoyed being scared a little bit—an attitude I believe began in the tenth month of my life, when my mother threw me into the ocean like a sack of garbage and stood by expressionless in a dinghy boat watching me go under, sputtering, slashing, and screaming. My pitiful struggle for life seemed not to affect her; she look calmly on while I clawed at the water, stricken with panic. Even as I gasped desperately on the way down for the last time, she made no move to help. Suddenly, mercifully, my father's hands scooped me up, held me above the water for a moment, then passed me to my mother—who promptly threw me back into the ocean again. (pp. 7-8)

On many occasions throughout his autobiography, Poitier demonstrates his willingness to take risks. It cannot be proved that the drowning incident at 10 months of age caused his characteristic risk-taking behavior, but it is clear that Poitier possessed a need to tie things together, to provide explanations for his characteristic behavior stemming from childhood experiences.

---

playing only a limited role, because the content and structure of orientations toward others are formed early in life. Although the dominant script can be changed (through the therapeutic benefits of transactional analysis, of course!) Berne believed that some kind of intervention like this was necessary for the change to happen. Ironically, there is some anecdotal evidence that Berne felt that he too was playing out a tragic life script—one that called for him to die at an early age of a broken heart. Berne's death occurred when he was 60; he died of coronary disease (Steiner, 1974).

As implied earlier, the proposal that life scripts are "relentless"— a favorite description by their advocates—is extreme. As will be illustrated through the dialectical approach later in this chapter, many individuals struggle to free themselves of their life scripts even without therapeutic intervention. Also, there are even script theories, specifically Sylvan Tomkins's (1979), that explicitly reject Berne's assumption of the inevitability of a life script dominating one's life until death.

STAGE THEORIES OF ADULT DEVELOPMENT

The second major conceptualization of adult personality development is the stage theory formulation. Erik Erikson (1959, 1963) gave impetus to a stage-oriented explanation that extended development throughout the life span by building on Freud's theory of psychosexual development and by generating a theory of eight stages of development. Erikson's theory serves in major ways as a prototype of a stage theory, in that each successive stage or period is not only qualitatively different, but is discontinuous with the next. A crisis, or critical choice in each, leads eventually to a relatively abrupt termination of each period, even though transition to the next stage or period may take several months or even years. The stages build on each other, and the way in which each crisis is resolved, affects the person's ability to attack successfully the conflicts of the next stages. Each new stage is seen as a wholly new level of structural integration. According to Erikson, then, personality development proceeds by "critical steps—critical being a characteristic of turning points, of moments of decision between progress and regression, integration and retardation" (Erikson, 1963, pp. 270-271).

As an example of a stage theory conception, Erikson's approach reflects at least three major differences from the early formation viewpoint reflected by life script theory. First, the mold is formed less concretely in childhood, although certainly the way that the initial trust-versus-mistrust conflict (described in Chapter 3) is resolved affects all future development. Second, stage theories propose tasks that we feel pressured to do at various ages. Third, Erikson acknowledges that the determinants of personality development extend beyond biological and family ones; the nature of society and its institutions are intrinsically intertwined with the stages of development; for example, parents and peers pressure us to form an identity in adolescence and to develop intimacy in young adulthood.

But what is common to these two conceptualizations is important. Erikson's writings can be interpreted as saying that the conflict or dilemma at each stage must be settled in one way or another before consideration of the task at the next stage—and, ideally, growth—can occur. This emphasis on resolution or closure seems to share the life script approach's assumption that the person develops a blueprint by which conflict is thwarted. In fairness, however, I should note that it is unclear whether Erikson unequivocally opts for a view that each stage's conflict must be resolved immediately; nowhere is he very explicit. The way that he expresses himself in *Childhood and Society*, first published in 1950, leads me to believe that at that time he assumed the resolution of conflicts was necessary. He discusses the absence of trust and "the firm establishment of enduring patterns for the *solution* of the nuclear conflict of basic trust versus basic mistrust" (1963, p. 249, italics added). His leaning toward the necessity of closure is also reflected in his statement that "basic conflicts can lead in the end to either hostile or benign expectations and attitudes" (1963, p. 251). But elsewhere he notes that earlier conflicts can resurface again much later in life.

Erikson's is not, of course, the only stage theory. It was chosen as an example for this overview, because it has been the most influential one, and Erikson, in his quest to test his theory, has been one of the founders of an approach to biographical analysis of personality called psychohistory. Erikson's stage theory is reviewed in Chapter 3 and the approach of psychohistory (better called, in this case, psychobiography) is critiqued in Chapter 4.

A number of other stage theories bear both resemblances and differences with Erikson's approach. One type, developed by Marjorie Fiske Lowenthal and her colleagues (Lowenthal, Thurnher, Chiriboga, & Associates, 1975), focuses on those transitions during adolescence and adulthood recognized by society as "major," such as graduation from school, marriage, parenthood, grandparenthood, and retirement. Because resultant changes in behavior or personality are expected in light of the social norms operating in our society, the explanatory concepts used by Lowenthal and her associates are more congenial with a sociological perspective than the psychological one emphasized in this volume.

Other examples of stage theories are evaluated in Chapter 5. Of particular usefulness here is the approach developed by Daniel J. Levinson and his colleagues (Levinson, 1978, 1980; Levinson,

Darrow, Klein, Levinson, & McKee, 1977), because Levinson's theory reflects the influence of an Eriksonian-type stage model mixed with an emphasis on polarities in adult personality development. This dialectical approach represents the third major way to conceptualize personality development in adulthood, and it is to this approach that we devote the next section of this overview.

DIALECTICAL APPROACH TO PERSONALITY DEVELOPMENT

A dialectical conception of human behavior has had a long history, but a short life within psychology. Among the subfields within psychology, its greatest impact has been upon developmental psychology; there, interest in a dialectical approach has advanced along with the recent focus on lifespan development. Although dialectical ideas are implicit in some of the most historic theories of sociology, social psychology, and personality—for example, in the work of Georg Simmel (1950) and Freud's tension between the superego and the id—only recently have these influential ideas been systematically interpreted within a dialectical framework. Applications of a dialectical analysis to personality have been rather infrequent, but Irwin Altman and his colleagues (Altman, Vinsel, & Brown, 1981) have developed a dialectical analysis of interpersonal relationships. By building on their work and relying heavily on their operational definitions of a dialectic, I want to specify what a dialectical conception of adult personality conveys.

The following assumptions are basic to this approach:

(1) Personality can be described as a collection of pairs of characteristics struggling for control within the individual; personality development reflects a striving toward the satisfaction or achievement of each of these forces, independently (perhaps even at the same time).

(2) These characteristics that are in opposition do not simply reflect a presence versus an absence, but rather each is an entity that has a quality of its own; the tug is between two different poles representing, for example, affiliation and privacy, rather than a presence/absence state of being hungry or not hungry.

(3) These contending characteristics are always in a state of tension; their relationship is cyclical and changing rather than stable. No matter how strong the pull from one motive or need at a given moment, some amount of the other oppositional force still exists and exerts an influence; thus—and perhaps this is the most important credo of the dialectical approach—the characteristic nature of the system is a never-ending struggle (Kimmel, 1980).

(4) In a dialectical analysis, a concept of balance or homeostasis is of no permanent value, because it is the nature of behavior always to be changing. In contrast to the two previous approaches that assume the resolution of conflict, a dialectical analysis would propose (to paraphrase Gail Sheehy, 1976) that the whole idea behind the nature of psychosocial development in adulthood is that things can never be settled once and for all. The dialectical view also contrasts with a biological conception that values homeostasis, or the return to a state of equilibrium after any crisis, as a fundamental survival mechanism.

(5) Change, in a dialectical analysis, can be assumed to be a cumulative process; that is, the long-term effects of conflicting forces may lead to a synthesis of opposites in the form of a new structural integration (Altman, et al., 1981). Adler (1952) proposes that this new synthesis can lead to changes that incorporate the original opposites but also yield something distinctively new. I will examine this claim in detail as a part of the consideration of Levinson's theory in Chapter 5. Yet it should be noted that there is an alternative view, held by some dialecticians, that dialectical processes do not necessarily culminate in this desirable higher-order synthesis; Immanuel Kant stated, for example, that certain dialectical opposites may not be resolvable, but may continue to exist as "irreducible contradictions" (Adler, 1927).

What are some examples of the oppositional bipolarities so central to a dialectical analysis? Altman and his colleagues (1981) were primarily interested in interpersonal relationships; with respect to the on-going relationship between two people, they proposed the dialectical concepts of openness-closedness and stability-change as most central. They also note that within social psychology, opposites include harmony and conflict, altruism and aggression, and competition and cooperation. But these authors note that social psychological research has mostly chosen to study one pole at a time, rather than the two in relationship with each other.

With regard to adult personality development, there are some bipolarities that are similar to Altman's interpersonal ones. Stability-change would seem to be reflected, for example, in Levinson's theory; as we will see in Chapter 5, it places emphasis on periods of entrenchment into a role, followed by questioning of one's outcomes, leading possibly to massive upheavals in one's personal and professional lives.

A conflict between individualism and being dominated by one's roles in life may reflect another dialectical issue. Again, the back-and-forth tasks of Levinson's theory are relevant. In certain periods, finding one's niche in the world of work or becoming an acceptable parent tug hardest at us; the role controls our behavior. But at other times not only must we escape the role or label, but our needs to be a unique individual take control (Snyder & Fromkin, 1980). Independence versus dependence and isolation versus community reflect other oppositional dimensions, to be elaborated on in Chapter 6.

Such pushes and pulls are certainly not foreign to life script and stage theories, either. What makes the dialectical conception different is its assumption that no stability is ever achieved. In the life script approach equilibrium is the goal; in Erikson's stage approach disequilibrium seemingly serves only to move the person toward resolution of the conflict. By contrast, Klaus Riegel (1976), a radical dialectician, proposed that developmental tasks are never concluded; "at the very moment when completion seems to be achieved, new doubts arise in the individual and in society" (p. 697).

As I mentioned earlier, among contemporary theorists, Daniel Levinson best reflects a synthesis of stage-theory and dialectical ideas, because Levinson specifies four polarities whose resolution is the principal task of men in mid-life. These are attachment/separateness, destruction/creation, masculine/feminine, and young/old; Levinson writes:

> Each of these pairs forms a polarity in the sense that the two terms represent opposing tendencies or conditions. . . . Both sides of each polarity coexist within every self. At mid-life a man feels young in many respects, but he also has a sense of being old. . . . He feels alternately young, old, and in-between. His developmental task is to make sense of this condition of in-between to become Young/Old in a new way, different from that of early adulthood. (Levinson, 1979, p. 197)

Levinson goes on to say, in a section most representative of his integration of these frameworks, "all these polarities exist during the life cycle. They can never be fully resolved or transcended, though some utopian thinkers have held out this promise" (1979, p. 198).

RECURRING ISSUES

Personal construct theory is correct; the world is too complex. It is expecting too much for any theoretical perspective to be entirely accurate and comprehensive as it seeks to explain our psychosocial development. I have already introduced attempts to integrate or synthesize contrasting perspectives. As each is examined in more detail in subsequent chapters, its contribution to an overriding conception of personality in adulthood will be specified.

It should be clear at this point that with regard to a number of issues, these conceptions differ. For example:

Is Biology Destiny?

As expanded in Chapter 2, the psychoanalytic viewpoint, in its original formulation, heavily relies upon biological origins for personality development in childhood. As a spin-off of a psycho-analytic view, the life script approach has little to say about heredity or constitutional factors. As stage theories extended the wellsprings of development beyond the first five years of childhood, emphasis shifted from biological to cultural determinants. (Biological consider-ations may reappear at the very final stage in older adulthood). The dialectical approach rejects the assumption from biology that homeostasis is desirable (or even attainable) with respect to personality development.

As Troll (1982) observes, among developmental psychologists who are interested in the early years of life, many have resolved the conflict between heredity and development by adopting an interac-tionist view. That is, "Neither heredity (biology) nor environment (experience) can be thought of apart from the other; both are intertwined from the first moment of conception " (Troll, 1982, p. 3).

Is the System an Open One or a Closed One?

I have frequently noted the complexity of the world that each of us faces each day. How do people regulate the input of new experience? Some people can be so open to new experience that they are constantly overwhelmed. Others can be so shut off to all outside stimulation that they live in worlds of autism or schizophrenia. For example, some people refuse to recognize changes in their wives or husbands and continue to interact with their spouses as they did when they first got married.

The goal, perhaps, is to regulate the input of new experience in a way that enables people to remain essentially stable over most of the rest of their lives, while being open to new experiences (Troll, 1982). But when are these regulating structures developed, and how much do these structures actually accommodate? And do these structures themselves change over adulthood? The developmental psychologist, John Anderson (quoted by Troll, 1982, p. 5), proposed that the aging person possesses a progressively more closed system. The last stage of Erikson's theory (see Chapter 3) takes a position—albeit a controversial one—on this issue.

Continuity Versus Abrupt Change

One conception of change in adulthood emphasizes that it is a gradual response to accumulating bits of information and experience (Troll, 1982). Interestingly, this is the way most people probably see their own lives. Often, when change seems to outsiders to be abrupt or dramatic—the shift to an entirely different line of work, or seemingly sudden breakup of a long marriage—the person will say, "Oh no, I've been leading up to this for a long time."

Some developmental psychologists agree; they conceptualize life as an unfolding process; Jaffe and Allman (1982, p. 3) say, "The life process consists of a somewhat orderly sequence of developmental stages and tasks, which are punctuated at each point by individual crises and difficulties." But others give the crises more prominence; Levinson's theory (see Chapter 5) views adulthood as alternating between periods of major upheaval and periods of quietude.

What Is "The Good Life"?

Each of the perspectives introduced in this chapter possesses implicit value judgments about what is the best adaptation to changing tasks and ages in adulthood. But there certainly are problems in determining what is "good." Smelser (1980, p. 22) notes:

Growth . . . is a relative concept. Like pattern, its presence or absence is dictated in part by the questions posed and by the scope of the life span considered. Whether or not a given process is regarded as growth depends also on the criteria by which the term is defined. Two investigators may agree on the empirical fact that in the later years of adulthood men and women become more resigned and conservative in a variety of ways. But whether this is to be interpreted as growth to some plateau of vision and wisdom or whether it is to be seen as defeat and retreat is unclear, and neither interpretation depends on the facts but on a framework for evaluation that the individual investigator uses.

To the mathematician, engineer, or physical scientist for whom "the facts speak for themselves," the value-colored nature of conclusions by adult personality theorists must be frustrating and elusive. Can there be any firm, objective, agreed-upon conclusions about the nature of development? I believe there are, but still we will see this issue recurring through virtually every chapter of this book. There is no easy solution to this problem. Values should be made explicit, of course, and sometimes they are not. When values are clearly articulated, people can choose between them. And sources of ideas should be identified. To some degree, theoretical concepts on this topic stem from the personal experience of the theoretician. (I consider this such an important point that a section of Chapter 2 is allocated to examples of this interaction.) But many of the ideas in this book, regardless of the individualistic nature of their origins, have stood the test of time and have been accepted by others.

More generally, many of the concepts and findings reported in this book may possess a "dated" quality. We are constantly reminded that we are living through a period of very rapid social change. Nuclear annihilation, a worldwide AIDS epidemic, and the threat from the "ozone layer" of the atmosphere were incomprehensible 50 years ago. At a more mundane level, the sex-roles of women and men (Chapter 8), our conceptions of work (Chapter 7), and the incidence of divorce (Chapter 9) are all changing, making many of the empirical findings presented here in need of updating and qualification.

2

PSYCHOANALYSIS AS AN EARLY-FORMATION THEORY

That "biology is destiny" clearly serves as a stronger assumption in Freud's psychoanalytic theory than it does in any other approach that seeks to conceptualize personality development in adulthood. Sigmund Freud was, of course, highly trained in physiology in medical school, and this orientation is reflected in his conception about the mainsprings for change in the child's development. Furthermore, his concept for the basic psychological energy, the libido, reflected principles from biology and physics.

This chapter examines psychoanalytic theory as a prototype of an early-formation theory. How does personality develop? Are characteristics manifested in adulthood determined by experiences in childhood? Is psychoanalytic theory validated by empirical evidence? If the theory is correct, how much personality change in adulthood is possible? These questions will be considered in this chapter. Also, because theories of personality development are human creations, a section of the chapter is devoted to the relationships between the lives of individual theorists and the constructs each developed to explain the lives of others.

BASIC CONCEPTS IN PSYCHOANALYTIC THEORY

One of the tasks for Freud, as of any personality theorist, was explaining the structure of personality. What are the basic building blocks in describing personality? How is it put together?

Personality Structure

Freud proposed that three systems within the person reflect different drives or motivations and these compete with each other for control of the person's behavior. It is important to recognize that these systems are concepts, not things; they are abstractions extracted from commonalities in behavior and inner experience.

Freud could not escape the conviction that in every person there is an aspect of untamed, animallike motivation. He conceived it to be there at birth—an instinctual set of demanding, selfish urges. This innate system he termed the id; he saw it as the reservoir of psychic energy and believed that it furnished all the power for the operation of the other two systems which developed later.

In young children, the id seems to rule, according to Freud's view. Young children, without restraint or regret, seek their pleasures and vent their unintentionally destructive impulses on the world. The id cannot tolerate tension; it seeks to discharge this tension immediately. This quest for immediate gratification is called the "pleasure principle."

But, in time, controls develop and restrain the operation of this primary process. At first, immoral and asocial behavior is inhibited only in the presence of disapproving and punishing adults. Later on, the individual internalizes these external controls. That is, they become his or her own and exert influence even when adults are not around to disapprove or punish. This system of controls Freud called the "superego," a construct that he defined as the *moral principle*, the conscience.

Right versus wrong is the only concern of the superego. While its drives are almost always in conflict with those of the id, the superego and id share a nonrational quality, a lack of concern with what is realistic or beneficial in the long run.

In Freudian theory there are two subsystems to the superego. In addition to the moralistic component, or conscience, the superego maintains an ego-ideal, a set of characteristics that the person seeks to attain for himself or herself.

The third basic system that seemed necessary to Freud to account for the behavior he saw is that of the ego. He found in his patients, as we have just noted, an array of primitive and unreasoning urges on the one hand, and rigid and sometimes equally unreasoning controls on the other. But he also saw the capacity to deal intelligently and rationally with reality. This reality principle is reflected in the actions of the ego. Freud saw the ego as something of an intelligent administrator concerned with keeping the person going in the face of the conflicting demands of the id and the superego and in the face of the demands of reality. But the ego may not be up to this; it may lose control. After all, according to Freud, the ego came into existence in order to advance the aims of the id, and all its psychic energy was derived from the id. (Not all of Freud's later followers agree with this last proposition.)

Three principal elements, then, participate in the lifelong drama that Freud saw enacted within the person. The three components of personality are: the selfish, now-centered id; the rigid, un-compromising voice of morality, the superego; and the sometimes weak but sometimes clever compromiser and arranger, the ego. The central theme of the play is conflict; in fact, originally, Freud explained pathology and mental illness as caused by these structural conflicts. In general, he portrayed an everlasting and irreconcilable conflict between good and evil, between superego and id. (Contrary to his public image, Freud was essentially a moralistic person. His view of human nature was negative, and he felt that it is the function of society to restrain people from their basic selfish impulses.)

The opportunity for the ego to grow strong is rooted both in hereditary factors and in the experiences of the child. As noted in Chapter 1, in Freud's view, personality is largely formed by the end of the fifth year, and later growth consists mainly of elaborating the structure (Hall & Lindzey, 1970, p. 50). Thus, the opportunities for the ego to develop control are tested by challenges to the young child as a result of biological changes during the early years.

Stages of Psychological Development

The previous section reflected Freud's assumption that certain inborn motives propel humans and determine the direction that behavior will take (Freud, 1917/1963; 1933). Attempts to satisfy these motives formed the groundwork for the emergence of personality characteristics that, according to Freud, would continue into adulthood. The energy expended in satisfying motives is a psychological or psychic energy called "libido." This can be thought of as much like physical energy in that we have only a certain amount of it at any given time. Hence the more energy that is devoted to one activity, the less there is available for another. Freud saw normal development as a process of redirecting the libido toward different goals as the person matures. Difficulties arise when psychic energy needed to work out problems in the present must be spent instead to achieve goals that should have been achieved in an earlier stage of development.

According to Freud, as children grow older they go through predictable and clear-cut stages of personality development. (Yes, Freud was a stage theorist; he did not, however, qualify for the second approach propounded in this book, because his stages did not extend into adulthood.)

Each of Freud's stages is centered on that part of the body that occupies the child's thoughts most at a particular developmental period. The first stage, which occurs during the child's first year, is the oral stage. The mouth during this stage is the center of the infant's universe, for it is used to ingest food and to express displeasure. Thus, the infant's libido is directed toward the satisfaction of its oral needs (sucking, then swallowing, then biting). If these needs are satisfied, the child can shift his or her psychic energy toward a concern appropriate for the next stage. (That is, weaning is successful not only functionally, but also psychologically.) If oral needs are not fully satisfied, fixation occurs. This can result from improper weaning, an unsatisfactory feeding schedule, oral overindulgence, fears and anxieties, or other reasons. In fixation a certain amount of psychic energy remains devoted to the satisfying of an earlier need even though the child has moved on to confront the tasks of a later stage of development.

If fixation has occurred, the adult's personality and behavior reflect the continued lack of satisfaction of this need. For example, if a man became fixated at the oral stage, he might be very talkative, chew gum constantly, or smoke. He might seek out an occupation that permits him to talk excessively—such as salesperson or professor—or he might be sarcastic or biting in his conversation.

That is, fixation could occur as a failure to satisfy either sucking needs (early part of oral stage) or biting needs (later part of the stage) or both. The concept of fixation is a prime example of Freud's relating personality factors to biological needs. But he also recognized that the child's environment would influence the degree of satisfaction or fixation.

The second stage in Freud's theory of personality development is the anal stage; here the 2-year-old or 3-year-old child, going through the self-discipline of toilet training, is learning self-control.

Society places great emphasis on achieving "proper" toilet training. Again, we have a choice point, in that the child-rearing practices of the parents can lead either to fixation or to a shifting of the child's libidinal energy to other concerns. Hall and Lindzey (1970) indicate some of the outcomes of toilet-training methods that Freudian theory would predict:

> If the mother is very strict and repressive in her methods, the child may hold back his feces and become constipated. If this mode of reaction generalizes to other ways of behaving, the child will develop a retentive character. He will become obstinate and stingy. Or under the duress of repressive measures the child may vent his rage by expelling his feces at the most inappropriate times. This is the prototype for all kinds of expulsive traits—cruelty, wanton destructiveness, temper tantrums, and messy disorderliness, to mention only a few. On the other hand, if the mother is the type of person who pleads with her child to have a bowel movement and who praises him extravagantly when he does, the child will acquire the notion that the whole activity of producing feces is extremely important. This idea may be the basis for later creativity and productivity (Hall & Lindzey, 1970, p. 51).

Thus are the traits of adulthood supposedly laid down during the anal stage.

The next stage of development, the phallic stage, usually occurs when the child is 3, 4, or 5 years of age. At this time, interests in one's genital organs come into prominence. (It is a manifestation of Freud's male bias that even while he tried to explain the development of each sex, he chose as the title for this stage a reference to the male sex organ, the phallus.) At these ages, masturbation and other kinds of self-stimulation may occur. The child may develop feelings of jealousy toward the parent of the same sex and feelings of affection for the parent of the other sex. During this period a boy, according to Freud, "rather naively wishes to use his new-found source of pleasure, his penis, to please his oldest source of pleasure, the mother" (Schaeffer, 1971, p. 12). He envies his father, who is occupying the position he craves and is doing the thing he wishes to do. Freud called this the Oedipus complex, after Oedipus, the mythical king of Thebes who killed his father and married his mother.

According to psychoanalytic theory, attitudes toward the other sex and toward people in authority are largely influenced by the Oedipus complex and the person's way of resolving it. A boy's fear of his father—a part of which is castration anxiety—may lead to a repression of the sexual desire for his mother. Through repression, the unacceptable desire is removed from conscious awareness to an unconscious level of the mind. At the same time, the boy comes to identify or align himself with his father. This identification gives the boy some vicarious satisfaction of the sexual drives that he cannot satisfy directly. If fixation occurs, in later life the male may seek as companions and sexual partners women who resemble his mother. Or he may carry over into adult life feelings of anxiety and self-doubt rooted in guilt about his sexual fantasies in childhood.

As he sought to explain the development of sexual orientation in females, Freud could not apply the same explanation, because both boys and girls start out attracted to the mother, the caregiver and source of benefits. He struggled over an explanation, and the resultant one was neither satisfactory to him nor acceptable to feminists (as we will see in the next section). According to Freud, after the girl's original identification with her mother, she comes to blame her mother for the fact that she lacks the genitals of boys. She wishes she had a penis; she feels ashamed that she doesn't, and she feels inferior. Her feeling of deficiency extends to her whole self-concept. She concludes that she has already lost her penis, and she blames her mother for depriving her of this organ. In the process she comes to devalue her mother.

This state, called penis envy, generates a shift in attraction to her father, called the Electra complex. Electra was the mythical woman who incited her brother to kill her mother and her mother's lover. The transfer of love to her father occurs because he has the valued organ which she aspires to share with him. She gives up clitoral masturbation and represses a good deal of her sexual impulses in general. She becomes more passive, more "feminine." Freud proposed that this lack of a penis is compensated for when the girl grows up and has a baby, especially if it is a boy baby. Later in childhood, the girl again develops a feminine identification with her mother in a manner that Freud does not specify very clearly. Freudian theory has difficulty in explaining female development in biological terms. Perhaps that is one of the reasons why the examples Freud used were usually male-oriented, even though the vast majority of his patients were females.

The next of Freud's stages is the latency period. Between the ages of about five and the onset of puberty, the child's libido is tame, partly because the child represses unacceptable desires for the parent of the other sex. Sexual interests are replaced by interests in school, sports, and friends. Freud felt that it was biologically determined that not much was to happen developmentally during these years, so he had little to say about them.

After this uneventful latency period, a person moves into the genital stage. The adolescent develops overt sexual interests. Concern is directed toward the biological goal of reproduction; that part of the libido that is not still being devoted to earlier selfish needs may be channeled into love and into a genuine concern for others. Only those people who have most of the libidinal energy available for this stage can become realistic, well-socialized adults.

But many adults, said Freud, have so much of their limited psychic energy still allocated to the satisfaction of the earlier needs that they have little left for the development of altruistic motives. They remain narcissistic or self-loving. Their "love of others" may be based on the ways these others remind them of themselves.

VALIDATION OF FREUD'S THEORY

One of the major contributions of Freud's writings to understanding of personality development was its comprehensive structure and richness of concepts. Some of his critics would begrudgingly acknowledge that this was Freud's only positive contribution; other critics would not even grant him that!

Whether one concludes that our understanding has or has not been advanced by psychoanalytic theory, it can be agreed that

Freud took a narrow view about attempts by others to substantiate his theory. When Saul Rosenzweig wrote Freud in 1934 about his attempts to validate Freud's hypotheses about repression through experimental procedures, Freud responded (on a postcard!), "I cannot put much value on these [attempts at] confirmations, because the wealth of reliable observations on which these assertions rest makes them independent of experimental verification." He added gratuituously, "Still, it can do no harm" (quoted by MacKinnon & Dukes, 1963, p. 703).

These "reliable observations" on which Freud based his theory were, of course, the statements and nonverbal behavior of patients undergoing psychological treatment (Hall & Lindzey, 1970). He carried out no experiments or controlled observations; he gave no personality tests and used no quantitative measures. But Freud did check for internal consistency; he did bring a critical attitude to his data; and he made an intensive study of single cases. Again and again he revised his theories in light of new observations. However, he did not revise enough, in the view of some of his critics; in 1984 it was claimed by Jeffrey Masson that Freud covered up some of his most sensational findings; Box 2.1 describes these claims in detail.

Empirical studies have examined virtually every aspect of psycho-analytic theory (Fisher & Greenberg, 1977). One focus here is on the assumption of early formation and the centrality of fixation in determining our personality as adults. Note that the hypothesis that adult personality patterns and characteristics derive directly from infant and childhood experiences is ingrained in modern thought; Freud tried to translate this platitude into a scientific finding (Stannard, 1980). Freud proposed specific childhood experiences that were related to specific adult character patterns.

But empirical research that focuses on specific linkages has failed to show the presence of these predicted relationships. Using objective measures of adult personality and correlating them with accounts of activities during early childhood has produced no consistent indication of a relationship (Sears, 1943; Orlansky, 1949; Eysenck & Wilson, 1974), although there are a few isolated studies that find relationships between particular measures, such as age at weaning and optimism/pessimism in adulthood (Goldman-Eisler, 1951). In reality, many of these empirical studies contained disabling methodological limitations (Cairns, 1983) and their results had little impact on the psychoanalytic perspective (Leichtman, 1987). In a

BOX 2.1
Freud and "The Seduction Theory"

In 1984 Jeffrey Masson, a psychoanalyst, claimed that Freud was a coward who tried to cover up his most explosive findings (Miller, 1984). Back in the late 1800s, Freud had speculated that all hysteria could be traced back to actual childhood sexual traumas, such as incest and rape. But Freud later claimed he rejected this explanation because of an increased awareness that some of the "seductions" his adult patients reported were, in fact, fantasies. He came to place more emphasis on the theory that all children have sexual fantasies and sexual urges long before puberty. This was, of course, one of Freud's ground-breaking conclusions.

But Masson proposes that Freud rejected his earlier idea because he feared professional rejection and isolation if he were to continue publicizing it. It was "a personal failure of courage," Masson says.

Critics of Masson say that Freud didn't suppress his own earlier hypothesis; he simply treated it as an open empirical question. Some neuroses of adulthood stem from having been raped or seduced when a child; some not.

In his introductory lectures, first published in 1916, Freud (1966) acknowledges:

> Phantasies of being seduced are of particular interest because so often they are not phantasies but real memories. Fortunately, however, they are nevertheless not real as often as seemed at first to be shown by the findings of analysis. . . . You must not suppose, however, that sexual abuse of a child by its nearest male relatives belongs entirely to the realm of phantasy. Most analysts will have treated cases in which such events were real and could be unimpeachably established. . . . Up to the present time we have not succeeded in pointing to any difference in the consequences, whether phantasy or reality has had a greater share in these events of childhood. (p. 370)

Furthermore, it would seem that Freud's later view, that of infantile sexuality, was much more objectionable to people in the Victorian era than would have been a revelation of rape. The innocence of childhood has always been one of our cherished illusions.

For those and other reasons, it would seem that Masson is

BOX 2.2
Object Relations Theory

The conceptions used in this chapter reflect Freud's own thinking about the ways that individuals' childhood experiences color their present behavior and relationships. In that sense these ideas are part of the classic Freudian model. Given that Freud began his writing in the last two decades of the nineteenth century, some of these ideas are 100 years old. More recently, some adherents to the basic guidelines of psychoanalytic theory have chosen to alter this mainstream viewpoint in several ways. Among these revisionists, those who emphasize *object relations* theory are most important for the focus of this book.

As St. Clair (1986), the author of a recent text on psychoanalytic theory, notes: "Object relations means interpersonal relations. The term *object*, a technical word originally coined by Freud, refers simply to that which will satisfy a need. More broadly, object refers to the significant person or theory that is the object or target of another's feelings or drives. Freud first used object in discussions of instinctual drives and in a context of early mother-child relations. In combination with *relations*, object refers to interpersonal relations and suggests the inner residues of past relationships that shape an individual's current interactions with people" (St. Clair, 1986, p. 1, italics in original).

So it can be seen that object relations continues the focus on the effects of past experiences (here, the emphasis is on past relationships) on shaping of personalities. Yet there are differences, not the least of which is the proposal that the main motive a person has is for a relationship, not the satisfaction of a biological instinct. St. Clair (1986) provides us with a clever distinction between the two approaches by interpreting the "case study" of Cinderella through the constructs of each. Let us suppose, he proposes, that Cinderella seeks the assistance of a psychoanalyst because she is experiencing conflict in her marriage with the prince. He observes that "A traditional Freudian might investigate Cinderella's repression of her sexual instincts and unresolved Oedipal feelings that she had for her parents. This therapist or analyst would analyze Cinderella's problems in terms of defenses and conflicts between the structures of the ego and the id" (1986, p. 3).

In contrast, notes St. Clair, a psychoanalyst committed to the object relations perspective:

> . . . would note that Cinderella suffered early psychological deprivation from the loss of her mother. Possibly this loss caused Cinderella to make use of the psychological defense mechanism of splitting, by which she idealized some women (such as her fairy godmother) and saw other women as "all bad" (her stepsisters and stepmother). She idealized the Prince despite knowing him for only a short time. A marriage based on such distorted images of herself and others is bound to run into problems as she sooner or later must deal with the Prince as a real person with human flaws. In object relations theory, the issue would center on the discrepancy between Cinderella's inner world and the persons and situations of the actual world. (St. Clair, 1986, p. 3)

As St. Clair notes elsewhere, "Psychoanalytic theory has historically progressed by a lively process of refining and clarifying early fertile concepts and their implications without necessarily abandoning any of them" (1986, p. 20).

more general sense, though, there is empirical verification for a psychoanalytic assumption that the kind of attachment that people form with their parents during childhood colors the nature of romantic relationships they have as adults (Hazan & Shaver, 1987).

Critics complain that Freudian theory is so general that it can't be pinned down enough to be empirically tested. But Nevitt Sanford (1980), a wise observer, has a different perspective on the difficulties in operationalizing psychoanalytic concepts. He writes, "The question is often put as to why Freud's theoretical scheme has persisted [more or less unmodified] for so long. Sixty years is a long time for a theory in science . . . I think it ought to be conceded that the general theory has lasted because it was well conceived in the first place, and because it has been increasingly validated by objective studies and by clinical utility as the years have gone by." (pp. 250, 251).

He goes on to observe: "No one will deny that the things Freud was talking about are things of perpetual, often consuming, interest. In conceptualizing them he seems to have made them just hypothetical enough, and just remote enough from anything directly observable, in order to insure the perpetuation of his theory; we cannot ignore his formulations, nor can we disprove

---

BOX 2.3
Psychoanalysis and Developmental Psychology

In the last decade, followers of psychoanalytic explanations have intensified their examination of concepts and theories from developmental psychology (Leichtman, 1987). Influential in this effort is psychiatrist Daniel Stern's (1985) book, *The Interpersonal World of the Infant*, "a work which draws on contemporary psychological research to construct a picture of the subjective experience of young children that contrasts sharply with the most influential theories of early development" (Leichtman, 1987, p. 1). For example, he reports findings leading to a conclusion that infants are born with a strong biological predisposition toward social relationships and thus rejects the self-centered id as "normal." He also extends the object-relations focus described in Box 2.2 backward, to the first two years of life, concluding that the infant and caretaker share efforts to achieve "affective attunement." He also questions the prominence of oral needs in shaping later experiences.

---

them. The concepts can be defined operationally, in the modern sophisticated sense; and so they cannot be dismissed as vagaries of the imagination; yet it is extraordinarily difficult to devise any critical tests of them" (p. 251).

Although Sanford's perspective generally is justified, many would respond that Freudian theory has not remained rigid, despite criticisms that it has. Recent followers have provided new emphases, as Box 2.2 and Box 2.3 reflect.

KAREN HORNEY'S MODIFICATION OF PSYCHOANALYTIC THEORY

As we know, Freud had many followers, some of whom developed their own theories of personality, albeit relying on his basic framework. In this and the next section are described two of these that I consider particularly relevant to the theoretical perspectives of this book.

Karen Horney (1950) proposed that neurosis resulted from a person's losing the thread of his or her guiding direction. Becoming too concerned with pleasing others, neurotic persons forget their own deepest satisfactions and needs. Horney's perspective is reminiscent of the life script approach described in Chapter 1; these two conceptions are similar in their assumption that the child forms a long-lasting style of responding to others, as a result of anxiety.

Basic anxiety, for Horney, is the feeling the child has of being isolated and helpless in a potentially hostile world. Anything that disturbs the security of children in relation to their parents produces basic anxiety. A person can become neurotic, and hence anxious, if he or she is raised in a home that lacks security, trust, love, respect, tolerance, and warmth. Conflict, then, is not inevitable, not built into human nature (as Freud believed); rather, conflict arises out of social conditions.

Horney theorized that people develop strategies by which to cope with the feeling of isolation and helplessness; this is done to minimize the anxiety of coping with others. One possible style or orientation toward others she called "moving toward people." This is the self-effacing solution to basic anxiety, in which the person shows dependency on others and seeks love from them. The person may become undemanding and be content with very little. Out of the desire to minimize the anxiety of coping with others, such persons may let others tread on them; afraid of being deserted and left alone, they avoid conflict.

"Moving away from people," a second type of strategy, is quite different. Here, the person becomes coldly aloof and withdrawn from any genuine interaction with significant others. A "lone wolf," such a person may reflect either resignation or rebelliousness. Whichever, there is a lack of commitment to others; the credo seems to be, "If I withdraw, nothing can hurt me."

The last type of strategy, "moving against people," reflects an orientation toward mastery and power. Hostility is a stronger component here, and this hostility may lead to a need to exploit others. The person seems to believe, "If I have power no one can hurt me."

Horney believed that normal people integrate these three styles, but that neurotic persons, because of their greater degrees of anxiety, must use artificial or irrational solutions. Thus the latter type consciously recognizes only one of the tendencies and denies or represses the other two, that is, like the follower of a life script, the neurotic person is locked into a rigidly unshakable coping technique.

CARL JUNG'S ANALYTICAL PSYCHOLOGY

Carl Jung was one of the most innovative of Freud's followers. Even though he had been handpicked by Freud to become his "successor," Jung's ideas came to deviate from Freud's to such a degree that their relationship disintegrated.

The following is only a selection of Jung's rich and extensive ideas, included particularly because Jung serves as a transition figure. Trained in an early formation framework, Jung was among the first to extend conceptions of childhood into adulthood. Many of the concepts described in Chapters 3 and 5 reflect his ideas as a source. Another of Jung's relevant contributions was the distinction between the anima and the animus; as we will see, these provide a dialectical flavor, and are manifested in contemporary views of personality development, especially Daniel Levinson's (Chapter 5).

Jung proposed that in the late thirties or early forties a radical transvaluation occurs. Youthful interests and pursuits lose their value and are replaced by new interests that are more cultural and less biological. The middle-aged person becomes more introverted and less impulsive; wisdom takes the place of physical and mental vigor. Jung believed that this shift was the most decisive in the person's life.

In introducing the concepts of the animus and the anima, Jung emphasized that there is both a masculine and a feminine side to personality, regardless of which sex you are. In most men, the anima is suppressed, and in women, the animus is less expressed. But recognition of the presence of both, and release of these values, gives the person completeness. Yet there is a tension between these two sets of values. One is more unconscious but is striving for expression; the psychoanalytic analysis of the life and character of Lewis Carroll, author of *Alice in Wonderland*, reported by Greenacre (1955), provides an illustration. The opposition of conscious and unconscious forces, as viewed by Jung, formed a kind of dialectic.

Jung's conception of anima and animus in competition for expression was a significant recognition of polarities in personality development and expression.

THEORIST'S LIVES: DO THEY DETERMINE THEIR THEORIES?

The theories and constructs represented in this book are human constructions. For example, as pointed by St. Clair, "The components of personality—the id, ego, and superego—are conceptualizations that exist only in writings about personality and are distant from people's experience of themselves" (1986, p. 3). If we really believe our own theories, especially, that each of us comes to perceive the world through certain constructs, we must conclude that "universal" psychological theories often have a subjective origin. That is the theme of a provocative book titled *Faces in a Cloud*, by Stolorow and Atwood (1979). My view is that this subjectivity is inevitable and not necessarily undesirable; the degree to which theories receive acceptance by others is partly determined by whether the theoretician's subjectivity reflects the orientation of others. Stolorow and Atwood note that "Every theory of personality constitutes a system of statements regarding the meaning of human life in the world. Each theory is founded upon distinctive images of the human condition and the essential relationships between man and the world. These images are, at least in part, subjective and pretheoretical in origin; rather than being results of impartial reflection upon empirical facts accessible to everyone, they are bound up with the theorist's personal reality and precede his intellectual engagement with the problem of human nature. . . . The personality theorist is a person and therefore views the world from the limited perspective of his own subjectivity" (1979, p. 17).

The term *personal reality* in the above quotation reflects George Kelly's assumption that each of us construes the world through idiosyncratic constructs. Furthermore, Stolorow and Atwood note that these views of the world develop prior to theorists' theories. Reading this quotation, George Kelly would have noted that theorists only do what all of us do, with two important exceptions: (1) they systematize their view of people in general, and (2) they seek to apply their construct system beyond just themselves, to people in general.

Where do theorists' constructs come from? Largely from their own experience. Although Freud certainly based his theories on the reports of his patients, his fundamental structure came before, and came from his quest to fathom his own nature. Stolorow and Atwood conclude that "personality theorists tend to rely upon their own lives as a primary source of empirical material. . . . No theorist offers definitive statements on the meaning of being human unless he feels those statements constitute a framework within which he can comprehend his own experience" (1979, p. 18).

I have argued that this development is natural and progressive. Theorists whose theories do not jibe with the ways that their audiences construe the world will not find acceptance for their theories. Stolorow and Atwood note the necessity of a common framework: "Other persons, in their reactions to theoretical ideas, are similarly subject to those influences" (1979, p. 18). Just like theory generation, theory acceptance is not entirely a rational act. A person's "eventual attitudes toward the material will be profoundly affected by its degree of compatibility with his own personal reality" (Stolorow & Atwood, 1979, p. 19).

Examples of the correlation between theorists' lives and their theories, while representing anecdotal evidence, are so prevalent that they lend strong credence to Stolorow and Atwood's propositions. In the following sections we examine Freud and Jung from this perspective. (Erik Erikson's life also impressively illustrates how theory derives from personal experience, but this example will be saved for Chapter 3, on Erikson's perspective.)

Freud's Life and His Theory

Sigmund Freud was born in 1856. His father, mother, and an older half-brother were the other family members. Another half-brother, Emanuel, was married and lived nearby. Emanuel's son, John, was to become Freud's first playmate.

As his mother's own first child, Sigmund Freud was her indisputable favorite. A prophecy had told her that she would bring a great man into the world, and the whole family was often reminded of this. Later, after Sigmund had several siblings, his younger sister was practicing her piano lessons, but the sound was so disturbing to young Sigmund that he insisted that the piano be removed, and his mother—despite her strong musical interests—agreed to do so (Fromm, 1959). As an adult, Freud (1952) once wrote, "A man who has been the indisputable favorite of his mother keeps for life the feeling of conqueror, that confidence of success which often induces real success" (p. 367). So be it.

But when Sigmund Freud was 11 months old, a younger brother, Julius was born. No longer was Sigmund the sole recipient of his mother's adoring care. Freud reacted with jealousy (Fromm, 1959). In Freud's lecture on "femininity" in New Introductory Lectures, he wrote, "It is a remarkable fact that a child, even with the age difference of only 11 months, is not too young to take notice of what is happening, when two children are so close that lactation is prejudiced by the second pregnancy" (quoted by Stolorow & Atwood, 1979, p. 65). The choice of "11 months" seems not to be a coincidence.

Eight months after birth, Julius died. Sigmund Freud, then age 19 months, blamed himself for his brother's death. He later described his self-reproach in detail. But he never expressed any feelings of betrayal or disappointment toward his mother—only very positive feelings; Freud was never able to acknowledge the ambivalent feelings that he possessed about his mother. Stolorow and Atwood believe that Freud developed hostility toward his mother but was unable to express it; "The central conflict in his emotional life had thus been established; namely, the conflict between an intense possessive need for his mother's love and an equally intense, magically potent hatred" (p. 52). But, in their view, he repressed the enraging disappointing qualities, and saved himself from the dreaded fear of losing her. This is reminiscent of Horney's "moving toward" interpersonal style. It is true that after Freud became an adult, he visited his mother every Sunday for 50 years, and had her over every Sunday for dinner.

Regarding his other early ties, especially those with his father, Freud's feelings were ambivalent; he was able to express both love and hate toward his father. Erich Fromm (1959) recounts an example, a story Freud's father told him when Sigmund was 12:

When he (the father) was a young man, a Gentile had knocked off his fur cap and then shouted at him: "Jew, get off the pavement!" When the little boy asked indignantly, "And what did you do?"; his father replied, "I went into the roadway and picked up my cap." Freud, in relating this story, continued: "This struck me as unheroic conduct on the part of the big strong man who was holding the little boy by the hand. I contrasted this situation with another which fitted my feelings better, the scene in which Hannibal's father, Hamilcar Barca, made his boy swear before the household altar to take vengeance on the Romans. Ever since that time, Hannibal had a place in my fantasies." (Fromm, 1959, p. 57)

Every theory has to make decisions about the locus of causation in regard to psychological development. Stolorow and Atwood note that in Freud's theory of psychosexual development "The sources of evil were located not in the parents (in particular, the mother), but in the child himself, in his own sexual and aggressive impulses, which emerge according to an innate biologically prede- termined sequence in relative independence of environmental influence" (1979, p. 63). According to Fine (1973), this emphasis reflected Freud's wish to exonerate his parents, especially his mother. That is, by his choice to locate "badness" within the child, Freud "absolved his mother from blame for her betrayals of him and safeguarded her idealized image from invasions by his un- conscious ambivalence" (Stolorow & Atwood, 1979, p. 63). Thus did he ward off his unconscious hatred of his mother.

Carl Jung's Life and His Theory

We find in Carl Jung's life other examples of the continuity between personal issues and later theoretical constructs. One overriding feature of Carl Jung's development as a child was his secret involvement in a world of religious fantasies (Stolorow & Atwood, 1979). In his autobiography, Jung (1961) refers to his secret world as "the essential factor of my boyhood" (p. 22).

At the age of 3, he was taught to say the following prayer before going to sleep each night:

Spread out thy wings, Lord Jesus mild,
and take to thee thy chick, thy child,
If Satan would devour it,
No harm shall overpower it,
So let the angels sing.

The second phrase ("and take to thee thy chick") was confusing, and Jung thought that Jesus swallowed children. This view was supplemented by the child's observations of funerals and burials.

One day, playing outside, he saw a man in a strange black garment and broad hat coming down the hill toward him. The young Carl Jung rushed into the house and hid in the darkest corner of the attic. He was frightened for days, and it was years before he could set foot inside a Catholic church.

Those, and other religious dreams with frightening connotations, doubtless contributed to the emergence of his concept of the two-sided nature of God. In fact, this splitting process—dividing objects into positive and negative components—became a generalized feature of not just Jung's world view, but also his conception of the nature of personality. Stolorow and Atwood (1979) state, "The world had been revealed in his mind as a polarized tension between above and below, omnipotent good and omnipotent evil. . . . We can therefore discern in these images an early source of Jung's later obsession with the reconciliation of opposites, the problem of wholeness, and integration" (p. 93).

During his childhood, Jung shared his "secret" with no one. His was a lonely existence; he had no siblings until he was 9; and at school he alienated himself from others. He came to see himself as possessing two separate personalities: "Personality No.1," as he called one of these components, was the outer self which was known to his parents and other persons. "'Personality No. 2,' on the other hand, was a hidden self which was unknown to others and which entertained secret fantasies about the ultimate mysteries of the cosmos" (Stolorow & Atwood, 1979, p. 98).

Jung's entire adulthood was obsessed with the competitions and contradictions between the two sides of his personality. His choice of psychiatry as a career was a compromise between these two self-images.

Given this perspective, it is quite understandable that one of Jung's major contributions to personality theory would be his emphasis on the bipolar nature of self-images. Staude (1981) observes:

> Jung was fascinated with polarities, probably in part because of his own split nature. He viewed development and the transformation of psychic energy as being a result of interaction among polarities in the

psyche, such as male/female, light/dark, individual/collective, etc. He found that developmental work with any one polarity usually opened out into other polarities. In his view dialectical-development conflicts within the psyche were transcended when both sides of the polarity were owned and acknowledged. In the course of the individuation process, in Jung's view, there is a gradual shift in the center of personality from the ego to the self, but neither side of this polarity is ever abolished; they remain in dialectical interplay. (pp. 100-101)

Following his conception of himself as two people, Jung did his dissertation on an interpretation of the personality development of Helene Preiswerk. She became the first example of what he came to call the law of enantiodromia, or polar reversal. Staude (1981) reports: "She went from one pole to another, her general weakness and silliness and her willingness to cheat, to the opposite pole where she was expressing the best in herself. . . . From this case he generalized another psychological law: in order to advance to a higher state of development we often have to commit some mistake so terrible that it may threaten to ruin our lives" (p. 29).

As noted earlier, Jung was one of the first theorists on adult personality to write about mid-life crisis. Again, his own experience was related to his perspective. During World War I, Jung experienced an internal war and revolution of his own. He questioned everything he had done and believed in previously. "He went through a process of breakdown and transformation that we have since come to know, partly through his writings, as the mid-life transition" (Staude, 1981, p. 44). Prior to that time, he had appeared to be quite successful. In 1911 he had a stable marriage and family, and a flourishing private practice as a psychiatrist. He was the acknowledged heir-apparent to Freud.

But, approaching the age of 40, he broke with Freud, marital infidelities threatened his marriage, and he established a sexual relationship with a former patient that was to last almost 40 years. He convinced his wife and his mistress that he needed both of them; his wife, Emma, provided the motherliness he missed in his own mother, whereas his mistress, Antonia Wolff, fulfilled the "female inspiration" for his creative work. He even had his mistress as a regular guest for Sunday dinner with his family.

Jung's mid-life crisis has been interpreted in various ways, "as everything from a heroic conquest of the unconscious to a psychotic breakdown. From his memoirs and sympathetic biographers it appears that Jung voluntarily made a conscious decision to confront the imagery of the collective unconscious at mid-life" (Staude, 1981, p. 47). That is, he saw the "quest for meaning" as the task of the second half of his life.

CONCLUSIONS

Readers may have varying reactions to the claim and purported demonstration that the ways that theorists view their own lives influence the theories they advance. For me, the claim is not disturbing. It reemphasizes three points:

(1) There is no agreed-upon reality, when we consider human experience. That is, there are many ways of explaining human development that possess some validity.
(2) Subjectivity in generation of theoretical constructs is virtually inevitable; only humans can create explanations for human experience, and no one can, himself or herself, develop without having to interpret the world through certain limited constructs.
(3) Theories survive or fail based on their acceptance by others. The very fact that the theories described here remain in the literature is an indication that, although their origin was partly subjective, they deal with experiences of enough commonality to be helpful in explaining personality development in others.

3

ERIKSON'S THEORY OF PSYCHOSOCIAL DEVELOPMENT

That type of approach that sees personality developing through a series of stages dominates this and the next two chapters. After evaluating Erik Erikson's conception in this chapter, we examine in Chapter 4 the utility of psychobiography as an explanation of personality, and in Chapter 5 other major explanations that rely on psychosocial stages. Although different stage theorists highlight different qualities, they possess a similarity in basic perspective. In general these conceptions view each stage or period as qualitatively different, with relatively abrupt shifts from stage to stage. Each of these stages is assumed to build on the earlier ones, and a successful reaction to the crisis or major task of each stage, in effect, gives the person the capabilities necessary to attack the conflicts of the next stages. Thus, each new stage provides a wholly new level of structural integration. But an unsuccessful or inadequate resolution of one "crisis" hinders the growth preferred at each subsequent stage unless some special intervention occurs (Dacey, 1982).

ERIKSON'S BACKGROUND AND
INTELLECTUAL DEVELOPMENT

Erik Erikson's life is so unique and so illustrative of Chapter 2's conclusion that theorists' concepts derive from their own experiences, it is worth detailed review.

Erikson's Life

The man who is now named Erik Homburger Erikson was born in 1902 in Frankfurt, Germany. He grew up in Karlsruhe, in southern Germany, as the son of a pediatrician, Dr. Theodor Homburger and his wife Karla, formerly named Abrahamsen. Erikson's mother was a native of Copenhagen, Denmark. The circumstances of Erikson's birth are not fully known. Elkind (1982) notes that "Not long after his birth his [real] father died" (p. 14). But this may be a rather sanitized version; Erikson has been reluctant to reveal the facts of his early life. Only when he was in his seventies did he state the following: "All through my earlier childhood, they kept secret the fact that my mother had been married previously, and that I was the son of a Dane who had abandoned her before my birth" (Erikson, 1975, p. 27).

Erikson has described his stepfather as coming from "an intensely Jewish small bourgeois family" and that his mother was a "Dane." We do not know whether his mother was Jewish. At any rate, he was brought up in a family that actively participated in Jewish traditions. He attended public schools, and religious services at the synagogue. The young Erik Homburger (for that was his name at that time) felt like an outsider in both settings. He says that he was "referred to as a 'goy' in his stepfather's temple while to his schoolmates he was a 'Jew.'"

Adolescence was not an easy stage for him; he says that "like other youths . . . I became intensely alienated from everything my bourgeois family stood for," but as Roazen notes, Erikson has not clarified for us what he was rebelling against. He was not a good student; he recalls that he was "selectively attentive."

Elkind (1982) tells us that Erikson's stepfather urged him to become a doctor, a pediatrician, like himself. But young Erikson deliberately chose to be different. After graduating from the "gymnasium," the German equivalent of high school, he enrolled in art school. Then he began to wander through Europe, earning a meager keep by painting portraits.

The summer of 1927 was a critical period for Erikson. He had been working in Vienna, painting children's portraits. At the age of 25, he had not yet established any firm professional goals. An old school friend was at that time the director of a small progressive school in Vienna that had a tie-in with Anna Freud, who, like her father, was a practicing psychoanalyst. Many of the children in the school were in a therapeutic treatment program under Anna Freud's direction. Erikson had served as a substitute tutor at the school, and it was clear to all concerned that he—in contrast to most men at the time—was very good at communicating with small children. So Anna Freud asked him whether he'd consider becoming a child analyst—a profession that was only beginning and that he had not even heard of. He agreed to, and became a patient in analysis with Anna Freud. (All psychoanalysts, then and now, were required to be psycho-analyzed themselves.) Although Erikson also received a Montessori diploma, his psychoanalytic training remained his basic professional experience. Among influential theorists in adult development, he is unique in that he not only lacks a M.D. or Ph.D. degree, but he is also not even a college graduate. But even after his "adoption" by the Freudian circle, Erikson still considered himself fatherless (Roazen, 1976, p. 98).

Erikson remained in Vienna until 1933, when he and his wife moved to the United States. He hoped to establish himself among psychoanalytic circles and continue to practice, but he was discour-aged by Freud's leading disciple in the United States, A. A. Brill of New York City. Hence he enrolled as a student in the graduate program in psychology at Harvard University, but he failed his first course. Roazen (1976) concludes that "His 'failure' can be attributed to his unwillingness to accede to what may have seemed to him some of the unnecessary demands of academic psychology, and in later years the Harvard psychologist Edwin Boring was embarrassed about how Erikson had fared in his department" (p. 8).

It was not until 1960, at the age of 58, that he changed his name from Erik Homburger to Erik H. Erikson. Why didn't he revert to his natural father's name? Roazen (1976) observes that "His choice of a last name is obviously significant. One story has it that his children were troubled by the American tendency to confuse 'Homburger' with 'Hamburger,' and that he asked one of his sons for an alternative; being Erik's son he proposed 'Erikson'" (p. 98). Although such a procedure is a Scandinavian custom, it also connotes, intentionally or not, that Erikson is his own father, self-created. Observers have been both mystified and critical of the name change. Roazen (1976) concludes, "Whatever else this name change may have meant to him, it was also an act of repudiation of his German-Jewish stepfather, as well as the mother who had secured a legitimate name for her son" (p. 99). Erikson now claims that the name change was a family decision, taken with his stepfather's approval. He has also written that he "kept my stepfather's name as my middle name out of gratitude." But it is also relevant to note that Erikson, who was raised in a Jewish family, became a devout adherent of Christianity about the time of his name change (Dacey, 1982).

How Erikson's Theory Differs from Freud's

Although Erikson's training and original theoretical orientation were in what is now called classical psychoanalysis, his evolving conception of the nature of personality reflects significant differences from Freud's view. Erikson is more positive in his orientation, placing his emphasis on understanding self-healing more than self-deception. He elevated the status of the ego, proposing that it has a psychic energy of its own. In keeping with Freud's original conception, Erikson believes the ego is largely unconscious, but unlike other post-Freudians, Erikson emphasizes that the ego has a unifying function, ensuring coherent behavior and conduct. Thus, as Roazen (1976) observes, the job of the ego "is not just the negative one of avoiding anxieties but also the positive role of maintaining effective performance" (pp. 23-24). In a recent collection of articles (Schlein, 1987), Erikson asks: "If we know what can go wrong in each stage, can we say what should have gone and can go right?"

Erikson (1963), writing 50 years after Freud, also saw a different type of concern facing most of his patients. He has written: "The patient of today suffers most under the problem of what he should believe in and who he should—or indeed, might—be or become, while the patient of early psychoanalysis suffered most under inhibitions which prevented him from being what and who he thought he knew he was" (p. 279).

Third, Erikson objected to the biological orientation of classical psychoanalysis. He believed that, more than biology, society "guides and narrows the individual's choice" (Roazen, 1976, p. 34). As we will see, the cultural environment has inputs into each of the life crises that serve as the guideposts in Erikson's developmental theory. For example, the "adolescent crisis of intimacy versus role refusal could be triggered by the sociological fact that during these years the adolescent is being asked to assume positions of role responsibility in the 'adult world'" (Smelser, 1980, p 13).

Of course, Erikson's most apparent and influential difference from Freud was his extension of psychological development beyond childhood. Although his concept of the identity crisis, occurring in late adolescence, is his most widely known contribution, his theory contributed to recent investigations of the "mid-life crisis" and similar issues in adulthood.

ERIKSON'S STAGE THEORY

Erikson proposed that eight stages described the pattern of personality development from infancy through old age. (In the sexist language commonplace at the time, Erikson unfortunately christened these "the eight stages of man.") At each stage, a psychosocial "crisis" (Erikson's term) faced the individual; this crisis—really, a choice point—led to subsequent development going in either one direction or another. A favorable resolution of the crisis leads to the acquisition of a virtue at that stage.

As is indigenous to stage theories, Erikson saw these choices as building on previous ones. His epigenesis principle would ask, for example, if a person chooses isolation as a way of resolving the crisis at Stage 6, how he or she develop generativity, instead of self-absorption, at Stage 7? We will illustrate the impact of the epigenetic principle as we explore each stage in sequence.

Stage 1: Trust Versus Mistrust

Erikson saw this stage as the foundation, and hence by far the most important stage (Dacey, 1982). Trust, he viewed in a broad sense—learning what to expect in the world. Acquisition of trust meant not so much a belief that the world is safe as that it is orderly and predictable. Hence, trust involves negative as well as positive expectation. Acquisition of trust means learning that a dangerous person can be trusted to be dangerous, just as much as it means that a care giver can be "trusted" to reappear, to provide (Dacey, 1982). In an interview with psychologist Richard I. Evans (1967, p. 15), Erikson stated: "There is a correspondence between your needs and your world, this is what I mean by basic trust." In contrast, irregularity and inconsistent care can lead to the child experiencing anxiety and insecurity, and hence mistrust.

Regularity in one's early environment is desirable but so too is variation. Erikson felt that the development of a favorable ratio of trust to mistrust was ideal, leading to the acquisition of the virtue of hope. Complete regularity and predictability would not prepare the child for the vicissitudes of life, so a small amount of mistrust was desirable. In his interview with Richard I. Evans, Erikson said, "I use Mistrust in the sense of a readiness for danger and an anticipation of discomfort" (Evans, 1967, p. 15). Thus each of the eight life crises involves conflict between two opposing characteristics. By suggesting that the successful resolution of each crisis should favor the first of the two characteristics but still incorporate the second to some degree, Erikson proposed that the presence of some mistrust is healthy.

Stage 2: Autonomy Versus Shame and Doubt

The task of children 18 months to 3 years of age is to gain control and mastery over their bodies. As Dacey (1982) notes, "Erikson agrees with other psychoanalysts that toilet training has far more important consequences in one's life than just control of one's bowels" (p. 40). If children are encouraged to explore their bodies and their social and physical worlds, some degree of self-confidence develops (Dacey, 1982). If, on the other hand, they are consistently criticized for their inability to control their bowels, they feel ashamed and come to doubt themselves. They become reluctant to test themselves. Erikson has stated: "If in some respects you have relatively more shame than autonomy, then you feel or act inferior all your life—or consistently counteract that feeling" (quoted in Evans, 1967, p. 20). Again, at this stage are reflected three basic aspects of Erikson's conception:

(1) At least at the early stages, the environment created by the care giver strongly influences the way the conflict is resolved.
(2) The resolution is not an "all-or-none;" some amount of the undesired choice—here shame and doubt—not only can occur, but has some healthy effects.
(3) Following the principle of epigenesis, an undesirable resolution may negatively affect the choice at the next stage. For example, a child possessing more shame and doubt than autonomy will be at a disadvantage at the next stage, when the task is to develop initiative.

Successful resolution of Stage 2 leads to accomplishment of the virtue of self-control and will.

Stage 3: Initiative Versus Guilt

Building on whatever degree of competence they have acquired in Stage 2 to control themselves, children ages three to five now discover that they can have some influence over others in the family and to become successful in manipulating their surroundings (Dacey, 1982). Children may ask questions in order to develop knowledge and skills; initiative results as they feel more comfortable in responding. But parents and others can make them feel inept, and hence guilt results. As opposed to shame in the earlier stage, guilt is an internally generated response to failure, and its importance at this stage, as a response, is that it denies the child the resources to deal with crisis at later ages.

It is at this age that the super-ego emerges; family members serve as role models for the acceptable actions. Dacey (1982) notes, "If these role models are capable, effective people, the child will develop a sense of personal initiative" (p. 40).

For Erikson, acquisition of a sense of purpose is the ideal accomplishment at Stage 3. Children will have learned that they have to work to achieve goals.

Stage 4: Industry Versus Inferiority

Choices at Stage 4 occur during the elementary-school years (ages 5-12). One interpretation of the task at this stage is how to go beyond models and learn the elementary technology of the culture (Dacey, 1982). Children begin to explore the neighborhood; they expand their horizons beyond their families. By "industry" as a desired resolution, Erikson, I think, means "industriousness," or learning to complete something. A sense of accomplishment in making and building should prevail. If not, the child may emerge with a life-long sense of inferiority. Once again, effects of an unfavorable resolution of earlier crises may appear. The child may not be able to be industrious because, in Erikson's words, he may "still want his mother more than he wants knowledge" (quoted by Dacey, 1982, p. 40). That is, children may consider their eager productivity merely as a device to please their teacher (i.e., a substitute mother) and not something desirable in its own right. Children may perform in order to be "good little helpers," rather than really achieving the ideal accomplishment of competence or workmanship (Dacey, 1982).

Stage 5: Identity Versus Role Confusion

Erikson invented the term *identity crisis* to signify the crucial importance of ego identity for entrance to adulthood. We are all aware that people strive for identity, for a coherent self-image or "persistent sameness within oneself" (Erikson, 1959, p. 102) in which a set of beliefs and values are all of one piece. Should the adolescent fail in this quest, the danger he or she faces is identity confusion.

This is not an easy task. Erikson saw that desirability of a moratorium period for at least part of the time between ages 12 and 18; during this "time-out" the adolescent has a chance to experiment with a variety of identities, without having to assume the responsibility of the consequences of any particular one (Dacey, 1982).

Repudiation of other identities is part of the successful resolution of this crisis. Previous identities such as "daddy's boy" or "mama's little girl" must be relinquished. But the endeavor may not go smoothly; for example, negative identities may have an impact. Erikson (1974) stated: "Every person and every group harbors a negative identity as the sum of all those identifications and identity fragments which the individual has to submerge in himself as undesirable or irreconcilable or which his group has taught him to perceive as the mark of fatal 'difference' in sex role or race, in class or religion" (p. 20). Sometimes teenagers actually choose to live their negative identities, at least for a while. Persons with negative identities adopt one pattern of behavior because they are rebelling against demands that they follow the opposite pattern. An example would be "a youth who joins a gang of shoplifters, not because he wants to steal, but because down deep he doubts his masculinity and seeks to prove through dangerous acts of theft that he is not a coward" (Dacey, 1982, p. 44).

The undesirable resolution, identity confusion, was seen by Erikson as an inability to make choices. The adolescent may see himself or herself as inconsistent, a trait not valued in our society. Erikson believed that gender identity was a central component of ego identity. By refusing to establish a clear sexual identity, the adolescent risks identity diffusion (Huyck & Hoyer, 1982, p. 213).

More extensive theorizing and research has emerged from this stage than any other in Erikson's theory. Roy Baumeister (1986) has identified two types of identity crisis: *identity deficit,* in which the self has not formed enough of an identity, and *identity conflict,* in which the self is over-defined and too many incompatible aspects of the self coexist. Furthermore, James Marcia (1966, 1980) has analyzed the process of identity development at this stage. He proposes that two discrete processes must be experienced before mature identity is attainable. First, the adolescent must experience a crisis, in the sense that treasured beliefs are questioned, threatened, reconsidered, perhaps abandoned, or reestablished with a firmer foundation. Such a crisis could occur with respect to one's religious beliefs, one's life style, one's sexual preference, one's occupational plans, or other fundamental values. Second, the person must make a choice; that is, there must be commitment. Not all teenagers have experienced these factors. Building on these two qualities of crisis and commitment, Marcia generated four types of identity status in adolescents:

Status 1. Identity confusion (or diffusion): No crisis has been experienced and no commitment has been made.

Status 2. Identity foreclosure: No crisis has been experienced, but the person has made a commitment to a certain identity, usually that of his or her parents, perhaps even forced on the adolescent by his or her parents. For example, we do not know if George Bush reflects foreclosure or identity achievement, but the dedication in his autobiography (Bush, with Gold, 1987) —To "my mother and father, whose values lit the way"—reflects the adoption of his parents' perspective on the world.

Status 3. Identity achievement: The adolescent has explored

BOX 3.1
Testing Marcia's Identity-Status Concept

Marcia's identity-status conceptualization has generated a large body of research (Marcia, 1980), directed mainly at discovering correlates of each of the identity statuses. For example, in the area of anxiety, Marcia (1967) found that persons in a moratorium status were the most anxious of the four statuses, caused, he speculated, because of their "in-crisis" position. The same study revealed that persons in a foreclosure status were the least anxious of the four groups. In reviewing the literature on self-esteem and identity status, Marcia (1980) reports that among men, both achievement and moratorium status individuals generally scored higher on measures of self-esteem than did those in the foreclosure and diffusion statuses, but that persons in the foreclosure and diffusion statuses were more liable to change their evaluations of themselves, both positively and negatively, in response to external feedback than were those in the other two statuses. Among women, those in a foreclosure status scored higher in self-esteem, while those in the moratorium and diffusion statuses generally scored lower. Foreclosure individuals endorsed authoritarian values more often than did any of the other identity statuses (Marcia, 1966, 1967; Marcia and Friedman, 1970). Neuber and Genthner (1977) reported that men and women in the achievement and moratorium categories, especially when contrasted with those in the diffusion status, tended to take more personal responsibility for their own lives. Several studies have found no differences in intelligence among the identity status (e.g., Marcia, 1966; Marcia & Friedman, 1970). When cognitive styles were investigated, persons in the foreclosure and diffusion statuses were more impulsive, responding more quickly and making more errors, and those in the achievement and moratorium statuses were more reflective (Waterman & Waterman, 1974). In a study of the interpersonal style of each of the statuses, Donovan (1975) reported that individuals in the diffusion status were generally withdrawn, felt out of place in the world, and characterized their parents as distant and misunderstanding, while those in the foreclosure group appeared to be happy and described their homes as loving and affectionate. Persons in the moratorium status were volatile, seemed to thrive on intense relationships and exploration of their worlds, and appeared to have a stake in being attractive and visible people. Donovan found only two individuals in the achievement status in his study, and he described them as demonstrating nondefensive strength with a capacity to care for others in a noncompulsive, nonbinding way. In discussing the outcomes of investigations on identity states and their correlates, Raskin (1984) points out that, in spite of the fact that the methods vary from study to study, most results support the hypotheses being tested, suggesting that identity status as a construct is rather robust. In addition, Bourne (1978) acknowledges that one of the major strengths of Marcia's approach is the abundance of research that it has stimulated. (From Ellett, 1986, pp. 9-11)

---

several possible identities (life styles, collections of values, and so on) for himself or herself, one has been chosen, and a commitment has been made to it.

The last of these, Status 4, is clearly, for Marcia and for Erikson, the most desirable. It would produce the ideal accomplishment at this stage, the virtue of fidelity. Erikson is adamant about the validity of such a resolution; he has stated: "I would go further and claim that we have almost an instinct for fidelity—meaning that when you reach a certain age you can and must learn to be faithful to some ideological view" (quoted in Evans, 1967, p. 30). (See Box 3.1 for a summary of empirical research on Marcia's four identity statuses.)

A second type of theorizing and research generated by Erikson's identity stage is reflected in the work of Dan P. McAdams (1985, 1987). In contrast to Marcia's emphasis on the *process* of identity formation, McAdams examines the *outcome*. His main thesis is that "identity looks like a story and that, like all stories in literature and life, identity can be understood in terms of setting, scene, character, plot, and theme" (McAdams, 1987, p. 16). McAdams capitalizes on Erikson's (1959) conception that identity is a configuration of sorts; he proposes that this configuration takes the form of a narrative that integrates a number of identity elements, thus forming a life story.

Stage 6: Intimacy and Solidarity Versus Isolation

Moving beyond identity, persons in their twenties face the task of developing intimate relationships with others. Erikson proposed that intimacy should include mutuality of orgasm with a loved partner of the other sex with whom one is able and willing to share a mutual trust and with whom one is able and willing to regulate the cycles of work, procreation, and recreation (Erikson, 1963, p. 266). That value judgments abound in Erikson's conception is apparent. But for Erikson, intimacy is more than sexual closeness. In his interview with Richard I. Evans (1967, p. 48) he provided a useful definition: "Intimacy is really the ability to fuse your identity with someone else's without the fear that you are going to lose something yourself." Persons who have achieved intimacy can accomplish the virtue of fidelity, that is, they can commit themselves to a relationship and have the ethical strength to abide by such commitments even if sacrifices and compromises are called for. Erikson was fond of Freud's response to the question: What should a normal person be able to do well? "Lieben" and "arbeiten,'" or love and work.

The other resolution to the crisis at this stage, which Erikson sometimes called distantiation, is a readiness to isolate ourselves from others when we feel threatened by their behavior.

Erikson's distinction at this stage has been operationalized by Orlofsky, Marcia, and Lesser (1973), who identified five intimacy statuses: intimate, preintimate, stereotyped relationships, isolate, and pseudointimate. Whitbourne and Weinstock (1979) added a sixth status, merger, accounting for the situation in which individuals who have not achieved any individual identities form intimate relationships to compensate for their own lack of focus.

Stage 7: Generativity Versus Self-Absorption and Stagnation

Although Erikson proposed that the next stage spanned the broad range of ages of 25 to 65, the crisis would seem to occur in the thirties or forties. Once a person has achieved certain goals in life—marriage, seeing his or children develop, establishing a niche in the occupational world—there is a temptation to become self-centered. The individual may become bored, self-indulgent, and unable to contribute to society's welfare. He or she falls prey to stagnation. In Erikson's words, such people often indulge themselves as though they were "their own only child."

In contrast, generativity is the ability to be useful to ourselves and society. A person's productivity, at this stage, means being helpful to others; generativity is driven by a voluntary feeling of obligation to care for others. In the broadest sense, it is a reaching out, transmitting a concern for the next generation. It goes beyond caring for one's own children; the issue is now that of taking responsibility in the adult world. Erikson later said he used the term "generativity" because "I mean everything that is generated from generation to generation: children, products, ideas, *and* works of art" (quoted in Evans, 1967, p. 51). The achievement of generativity leads to the virtue of care, which includes "the care to do" something, to "care for" somebody or something, to "take care of" that which needs protection and attention, and "to take care not to do something destructive" (quoted in Evans, 1967, p. 53). McAdams, Ruetzel, and Foley (1986) have proposed that generativity reflects a combination of the needs for agency (expanding and asserting the self) and for communion (merging the self with a larger environment of which the self is a part) (Bakan, 1966). Generativity permits the mature adult to express power and intimacy at the same time.

Stage 8: Ego Integrity Versus Despair

The last crisis, according to Erikson, is coming to terms with one's own life. If integrity occurs, the person sees his or her life as well spent. The attainment of integrity is reflected in older persons who are reasonably satisfied with the achievements they have attained.

On the other hand, if despair is the resolution of the crisis at this stage, the person feels that he or she has made many wrong decisions (or no decisions at all). Life has lacked integration. Despair is often associated with anger that the person won't have another chance. There may be disgust, and contempt for others that disguises contempt for oneself.

ERIKSON'S CASE STUDIES

As a clinician, Erikson sought to study individual lives. The ways that specific persons chose to resolve the crisis of life provided opportunities to test his theory. Erikson prepared detailed biographical analyses of two internationally known persons, Martin Luther and Mahatma Gandhi, who—he concluded—illustrated choice points at two important stages in adulthood. In examining these analyses at this point, we anticipate the approach of psychobiography, examined in more detail in Chapter 4.

Erikson on Luther

Martin Luther was born on November 10, 1483. His father, Hans Luther, was a coal miner, who gradually achieved a moderate degree of prosperity. However, Martin Luther's memories of his childhood were of poverty and an upbringing that was strict and perhaps even harsh.

BOX 3.2
Luther and the Practice of Indulgences

An article commemorating the 400th anniversary of Luther's birth states:

Albrecht of Brandenburg, a German nobleman who had previously acquired a dispensation from the Vatican to become a priest while under age and to head two dioceses at the same time, wanted yet another favor from the Pope: the powerful archbishop's chair in Mainz. Pope Leo X, a profligate spender who needed money to build St. Peter's Basilica, granted the appointment—for 24,000 gold pieces, roughly equal to the annual imperial revenues in Germany. It was worth it. Besides being a rich source of income, the Mainz post brought Albrecht a vote for the next Holy Roman Emperor, which could be sold to the highest bidder.

In return, Albrecht agreed to initiate the sale of indulgences in Mainz. Granted for good works, indulgences were papally controlled dispensations drawn from an eternal 'treasury of merits' built up by Christ and the saints; the Church taught that they would help pay the debt of 'temporal punishment' due in purgatory for sins committed by either the penitent or any deceased person." (Ostling, 1983, p. 100)

In 1501, at the age of 17 or 18, he entered the university. He was obviously a brilliant student and his father hoped that he would become a wealthy lawyer.

In the middle of the spring semester of his first term in law school in Erfurt, on his way home, the 21-year-old Luther was caught in a tremendous thunderstorm and, in sudden fear of not surviving, made a vow to Saint Anne that if he survived he would become a monk (Spitz, 1973). Thus, despite his father's objections, he entered a monastery, took his vows, and was ordained as a priest in 1507. The following year he began to lecture at the recently founded university at Wittenberg.

Several years later he visited Rome on church business. Although he was overcome with emotion as he approached the center of Christendom, he much later was to talk about the upset and trauma at seeing how worldly and ostentatious Rome was. Despite his growing antagonism with the deviations of the Church, he progressed through the University hierarchy; in 1511, at age 28, he was appointed a professor at Wittenberg. But his frustrations with the Church came to a head in 1517 when, at the age of 33, he posted his 95 theses attacking the sale of indulgences by Church authorities. Word immediately spread throughout Europe of his action. An example of indulgences is provided in Box 3.2.

Luther refused to obey orders from the Church and began to attack the Pope, Leo X. The latter issued a statement condemning Luther's heresies; Luther publicly burned his copy of the message. Luther was henceforth excommunicated and the emperor of the Holy Roman Empire ordered him to appear for censure.

But Luther refused to recant. He spent the remaining 30 years of his life teaching, preaching, writing, and establishing what came to be called the Lutheran church. In his mature years, his productivity was immense. He wrote the equivalent of a pamphlet-length essay every two weeks; he traveled extensively, gave many lectures, as well as preaching every week. In the Peasants War (1524-1525) he supported the princes against the rebellious peasants, and thus lost much of the support he had had from the populace. At the age of 42, he married a former nun Katherine von Bora; they were to have six children before Luther died on February 18, 1546, at the age of 62.

Erikson used Luther as an example of the place of a moratorium period in forming an identity. In his interpretation of Luther's life,

Young man Luther: A study of psychoanalysis and history (1958), Erikson focused first on Luther's abrupt religious conversion as a young man and his decision to become a monk, thus bringing his own potential career as a lawyer to a sudden halt. As Roazen (1976) observes, "His training as monk was a form of 'indoctrination'; yet only that discipline gave Luther the breathing space, in Erikson's view, to find himself" (p. 78).

Psychoanalysis—and Eriksonian analysis—puts emphasis on the importance of a single event in the formation of character. In his book on Luther, Erikson has chosen the so-called fit in the choir as the pivotal event. During his early or mid-twenties, Luther supposedly fell to the floor of the choir loft in the monastery, raving, "Non sum! Non sum!" that is, "It isn't me" (or "I am not," depending upon which translation one prefers). Crosby and Crosby (1981), in a critical evaluation of Erikson's book, note that "the occasion which set off this apparent fit may have been the reading of Mark 9:17 where a father offered his son to Jesus: 'And one of the multitude answered and said, "Master, I have brought unto thee my son, which hath a dumb spirit".' To Erikson this event reveals a crisis in the development of Luther's identity—a protest by Luther of what he was not in order to break through to what he was to be" (p. 211). Erikson sees the fit as "both unconscious obedience to the father and implied rebellion against the monastery" (p. 38). That is, at the point at which this fit occurred, Luther "was, in short, at the crossroads of obedience to his early father and to his heavenly father. It was, in Erikson's famous phrase, a crisis of identity" (Crosby & Crosby, 1981, p. 211).

Others have interpreted this event somewhat differently, while still seeing it as reflecting part of an identity crisis. Dacey (1982) concludes that "Luther's greatness as a leader, says Erikson, was built partly on the enormous anger and unresolved conflict he experienced in his late teens. Luther's decision to become a monk was the assuming of a negative identity. The choice expressed his rejection of 15th century society rather than his devotion to Catholicism" (p. 45). The earlier decision to become a monk was an example of negative identity, and for Dacey, the "fit in the choir" is an indication of how difficult it was for him to be who he was.

But did the "fit in the choir" even occur? Luther never mentioned it. The only references to it were in publications that appeared after his death, and most of those were written by avowed enemies who might have been tempted to discredit Luther's stability (Stannard, 1980, p. 22).

For example, Spitz (1973) recounts that "the story is told, however, by Luther's archenemy and dedicated defamer, Johannes Cochlaeus, in his commentary on Luther's life and works published three years after Luther's death, or more that four decades after the event. It is told, moreover, to prove that Luther had secret commerce with a demon. Cochlaeus's whole book is so full of falsehoods that Cardinal Alexander warned against its publication, fearing that the reaction would make it counter-productive" (p. 196).

Erikson recognizes the weakness of this evidence; at one place he calls it an "alleged event." But he also says the fact that Luther never mentioned it may be a result of his having amnesia for the event.

Recall that if the "fit in the choir" occurred, it took place when Martin Luther was around 22 to 25 years of age. It was not until a decade later, in 1517, that Luther nailed his 95 theses to the church door in Wittenberg. However, Erikson felt that it was characteristic of original thinkers to experience long delays in reacting. This decision to protest against the Church and offer a different theology—as well as Luther's greatness as a leader—is partly based on the enormous anger and unresolved conflict he experienced in adolescence. Roazen (1976) put it this way: "Then around the age of thirty—an important age for gifted people with a delayed identity crisis—Luther's distinctive theology emerges" (p. 79).

Monkhood provided an extended moratorium. As his identity evolved, Luther was able to devote himself unequivocally to God, and turn all his anger toward the Pope.

Why so much anger? Because of the harsh treatment he received as a child. Erikson claims that Luther's father was brutal, malicious, and tyrannical, that Hans Luther beat young Martin. Erikson even interprets Luther's "harsh" image of the Heavenly Father as a projection of his image of his earthly father. But Erikson also admits that there are almost no facts about Martin Luther's childhood. According to Stannard (1980), there are only two mentions of beatings that Martin Luther received as a child, one by his father and one by his mother. And Spitz (1973) responds that "The idea that Luther's father was harsh with him as a regular thing is based upon one saying in the Tischreden of May 1532. . . . 'My father once whipped me so hard that I fled from him and felt ugly toward him [or, became sadly resentful toward him] until he gradually got me accustomed to him again " (p. 191). Furthermore, Spitz concludes that "Hans Luther was not harsh, drunken, or tyrannous, but rather tender and pious as well as stern and ambitious for himself and his son" (pp. 193-194).

Why was Luther great? For Erikson, it was his struggle "to lift his individual patienthood to the level of a universal one and to try to solve for all what he could not solve for himself alone" (quoted in Roazen, 1976, p. 83). Erikson acknowledges that Luther was a gifted but a troubled young man "who had to create his own 'cause' on which to focus his fidelity in the Roman Catholic world as it was then" (quoted in Evans, 1967, p. 42).

Erikson on Gandhi

For another of his book-length psychological analyses Erikson chose as his subject, Gandhi, the advocate of nonviolent protest in India. But here the focus was on generativity rather than identity; Erikson sought to understand the development of Gandhi's protest as an "ideological innovation in the context of his middle age" (Roazen, 1976, p. 122). As indicated before, the characteristic crisis of mid-life is that of generativity versus stagnation, with generativity defined as a concern for establishing and guiding the next genera-tion. Central to generativity is the orientation toward *care,* and in writing about generativity in *Gandhi's Truth,* Erikson (1969) reveals how it can be manifested in a bold, caring action:

> From the moment in January of 1915 when Gandhi set forth on a pier reserved for important arrivals in Bombay, he behaved like a man who knew the nature and the extent of India's calamity and that of his own fundamental mission. A mature man of middle age has not only made up his mind as to what, in the various compartments of his life, he does and does not *care for,* he is also firm in his vision of what he *will* and *can* take *care of.* He takes as his baseline what he irreducibly is and reaches out for what only he can, and therefore, *must do.* (p. 255, italics in original)

As the critical event in Gandhi's life, Erikson chose the textile strike of March 1918, the Ahmedabad incident. It was the first time that Gandhi fasted over a political issue, in order to publicize the fact that the textile workers toiled long hours in the mills and were pitifully underpaid. A year later, he led the first Indian nationwide civil disobedience. Gandhi was about 50 years of age; he was "in between things" in 1918. By fasting, his personal restraint became a force in itself, and clearly fasting is the opposite of Erikson's negative choice, stagnation, which is defined as indulging oneself to excess.

Gandhi's act of passive resistance was successful. Eventually the mill owners acceded, and the workers' wages were increased.

Interestingly enough, Gandhi, in his own autobiography, minimizes the importance of the Ahmedabad incident, as do most historians and biographers of Gandhi's life. If asked to pick the critical event in the formation of his character, most experts would select the shocking incident at Pietermaritzburg, South Africa, in 1893. Gandhi was 24 at the time. He had just arrived in South Africa a week before. After growing up in India, he had gone to England for training as an attorney. Now dressed in a suit, London cravat, and a stiff collar, he was traveling to his first job, seated in a first-class railroad car going from Durban to Pretoria, South Africa. At this time Gandhi was very conventional, very concerned about his appearance and pleasing others. But apparently he did not know about the rules about segregation of the races in South Africa. A white man entered his railroad compartment, and demanded that he leave. "Move your black ass back to third class or I will have you thrown off," he said. The police came, grabbed him, and rudely deposited him on a railroad-station platform, where he spent a cold night. This one act, Gandhi often said, changed his life. Gandhi remained in South Africa for 21 years, organizing the citizens to combat racial prejudice.

A Critique of Erikson's Theory

Erikson's approach has the virtue of being comprehensive and life span in its orientation. But it is not without its limitations. For example, it seems rife with value judgments. Is Erikson describing what *is* or what he hopes should be for good adjustment (Dacey, 1982)?

Furthermore, concepts are seldom if ever defined precisely

(Huyck & Hoyer, 1982, p. 216), and it is difficult to translate the concepts into operational definitions. In fact, Erikson is inconsistent about the necessity of epigenesis and the time-bound resolution of conflicts. Smelser (1980) observes:

> Erikson's model of adult development is a complex mixture of determinancy and indeterminancy (Erikson, 1950). On the side of determinancy, he envisions a definitive sequence of stages which follow on and build on one another. In addition, he suggests definite age ranges for the various stages of the life from infancy to old age, though—on the side of indeterminancy—he does not fix exact or unvarying chronological ages for each stage or the transitions between them. His theory of development is also lent determinancy by its principle of epigenesis—the principle that for a given developmental process to transpire, others have to have transpired before it, and that the resolution of any given prior crisis is not fixed for all time but must develop further at all subsequent stages. Yet at the same time the principle of epigenesis is not a completely fixed one; each developmental stage has a measure of its own autonomous dynamics." (p. 19)

That is, issues can surface again later. Elkind (1982) comments that the problem of basic trust versus mistrust "arises again at each successive stage of development" (p. 15). Questions of identity, thought to be resolved in the late teens, may resurface in the 40-year-old faced with a divorce (See Box 3.3 for an example.)

One salient type of critique of Erikson's theory is to question whether further stages are necessary. Several stages (particularly Stages 7 and 8) cover broad age periods. Several elaborations of Stage-7 issues are described in Chapter 5, in a section on the newer stage theories of Roger Gould and Daniel Levinson. Related to this criticism is the question whether the current stages cover all the relevant issues in personality development. Ryff and Heincke (1983) identified complexity along with generativity as a key personality issue of middle age. Jane Loevinger's (1976) construct of ego development proposes that with the maturity of middle adulthood the person may establish a highly differentiated view of life's goals and issues.

Greatest scrutiny to the adequacy of Erikson's last stage has been carried out by Robert Peck (1968), who has suggested a modification of this stage.

BOX 3.3
The Recurrence of Crises

Are conflicts resolved once and for all? As Elkind (1982) reports, "A child who comes through infancy with a vital sense of trust can still have his sense of mistrust activated at a later stage if, say, his parents are divorced and separated under acrimonious circumstances" (p. 15).

Elkind notes that this point was brought home to him in a very direct way by a 4-year-old patient he saw in a court clinic: "He was being seen at the court clinic because his adoptive parents who had him for six months, now wanted to give him back to the agency. They claimed that he was cold and unloving, took things, and could not be trusted. He was indeed a cold and apathetic boy, but with good reason. About a year after his illegitimate birth, he was taken away from his mother, who had a drinking problem, and was shunted back and forth among several foster homes. Initially he had tried to relate to the persons in his foster homes, but the relationships never had a chance to develop because he was moved at just the wrong times. In the end he gave up trying to reach out to others, because the inevitable separations hurt too much.

"Like the burned child who dreads the flame, this emotionally burned child shunned the pain of emotional involvement. He had trusted his mother, but now he trusted no one. Only years of devoted care and patience could now undo the damage that had been done to this child's sense of trust" (p. 15).

Within the eighth stage, Peck has elaborated two broad periods—middle age and old age—and within each, several "crises" (Troll, 1982, p. 19). Among middle-aged "crises," according to Peck, are:

(1) learning an appreciation of wisdom versus an appreciation of physical powers;
(2) learning to socialize human relationships rather than sexualize human relationships;
(3) developing cathectic flexibility versus cathectic impoverishment (That is, Peck felt it was valuable to be able to shift emotional investments from one person to another and from one activity to another);
(4) maintaining mental flexibility versus mental rigidity.

In contrast, Peck saw other crises during old age:

(1) ego differentiation versus work-role preoccupation. (Here Peck is referring to the desirability that retired persons shift their value systems so as to redefine their self-worth in terms of something other than their occupation.)
(2) body transcendence versus body preoccupation.
(3) ego transcendence versus ego preoccupations. As Peck, 1968, puts it: "The constructive way of living the late years might be defined in this way: to live so generously and unselfishly that the prospect of personal death—the right of the ego, it might be called—looks and feels less important than the secure knowledge that one has built for a broader, longer future than any one ego could ever encompass" (p. 91).

Perhaps that is a fitting final word on Erikson's encompassing theory too; we can view it constructively as not a final word, but a building block for the theory and observations that follow.

4

PSYCHOBIOGRAPHY AND PERSONALITY DEVELOPMENT IN ADULTHOOD

Chapter 3 portrayed Erik Erikson's analysis of life-span personality development through his concept of crises, or choice points. Eriksonian theory assumes that our active choices can affect the subsequent section of our lives and the adaptive styles we manifest. But how do others—watching our struggles from the outside— conceptualize and explain our reactions to crises and our choices? Biographers, writers of "personality profiles" in magazines, and even each of us who cares about our friends must consider this demand to explain. Two recent books portray contrasting solutions to the dilemma faced by the person who must describe and demarcate the life of another individual.

Bearing the Cross (Garrow, 1986) is a long (800 pages), detailed, heavily researched biography of Martin Luther King, Jr., with emphasis on that part of King's life beginning with the Montgomery bus boycott and ending with his murder in April, 1968. The author, David Garrow, took seven years to write the book, and in the process interviewed 200 people and incorporated into his narrative the contents of 500 interviews carried out by others. *Bearing the Cross* is a valuable, chronologically based description of the activities in the last 12 years of King's life.

But critics have consistently concluded that a much-needed integrative view of King is lost in the mass of detail provided by this book. Martin Luther King, Jr., was—even more than most of us—a frustratingly complex person whose life choices insisted on explanation. On the one hand, he was a man with vision, with the courage and character to combat immoral laws and with the galvanizing oratorical skills to rally others behind him. At the same time he was a philanderer whose sexual promiscuity placed the achievement of his goals in great jeopardy. At periods during the height of his effectiveness he drank heavily. How do we explain the psychological development and behavior of this complicated man? One of the book's reviewers notes that "Mr. Garrow presents the reader with the most complete dossier yet published on the life King led in hotel rooms and in his hideaway apartment in Atlanta. Yet he seems reluctant to integrate this material into a deeper understanding of why King continued his libertine pursuits even when it became clear that they might be used to destroy him" (Raines, 1986, p. 34). This all-too-vulnerable human being deserves some theory-based explanation of his behavior.

THE DEFINITION OF PSYCHOHISTORY AND PSYCHOBIOGRAPHY

Psychohistory seeks to fill the deficits in the above analysis. Erikson defined this approach as "the study of individual and collective life with the combined methods of psychoanalysis and history" (1974, p. 13). In a valuable review that serves as a structure for this chapter, Crosby and Crosby (1981) state: "We define psychohistory as a form of history which explicitly uses the concepts, principles, and theories of psychology to enhance our understanding of particular people and events in the past" (p. 196). Technically, *psychohistory* refers to the analysis of some historical event or phenomenon (such as the Salem witchcraft trials in Colonial New England, or the rise of Nazism in Germany) or the explanation of a particular culture or nationality. In contrast, *psychobiography* is usually reserved for the psychological exploration of a given individual's life, such as Martin Luther King, Jr., or—as we saw in Chapter 3—Martin Luther. (But, just to complicate things, "psychohistory" occasionally is used as a generic label for either the focus on events or on an individual's life.)

Since psychobiography's mission is in keeping with the thrust of this book—and because the first and most influential psychobiographical analyses were constructed by Freud and by Erikson—this chapter is directed toward illustrating the benefits and limitations of such an approach.

If some analysts of an individual's life, like author David Garrow, may be faulted for not supplying a structure for explaining their subject's life, might others have the opposite limitation, in that they go overboard in providing explanations that rest more on speculation and assumption than on data and observation? At least for some reviewers, a second recent book generates such an example.

Bernhard Goetz received instant, nationwide publicity as the "subway vigilante" when he shot four black youths in New York City a few days before Christmas in 1984. Two years later, a San Francisco Bay area psychotherapist and sociologist, Lillian B. Rubin (1986), offered a book-length biography and diagnosis of Goetz. Here are some excerpts from her book:

> As he struggled, as all adolescent boys must, with his developing sense of himself and his maleness, the issues of sexuality and identity would have been even more difficult for him than for the ordinary teenager. (p. 140)

> Unquestionably, Bernie's continuing problems with authority were born in childhood when he had to fight so hard to maintain some sense of his own integrity, his own autonomy. (p. 141)

The validity of these interpretations rests upon their sources. And these are limited because the author never interviewed Bernhard Goetz (who refused the invitation), nor his former wife. (The author did talk to Goetz's sisters.) It is true that some reviewers have been tolerant of Rubin's sweeping interpretations; Wray Herbert (1987, p. 80) wrote: "Like all psychohistories it is somewhat conjectural, relying heavily on distant memories of secondary sources." But others have been quite critical: "Rubin sometimes writes as if she had gotten inside his head" (Foreman, 1986, p. 3c), and "Some of it seems plausible and some of it is silly" (Johnson, 1986, p. 31). The latter reviewer observes, "For example, she speculates that there might have been a connection between the $5 that one of the teenagers asked Mr. Goetz for just before the shootings and the $5 that Mr. Goetz's father was alleged to have paid to fondle two young boys in a sordid scandal when his son was an impressionable 12-year-old" (Johnson, 1986, p. 31). We do not know for sure. But how often does psychobiography, in its quest for an explanation, let speculations and selective evidence override scholarship and a balanced review of the facts? We will see.

CAUSAL EXPLANATIONS OF INDIVIDUALS

The introduction to this chapter has implied that psycho-biography seeks to capture the essence of an individual's personality development. Crosby and Crosby (1981) classify psychobiographies as reflecting two types of explanations: *Causal* and *coherent whole*. Causal explanations are "those explanations which seek to account for adult behavior in terms of childhood experiences" (p. 199), as Rubin has done with Bernhard Goetz. In contrast, coherent whole explanations "aim to create a unified whole out of apparently divergent bits of data as they relate to the actions of persons or groups" (p. 199). To a limited degree, Garrow tried to do the latter in his biography of M. L. King, Jr.; at least he provided those "divergent bits of data" from which a composite portrait might be painted.

Generating either type of explanation is a challenging task but the development of a causal explanation is more so, because it asks *why* is the the person the way he or she is or was? In seeking to establish links between childhood experiences and adult behavior—a fundamental assumption of psychoanalytic theory described in Chapter 2—the quest for causal explanations faces several kinds of difficulties, particularly if the subject of the psycho-biography lived in earlier times. Especially with these circumstances, psychobiographers are forced to rely on letters, diaries, auto-biographies, memoirs, and similar personal documents. (The use of these in understanding personality development in adulthood is further described in Chapter 12.) And such materials usually devote scant attention to childhood. But even when the subject is alive, those people who were relevant to the subject's early years may no longer be.

Without access to direct evidence about the purportedly vital childhood experiences, psychobiographers have sometimes capitalized on what Crosby and Crosby (1981) justifiably label as two questionable devices. First, "they often substitute generalized clinical studies for the emotional states of their specific subjects. In so doing, they misapply the legitimate use made by analysts of clinical studies as supplementary guides to the therapeutic dialogue" (Crosby & Crosby, 1981, p. 200). Second, psychobiographers have relied too heavily on the psychoanalytic concept of the unconscious in explaining the sources of personality development. The following sections provide illustrations of these excesses.

Adolf Hitler and Causal Explanations

His evil regime caused the death of six million Jews and a devastating world war. Not surprisingly, Adolf Hitler has been one of the most frequently analyzed subjects by psychobiographers; one of the most comprehensive is a book by R.G.L. Waite (1977). In summary, Waite concludes that Hitler's adult behavior—his speeches, his late-night monologues—reflect an oral fixation, strongly lacerated with aggression. But, he proposes, Hitler also possessed anal character traits, including a compulsion for cleanliness and an obsessive concern about time.

But Waite then reasons backward in time, from the oral behaviors of adulthood, suggesting that there may have been serious interference in the feeding process when Hitler was an infant. And because of the anal character trait, Waite claims, it "may be assumed" that Hitler's mother was "particularly rigorous" in toilet training her children. But—regrettably—we don't know anything about Hitler's toilet training. Waite's interpretation remains unproved.

Furthermore, Waite relies heavily on the unconscious as an explanation of Hitler's behavior. As Crosby and Crosby (1981) conclude, "Of course, Hitler's behavior may well have been unconsciously motivated. But we simply have no way of knowing; we lack the vital evidence" (pp. 202-203).

As observers seek to understand Hitler's orientation, a major question centers on the source of his anti-Semitic feelings. In Waite's explanation, the family doctor, Edward Bloch, plays a prominent role. Dr. Bloch, a Jew, tried to treat the breast cancer that developed in Hitler's mother, but he failed, and she died. Hitler was a teenager at the time; he developed feelings of ambivalence toward the doctor, who also had begun to serve as a kind of father substitute for Hitler. The youth, according to Waite, appreciated the doctor's efforts but resented his failure. Perhaps also, what the young Hitler perceived as the doctor's "intimacies" with his mother—the frequent examination of her breasts—may have stimulated Oedipal feelings in her son. Waite concludes that he came to see Dr. Bloch as a "brutal mutilator" of his mother after the doctor performed a mastectomy. (Dr. Bloch had also tried to treat her with iodoform, which caused her to experience a severe and painful burning sensation.) But all this is speculation, and not very parsimonious speculation, at that. It could be just as plausibly argued that the function of Hitler's anti-Semitism was to manipulate and mobilize the feelings of the German populace and solidify Hitler's Nazi political party.

The criticism of Waite's approach does not mean that the search for understanding of Hitler's development should be forsaken—only that more sophisticated analyses are necessary. As Cocks and Crosby (1987) conclude, "Historians have turned away from the early easy conviction that Hitler could be understood in crude psychopathological terms alone; they have become increasingly sophisticated about the fascinating mixture of the rational and irrational, the conscious and unconscious within Hitler" (p. xi).

The "Why" of Richard Nixon

Richard Nixon continues to fascinate the American news media; a *Newsweek* cover in 1986 proclaimed, "He's back!" Nixon has been the subject of at least four book-length psychobiographies, as well as innumerable chapters and articles. As the topic for psychological analysis, Nixon possesses the virtue of being a contemporary figure, long in the public eye, and hence the focus of much written material, including observations and reminiscences by his associates and family. Nixon himself has written two books of memoirs, plus several other books. And, of course, there exists all kinds of official records, including even the White House tapes!

Alan Elms, a judicious exponent of the psychobiographical approach, calls President Nixon's informal farewell to his staff, upon his resignation in August 1974, "a psychobiographer's dream" Elms (1976) observes:

> With sweat and tears streaming down his face, Nixon praised the staff for not having robbed the public till and pitied himself for having to 'find a way to pay my taxes.' He remembered 'my old man' who moved from job to job and who sold 'the poorest lemon ranch in California ... before they found oil on it' but who was nonetheless 'a great man, because he did his job and every job counts up to the hilt regardless of what happens.' (p. 103)

Nixon said the following about his mother in that speech:

> Nobody will ever write a book probably about my mother. Well, I guess all of you would say this about your mother; my mother was a saint. And I think of her two boys dying of tuberculosis, nursing four others in order that she could take care of my older brother for three years in Arizona and seeing each of them die. Yes, she will have no books written about her. But she was a saint.

Elms (1976) points out that this was followed by "an odd combination of self-deprecation and implied self-praise" (p. 104) and then finally a set of "concluding homilies":

> Because the greatness comes not only when things go always good for you, but the greatness comes when you're really tested, when you take some knocks and disappointments, when sadness comes . . . Always give your best. Never get discouraged. Never be petty. Always remember, others may hate you, but those who hate you don't win unless you hate them. And then you destroy yourself.

An ironic message, coming as it does from Richard Nixon, we would all probably conclude. Elms proposes that "If a skilled psychobiographer had sat down to write a farewell speech for Nixon that would incorporate in dramatic form the major psychological themes of Nixon's life, he would have written just such a speech. That Nixon did it himself, apparently with little advance preparation and under great emotional stress, makes it one of the prize psychobiographical documents of modern times" (p. 104).

Whence came these themes? Psychobiographers looking for causal explanations concentrate on Nixon's childhood. Richard Nixon was the second son of a hard-working but frequently unsuccessful father and a Quaker mother. The latter, Hannah Nixon, everyone agrees, was the major influence on his life.

The death of children is a recurrent theme in Nixon's own childhood. He was almost killed in a wagon accident when he was three, and a serious illness almost led to his death at the age of 4. Again, during his senior year in high school, he was quite ill. (Yet as President he claimed that he had never been sick a day in his life.) His younger brother Arthur died suddenly of tubercular encephalitis when Richard Nixon was 12. Furthermore, Harold, his older brother, also died of tuberculosis when Richard was 19, after a long struggle in which his mother, hoping for a recovery, took Harold to Arizona for two years (not three, as President Nixon said in his farewell speech).

Nixon grew up in a small town in Southern California, and remained there to go to Whittier College, a small Quaker school. He once noted that Whittier "did not offer a course in political science in the years I spent there." (He added that he had received a good education, but that if he *had* been "exposed" to a political science course, he might have defeated John Kennedy in the 1960 presidential election.) But Fawn Brodie (1981), one of his psychobiographers, examined his college transcript and discovered that he had completed courses titled "Government," "The American Constitution," and "International Relations and International Law."

Richard Nixon worked hard in college, and continued to do so at Duke University Law School. But his career as a lawyer began with disappointment. Denied jobs with the Federal Bureau of Investigation or with any prominent New York City law firm, he was forced to return, shamefaced, to his hometown. There, his mother persuaded a family friend to take him into a local law firm (Elms, 1976).

After practicing law for five years in Whittier, Nixon migrated to the East Coast again, in 1942, shortly after World War II began. After struggling for eight unhappy months as a low-level government bureaucrat, he joined the wartime navy and served as a supply officer in the South Pacific. Returning to southern California at the end of World War II, he was persuaded to run for the U.S. Congress, thus initiating his 30-year political career.

The psychobiographers who seek to explain the "why" of Nixon's personality development range from fairly conventional to exceedingly negative interpretations. One of the most substantial is that by Bruce Mazlish (1973), a historian trained in psychoanalysis. As we would expect, Mazlish chooses to emphasize the influence from Nixon's early family life, by noting that Richard adopted one set of characteristics from his mother, and one set from his father— with a resulting clash between them. His "Protestant ethic" traits— emphasis on planning, hard work, and persistence—came from his mother, but Mazlish also describes the young Nixon as identifying with his father in a number of ways, including his love of argument, his interest in politics, his being a "loner," and his fear of failure.

Mazlish hypothesized that Nixon "sought to redeem his father by being successful" and used his mother's admirable traits in the service of that goal. He also identified more with his father's fundamentalist version of Quakerism than with his mother's pacifist and relatively liberal version. But the conflict between these led him to feel ambivalent about peace and war throughout his life.

In Mazlish's interpretation, Richard Nixon's brothers played important developmental roles in negative ways, because they aroused the "natural emotions of sibling rivalry." Each took their mother way from Richard, in one way or another. The deaths of two his brothers must have generated powerful emotional responses; Mazlish speculates that these were fear of getting tuberculosis and of dying, along with strong guilt feelings over having survived after experiencing the resentment toward them while they were alive.

Mazlish went on to speculate that Nixon's later pattern of seeking out crises—or at least basking in the glory of having coped with each crisis—was "partly motivated by the need to confront his death fears, repeatedly and constantly." Nixon's own childhood illnesses presumably intensified this fear of death. As a child he not only was severely ill, but he was clumsy and socially inept; he also apparently developed the notion that he wasn't terribly bright.

Mazlish concludes that Nixon reflects an almost classic case of compensation for inferiority. Nixon is a man with "an insecurely held self," driven to succeed and possessed by a need to "create crises, as a means of testing himself and assuring himself greater personal support."

Mazlish's conclusions might appear to some to be overgeneralized, but the other psychobiographers of Nixon have generated interpretations that are even more extreme. Eli Chesen (1973), a Phoenix psychiatrist, was aware of Mazlish's book and criticized it as too much of a classical psychoanalytic interpretation for the available data to support (p. 21). He also was critical of Mazlish's "tenuous theories of sibling rivalry followed by sibling guilt" (p. 69).

Chesen diagnosed Richard Nixon as a standard obsessive-compulsive neurotic whose every action is fueled by anxiety and fears about his own weakness. He described Nixon's father as a quite violent man who frightened Richard by his wrathful and authoritarian ways. Chesen portrayed Nixon's mother Hannah as loving but with an iron will and a sense of ambition. Richard Nixon, in this view, identified more with his mother than with his father, and her nature as a domineering matriarch led to "significant feelings of uncertainty about himself as a male" (p. 77), and an exaggerated concern with the task of proving himself manly. Chesen concluded that Nixon moved to "shut the world out" and seek total control over every situation because unconsciously he was helpless, dominated, and weak but didn't want anyone to know it.

Hostility is the key concept in the explanation of Nixon's personality development offered by David Abrahamsen (1977), a psychoanalyst who has also written extensively on the criminal mind. Nixon's unhappy childhood left him with such a reservoir of anger, bitterness, and repressed hostilities, and he was so guilt-ridden because of his unresolved Oedipal feelings toward his mother that "ultimately he willed his own destruction in the Watergate affair" (quoted by Anderson, 1977, p. 5). Abrahamsen believes that Nixon feared his father (described in his book as an angry, impulsive man who failed at almost everything he undertook); he also "was ashamed of his hand-me-down clothing, felt deprived of both love and material goods, and began to imitate the secretive, and manipulative behavior that his mother used to deal with her troublesome husband" (quoted by Anderson, 1977, p. 5).

But Abrahamsen (1977) goes on to conclude:

> Although he was unaware of it, the real poverty of his life was not economic; it was emotional. He covered up the lack of love and affection particularly from his father—a lack which was reflected in Nixon's later personal and professional life. This attitude toward his childhood is an important character structure. As an adult he wanted to give the impression that his home life was simple, even poor, difficult at times, but good, because the emotional involvement was too powerful for him to deal with. To protect himself from these

---

BOX 4.1
A Letter Written by Richard Nixon at Age 10

My Dear Master:

The two boys that you left me with are very bad to me. Their dog, Jim, is very old and he will never talk or play with me.

One Saturday the boys went hunting. Jim and myself went with them. While going through the woods one of the boys triped (sic) and fell on me. I lost my temper and bit him. He kiked (sic) me in the side and we started in. While we were walking I saw a black round thing in a tree. I hit it with my paw. A swarm of black thing (sic) came out of it. I felt pain all over. I started to run and as both my eys (sic) were swelled shut I fell into a pond. When I got home I was very sore. I wish you would come home right now.

> Your good dog,
> Richard

---

memories, he needed to construct an image of an orderly and harmonious home. When a person says his home is good when in fact it is not, he is distorting the truth to give a false impression. It is this need to push painful situations out of his mind, which became a vaunted Nixon quality. It was his way of rearranging reality so that he did not have to face up to and cope with his repressed anger and emotional stress of his early years. (p. 5)

Abrahamsen, describing it as a pathetic document, reprints Nixon's "My Dear Master" letter (see Box 4.1) written at age 10, in which a terribly unhappy child portrays himself as a victim of a hostile world.

The "faithful dog" metaphor is prolonged in Richard Nixon's stubborn courtship of Pat Ryan, during which, when she insisted on seeing other men, he would drop her off on dates and pick her up afterward. Abrahamsen thinks that Nixon was attracted to Pat primarily because she reminded him of his mother; she was (and is) a strong woman who could sustain him, as Hannah had.

Our fourth, and final, book-length analysis of Nixon's character development, by the late historian Fawn Brodie (1981) moves away from psychoanalytic concepts. Brodie concludes that Nixon has manifested a lifelong habit of deception. As a youth, Nixon is portrayed by Brodie as rigid and unable to make true friendships with members of either sex. He became addicted early to the habit of manipulating the truth, according to Brodie. He was compulsively driven to seek almost any elective success to compensate for his own sense of worthlessness.

Brodie's (1981) description of Nixon's parents is somewhat similar to previously described ones. Frank Nixon is portrayed as punitive and occasionally violent, a man who made scapegoats of his sons to palliate his own sense of missed opportunity. She speculates on whether his father ever kicked Richard, because "the theme of kicking, and being kicked, appears early in Richard Nixon's life and surfaces repeatedly" (pp. 44). She documents nine references that Richard Nixon made to kicking over a period of 50 years and an actual kick he delivered to a protester in Peru. Brodie describes his mother as saintly but somewhat less than truthful. She was frequently absent, she withheld affection, and she apparently never communicated an Eriksonian sense of trust and self-esteem to her son.

The viciousness of Nixon's often blatantly dishonest attacks on political opponents Brodie (1981) attributes to the "sinister theme of fratricide, running like a lethal shadow through Nixon's life" (p. 506). According to Brodie (1981), Nixon saw himself in fierce competition with Harold, his much adored older brother who died of tuberculosis when Richard Nixon was a freshman in college. She writes:

> One thing Richard Nixon could not do after his older brother contracted tuberculosis was to challenge him, since the threat of death had removed him as a natural antagonist. But he did challenge scores of other brothers, seeking . . . to defeat his opponents 'without annihilation.' . . . Later he would embrace a more dangerous object than winning—the irreparable destruction of an opponent. (pp. 105-106)

Freud's Venture into Psychobiography as Explanation

Although these four analyses of Nixon's psychological develop-ment contain some plausibility along with their similar interpreta-tions, they also reflect some of the problems in seeking causal explanations within the psychobiographical approach. These limita-tions extend back to the very first psychobiographical analysis,

Sigmund Freud's attempt in 1910 to explain the character of Leonardo da Vinci.

Despite what he wrote in his book, Freud was an admirer of Leonardo (Coles, 1987); he had no desire to harm the reputation of a great man. But Freud was perplexed by the inconsistencies in Leonardo's behavior; for example, he was known to possess a "feminine delicacy of feelings" (he was a vegetarian, and he had a habit of buying caged birds at the market and freeing them) but he also designed "the cruellest offensive weapons" of war. Likewise, he maintained an "insatiable and indefatigable thirst for knowledge" while showing a "frigidity" and a "cool repudiation of sexuality."

Freud proposed that Leonardo had engaged in the defense mechanism of sublimation; his persistent investigative orientation constituted an outlet for his repressed sexuality. But, wrote Freud, to substantiate this hypothesis we would "need some picture of his mental development in the first years of his childhood." The problem is that very little is definitively known about Leonardo's early life. (Freud acknowledged that.) Leonardo was apparently born in 1452, the illegitimate son of a notary and probably a young peasant woman. Freud quotes Leonardo's "earliest memory" from his scientific notes on the flight of birds:

> It seems that I was always destined to be so deeply concerned with vultures; for I recall as one of my very earliest memories, that while I was in the cradle a vulture came down to me, and opened my mouth with its tail, and struck me many times with its tail against my lips. (Freud, 1910, quoted by Coles, 1987, p. 85)

For Freud, this is a very diagnostic memory, or dream, because the tail of a vulture is interpreted as a "substitute expression" for a penis. To Freud, this is illustrative of a "passive" homosexual experience. The desire to suck on a penis may be traced to a reminiscence of sucking at his mother's breast.

Freud attributed the purported homosexual orientation to Leonardo's having spent life alone with his mother. He concluded that Leonardo was "emotionally homosexual." But the actual evidence for Leonardo's homosexuality is very thin; at the age of 24 he was anonymously accused, with three other young men, of homosexuality. The accusation was investigated and the charges were dismissed. No evidence exists that Leonardo had any adult sex life of any kind. Freud seemed to rely heavily on an 1895 biography of Leonardo da Vinci that contained an incorrect translation; the word "vulture" in the above quotation should have been "kite" (a small bird).

Erik Erikson as a Psychobiographer

Chapter 3 reflected the centrality of the psychobiographical method in the testing by Erik Erikson of his theory of development. Crosby and Crosby (1981) note that Erikson is generally considered to be the most effective exponent of psychohistory. He would seem to be ideally qualified to be a psychobiographer. Is he? Erikson (1958), in *Young Man Luther*, follows the common psychobiographical assumption, linking childhood experiences to adult behavior. Crosby and Crosby conclude that even though few facts are available on Luther's childhood, "Erikson believes he overcomes this disadvantage by using his clinical training which allows him to recognize major trends 'even when all the facts are not available' (Erikson, 1958, p. 50)" (Crosby & Crosby, 1981, p. 211). Erikson had delved into Luther's early life in order to substantiate his conclusion that Luther experienced a crisis of identity. He concludes that Luther's childhood was "somber and harsh" (1958, p. 47) and "intensely unhappy" (p. 53). Erikson portrayed Luther's father as brutal and stern and yet ambitious for his son; the relationship between father and son is crucial in Luther's analysis. But his sources are from Luther's later writings and reminiscences—not guaranteed to be accurate.

CRITERIA FOR CAUSAL EXPLANATIONS

The search for causal explanations dominates psychobiography. How can we tell whether a psychobiography presents a legitimate or convincing explanation for the life choices and accomplishments of its subject? Crosby and Crosby (1981) emphasize two criteria: proper evidence and sound inference. Furthermore, they state: "The psychohistorian should also be able to convince us that the temporally antecedent events are likely causative agents for the documented effects" (1981, p. 214). Also, competing explanations should be refuted.

In a masterful act of evaluative scholarship, Crosby and Crosby (1981) reviewed approximately 50 books and articles that provided causal explanations of the personality of individuals. Two-thirds of these used psychoanalysis as their theoretical reference point. Crosby and Crosby conclude that, as a group, these did a rather effective job of expressing principles clearly, but they were less successful in demonstrating "cause." They rarely offered alternative explanations. Only 9 of the 50 studies—less than 20%—received a positive evaluation.

COHERENT-WHOLE EXPLANATIONS

Not all psychobiographies seek to detect the reasons why the subject behaves in characteristic ways. Using the valuable structure provided by Crosby and Crosby, we note that some psycho-biographies aim to create a unified whole out of the divergent bits of data from a person's life. These psychobiographies have an advantage over those offering causal explanations, because they do not necessarily delve into the subject's childhood and thus have less of a problem regarding the scarce childhood information.

One strategy in developing a coherent-whole explanation is to look for repetitive patterns—that is, to determine whether, in the person's life, distinctive modes of behavior recur in certain types of contexts. If so, the psychobiographer may introduce a construct or constructs that make sense of the persons' behaviors (Crosby & Crosby, 1981, p. 219). Any hypotheses offered by the psycho-biographer should be specific enough that they can be refuted. As in the case of the earlier causal explanations, the psychobiographer should consider plausible alternative constructs.

An Example of a Coherent-Whole Approach

Woodrow Wilson is a case in point. Numerous analysts (for example, Hargrove, 1966) have noted that Wilson, throughout his career as Princeton University president, governor of the state of

New Jersey, and U.S. president, would turn disputes over policies into personal fights. He refused to compromise in matters in which he had an emotional stake if the conflict was with another man whom he saw as a rival. George and George (1956) conclude that when the rivalry was with a strong male authority figure, Wilson had a tendency to become self-destructive and rigid. When Wilson was president of Princeton University, he fought with the dean of the graduate school, Andrew West, over the construction of a new graduate center. Wilson, having been offered a compromise with West that would have met his terms for the financing and location of the center, refused. He behaved similarly when the U.S. Senate balked at his request that it ratify a peace treaty and his plan for U.S. participation in the League of Nations (a forerunner of the United Nations) after World War I. Hargrove (1966) writes: "Historians agree that Wilson blundered in his fight with the Senate and finally killed his own idea of the League. It was a fight with West all over again. He translated a substantive fight into a personal one and so structured the situation that he would have to lose unless his opponents would bend their wills to him completely. . . . He had never been able to work well with men of the same stature as himself, and he saw this mission as peculiarly his own." (p. 51)

The psychobiography of Wilson by George and George (1956) is propelled by Harold Lasswell's (1930) claim that individuals seek power in order to overcome poor estimates of themselves. George and George "piece together, in an intelligible psychological whole, Wilson's love of constitutional writing, his desire for strong leadership, his constant need for reassurance, and his stubborn refusal to compromise in certain situations to show that, for Wilson, power compensated for low self-esteem" (Crosby & Crosby, 1981, p. 220).

Another example of a coherent-whole approach is described in Box 4.2.

Evaluation of Coherent-Whole Explanations

Coherent-whole explanations seek to answer the question "What is this person like?" Crosby and Crosby (1981) suggest the following criteria in evaluating the accuracy of these explanations:

BOX 4.2
Bushman on Benjamin Franklin

Crosby and Crosby (1981) conclude that perhaps the most promising of any of the coherent-whole explanations is R. L. Bushman's (1966) article that deals with Benjamin Franklin's widely recognized tendency to be conciliatory. In doing so, Bushman completely avoids references to Franklin's unconscious or to events in his childhood. Instead, he focuses on the correlation between Franklin's personal traits and his political behavior.

For example, Franklin (1961) writes in his autobiography;

> When about sixteen years of age I happened to meet with a book written by one Tryon, recommending a vegetable diet. I determined to go into it. My brother, being yet unmarried, did not keep house but boarded himself and his apprentices in another family. My refusing to eat flesh occasioned an inconvenience, and I was frequently chided for my singularity.

> I made myself acquainted with Tryon's manner of preparing some of his dishes, such as boiling potatoes or rice, making hasty pudding, and a few others; and then proposed to my brother that he would give me weekly half the money he paid for my board, and I would board myself. He instantly agreed to it, and I presently found that I could save half of what he paid me. This was an additional fund for buying books. But I had another advantage in it. My brother and the rest going from the printing house to their meals, I remained there alone, and dispatching presently my light repast (which often was not more than a biscuit or slice of bread, a handful of raisins or a tart from the pastry cook's, and a glass of water) I had the rest of the time till their return for study, in which I made the greater progress from that greater clearness of head and quicker apprehension which generally attend temperance in eating and drinking. (pp. 29-30)

Bushman notes that this was an advantageous arrangement for all concerned. A similar pattern can be found in Franklin's behavior as a diplomat and public servant; he was an expert negotiator and reconciler of conflicting viewpoints. Numerous examples abound, both in his role during the Constitutional Convention and his representation of the United States as an emissary to France.

Bushman concludes that Franklin's personal desire to avoid hostility motivated him to select negotiating roles throughout life.

(1) How well does the psychobiographer document the behaviors he or she seeks to explain?

(2) How well does the psychobiographer demonstrate that the behaviors documented were an expression of the subject's own adjustment or personality and not simply the response to a situation or a role the person is playing?

(3) How appropriately and effectively are psychological constructs and theories used?

(4) Are alternative explanations explored?

Crosby and Crosby apply these criteria to 56 books and articles that provide coherent-whole explanations of individuals' lives; all the subjects were political figures. Some 60% of these works used psychoanalysis as the theory-based explanation. Exactly half of these (28 to 56) were rated favorably by Crosby and Crosby on these criteria, as compared with only 20% of the causal explanations. Most psychobiographers who use coherent-whole explanations show that the subject behaved consistently and many demonstrate that the behaviors are distinctive and not inevitable. But these usually did not consider plausible alternative explanations; they are refuted in only about 10% of the studies.

Attempts to Explain a Specific Event or Pattern in a Person's Life

---

More limited than the previous approaches is the effort to explain a particular action or event in an individual's life. An example is Robert Sears's (1979a) analysis of Mark Twain's letters and stories.

Like all writers of fiction, Mark Twain may be assumed to reflect personal issues in his stories and other fiction. But these personal fears and misfortunes may or may not be heavily disguised. Binion (1978) offers the example of Henrik Ibsen:

Inquiry on him would almost have to begin with his impregnating a servant girl when he was eighteen. This misadventure looms even larger behind his later dramas than the two unsettling circumstances of his childhood: his rumored illegitimacy and his father's financial ruin. All three come into The Wild Duck practically undistorted in the back drop of the sorry mènage of a photographer and dreamer (read:

naturalist and poet). Tragedy ensues when an idealistic illusion-destroyer (Ibsen again) drags the old misadvantage upstage center. Ibsen took his own hint here and returned to distinguishing his experience of the unwanted child again and again until his last heroine went mad from reliving it again and again in disguise. Here, in *When We Dead Awaken*, the child is a statue for which she had posed in the nude. Traumatized by the sculptor's mere thanks for the chaste episode, she relives it in reverse as a nude artist who teases men to despair. (p. 315)

Sears attempted to demonstrate the effects of an early experience of loss of love upon the letters and novels written by Mark Twain. Sears was aware of many facts in Samuel Clemens's boyhood that could lead to the development of separation anxiety: the presence of a mother who mixed love and rejection; the deaths of a brother and a sister before he was 10 years old; and his father's death when he was 12 years old. Later, when Samuel Clemens (Mark Twain) was an adult, his first-born son died at the age of 18 months.

Sears has content-analyzed those letters written by Mark Twain between 1868 and 1904 as well as the novels he composed over that period. Thus Sears (1979) was able "to match the peaks and valleys of (Twain's) suppressed feelings with the events of his adult life" (p. 100). Sears concludes that the analysis of letters in combination with fiction writings provides additional understanding of a long-standing fear, "because fictional expression is under less conscious control than are direct communications such as letters" (p. 102, 104).

Similarly, William McKinley Runyan (1982) chooses one dramatic event in the life of painter Vincent Van Gogh—his cutting off of part of his ear—and illustrates various explanations for the motive behind this act.

CRITICISMS OF PSYCHOBIOGRAPHY

Throughout this chapter we have alluded to criticisms of the psychobiographical approach. It is appropriate now to systematize and evaluate these criticisms. The following structure relies on Stannard's (1980) exceedingly critical review of psychobiography.

Errors of Fact

Psychobiographers sometimes create "facts" to fill gaps in the historical record. Erik Erikson's use of Martin Luther's "fit in the choir" (see Chapter 3) is a highly questionable "fact," the importance of which is compounded by the central role that Erikson gives it in explaining Luther's mid-life crisis. Freud's use of a mistranslation of "vulture" also qualifies here.

Errors of Theory

Previously we described some of the theory-related exaggerations in causal explanations. One example, again from Waite (1977), will suffice: "Because Hitler's hatred of the Jews was monumental, his feelings of guilt and self-loathing must have been great indeed" (p. 424). Does the mechanism of projection exist, as this statement assumes? A detailed review of empirical evidence by David Holmes (1972, 1974) questions the broad applicability of projection as an explanation.

Errors of Culture

Psychobiographers sometimes reflect what we may call "psychological imperiousness" or psychological overdetermination; that is, they explain an individual's behavior on the basis of the person's unique internal qualities and experiences—such as the individual's personality, talents, and childhood experiences. A more parsimonious explanation may stem from the culture or society in which the person has lived. Freud took as evidence of Leonardo da Vinci's gentleness his habit of buying and freeing caged birds. But this procedure was a very old and popular folk custom that was believed to bring good luck.

Similarly, Fawn Brodie (1981), in *Thomas Jefferson: An intimate history*, makes much of Jefferson's involvement with a young slave, Sally Hemings. Brodie notes as evidence of his preoccupation that on a trip through Holland, Jefferson makes eight references to the land as "mulatto." But "mulatto" was commonly used in eighteenth century America to describe the color of the soil.

But explanation is not an "either/or." Inner personality and outer society interact and integrate. The philosopher of history Hans Meyerhoff (1987, p. 26) observes: "The fate of the libido is always decided in a concrete historical situation. This does not mean that the psychological processes do not have their own 'inner logic'; what it does mean is that outside conditions, both social and ideological, are built into the psychological structure of man."

Errors of Reasoning or Logic

Stannard (1980) claims that psychobiographers frequently fall victim to a "common error" in historical writing: *post hoc, ergo propter hoc.* That is, if event B followed event A, then B must have happened *because of* A. But he proposes that psychobiographers go even further: "So long as B is found to exist, it is *assumed* that *A must have happened* since B is a psychoanalytically posited consequence of A" (p. 24, italics in original). Examples of Waite's analysis of Hitler, reported under Causal Explanations of Individuals in this chapter, reflect this type of circular reasoning.

Further Criticisms

Noting that "up to now, psychohistory has put its worst foot forward" (p. 243) the excellent review by Crosby and Crosby (1981) notes other kinds of criticisms, including methodological flaws, vagueness of definition, and simplistic approaches in a different sense from the earlier criticisms in that a handful of early determinants may be relied upon for a "complete" explanation.

One of the personally most aggravating tendencies in many psychobiographical analyses is the emphasis they place on pathological explanations for the individual's behavior. Even altruistic or socially beneficial acts by successful people are portrayed as the result of personality malfunctions or deviations. As Coles (1987) observes, psychopathological labeling can become a device for moral condemnation or clumsy debunking. The reader legitimately asks, are there not any well-adjusted people out there? Are all significant actions in history (Lincoln's freeing of the slaves, Florence Nightingale's work with hospitalized soldiers) explained only by relying on failures of healthy childhood experiences to occur?

An extreme example of the tendency to provide negative explanations is Freud and Bullitt's (1967) posthumous psycho-biography of Woodrow Wilson. In the book President Wilson's virtues are portrayed as weaknesses and his visions as the fruits of compulsion. His idealization of the League of Nations is interpreted by Freud and Bullitt as evidence of a passive feminine relationship between Wilson and his father (L. F. Brown, 1967).

RESUSCITATING PSYCHOBIOGRAPHY

The general stance of this chapter has been one of criticism toward psychobiography. That is regrettable if it becomes a final verdict, for the approach holds promise if it is carefully applied. Concerned critics like Crosby, Cocks and Crosby, and Elms have made a number of suggestions for strengthening the procedure:

(1) Recognize the limits of the approach (Cocks & Crosby, 1987, p. x).
(2) Pay attention to the suitability of their subjects for investigation. For example, in analyzing Martin Luther's life, there is little information available about his childhood. As Elms (1976) puts it, "Don't move very far out in front of your data" (p. 94).
(3) Reexamine reliance on classical psychoanalytic theory. As described in Box 2.2, revisions have focused more on the mother-child relationships than on the role of the id and the fixations of psychosexual stages emphasized by Freud originally. Cocks and Crosby (1987, p. xi) conclude that "The evolution within the various schools of depth psychology in the 1920s and 1930s toward a greater emphasis on ego functions, character, and object-relations operating throughout an individual's life, rather than on id impulses buried deep within the psyche and childhood, has offered the psycho-logically attuned historian greater interpretive flexibility."
(4) Preconceptions and biases of psychobiographers need to be ack-nowledged. Occasionally, these works clearly are motivated by the authors' hostility and vindictiveness toward their subject (Elms, 1976, p. 95).

But even when these do not exist, psychobiographers should be explicit about their methods. For example, Erikson employs the method of "disciplined subjectivity," and he develops this concept in *Young Man Luther* and *Gandhi's Truth,* as well as more theoretical articles. But as Strozier (1976) concludes, Erikson never precisely defines what he means by "discipline." He does state that psychobiographers must be "reasonably clear about" the stage and conditions of their own lives when they involve themselves in the historical lives of others (Erikson, 1968).

Despite these qualms, much can be learned from psychobiography. J. W. Anderson (1981) reflects our view eloquently: "It seems to me that if psychology has anything to say about people— their complexities and their accustomed patterns and motivations—then biography is an area to which understanding should be applied" (p. 265). Psychologists should not neglect this avenue as a means to help us make sense of the development of individual lives.

5

CONTEMPORARY STAGE THEORIES

As Chapters 3 and 4 demonstrate in detail, Erik Erikson's stage theory has served as a foundation for systematic thinking about personality development in adulthood. This chapter illustrates how the Eriksonian influence is an indirect one also; the more recent theories—described in this chapter—are, in a sense, laboratories of Erikson's ideas. The systematic writings of Robert Havighurst, Roger Gould, and Daniel Levinson contribute to the intensive investigation of adult development that has surfaced in the last 15 years; empirical tests of their theories are beginning to appear.

ROBERT HAVIGHURST: AN EMPHASIS ON LIFE TASKS

Robert Havighurst (1972), an educational psychologist, was struck by the notion that every society seems to generate a rather explicit timetable for the accomplishment of various life tasks (Huyck & Hoyer, 1982). Building on Erikson's approach, he identified what he called specific developmental tasks (see Box 5.1). As an educational psychologist, Havighurst was particularly interested in

---

BOX 5.1
Havighurst's Proposed Developmental Tasks
(Adult Periods Only)

Ages 18-30:

    (1) getting started in an occupation
    (2) selecting a mate
    (3) learning to live with a marriage partner
    (4) starting a family
    (5) rearing children
    (6) managing a home
    (7) taking on civic responsibilities
    (8) finding a congenial social group

Ages 30-60:

    (1) assisting teenage children to become responsible and happy adults
    (2) achieving adult social and civic responsibility
    (3) reaching and maintaining satisfactory performance in one's occupational career
    (4) developing adult leisure-time activities
    (5) relating to one's spouse as a person
    (6) accepting and adjusting to the physiological changes of middle age
    (7) adjusting to aging parents

Ages 60 to end of life:

    (1) adjusting to decreasing physical strength and health
    (2) adjusting to retirement and reduced income
    (3) adjusting to death of one's spouse
    (4) establishing an explicit affiliation with one's age group
    (5) adopting and adapting social roles in a flexible way (such as expansion in family, community, or hobbies, or a slowdown of all activities)
    (6) establishing satisfactory physical living arrangements

---

helping the schools prepare individual students to deal with developmental tasks, but he extended his analysis through adulthood, also.

According to Havighurst, a developmental task arises at a certain period of life because of a combination of physical maturation and cultural pressure. He identified six to eight tasks for each period in life; Havighurst's system resembles Erikson's in that it is age-graded; that is, one in which people expect particular life events to occur at specific ages. Whether age should be used as such a precise indicator is controversial; the issue will be faced later in the chapter.

A further similarity with Erikson's approach is that Havighurst viewed that these tasks, once accomplished, made development firm and secure (Huyck & Hoyer, 1982).

Havighurst's conception is, of course, very simplified (Huyck & Hoyer, 1982). Additionally, like Erikson's, it often seems to blend "typicality" with "normality"; it assumes that all people marry and have children. Furthermore, there is no recognition that the consequences of being "out of phase" may be beneficial rather than harmful (Huyck & Hoyer, 1982, p. 219), as in the case of a woman delaying her first child until after establishing a professional career, or a man in his fifties, divorced, remarried, and starting a second family.

The term *out of phase* implies that there is a "right time" for achievement of these tasks. Increasingly the effort to peg development to specific ages is being criticized. Bernice Neugarten (1979; Neugarten & Neugarten, 1987), a leading authority on adult development, has argued that our society is becoming an age-irrelevant one, in which chronological age is not and should not be used as a criterion for expecting a particular kind of behavior. The schedules of our lives are so varied that, according to Neugarten, a single timetable is impossible to specify. As just one example of variation, different cohorts (a *cohort* is a group of people born in the same years or time period) move through the life course on different schedules (Rosenfeld & Stark, 1987).

ROGER GOULD AND REJECTING THE MYTHS OF EARLIER AGES

That people move through stages during adulthood generated its greatest impact upon the public through the publication of Gail

Sheehy's *Passages* in the mid-1970s. Sheehy, a professional journalist, used the work of Roger Gould and Daniel Levinson as support for her conclusions. These two theorists may be considered the "gold dust twins" of contemporary stage-theorizing, for they started collecting data at about the same time (the late 1960s)—one on the East coast and one on the West coast—and they both published influential books reporting their findings and theories in the late 1970s. Although each classifies adults into age-graded periods and each sees qualitative differences in the relevant issues at different periods during adulthood, Gould and Levinson also have different contributions to make to theorizing. And each has ideas worthy of further investigation.

Gould's Theoretical Background and Major Thesis

Roger Gould is a psychiatrist trained in a psychoanalytic perspective. His writings reflect a combination of classical psychoanalytic theory, with its reliance on biological determinants, and object-relations theory (see Box 2.2), placing emphasis on the child's interaction with his or her mother. "Every child is born with an 'insatiable biological drive' to have what it cannot have, the total attention and love of its mother," states Gould (quoted in *Time* magazine, August 14, 1978, p. 69). Consciousness in childhood, replete with a strong residue of anger, grows out of this "basic fact of biological helplessness and immaturity" (Gould, 1978, p. 18).

Thus, for Gould, the person's basic developmental task—recurring throughout life—is to shed *major false assumptions* in order to achieve further levels of adult maturity. Different myths are predominant topics for renunciation at differing ages; thus does Gould structure growth around developmental periods, or stages.

Gould's Developmental Periods

Gould organizes adult development through six major periods, spanning the ages of 16 to 60. Age, in and of itself, is an important marker for Gould; he states: "My data suggest that not only does adulthood consist of a series of tasks to be performed, but there exists an actual time clock that is thoroughly universal and thoroughly regular, which defines the task at hand. The fact that you're 40 or 43 years old, for example, really does affect the way you view life and the decisions you make. When you reach 50, your perspective changes" (Gould, quoted by Walker, 1974, p. 20).

What are the myths that, for Gould, the developing person must shed? For the ages of 16 to 22, the developmental task is "leaving our parents' world" and the major false assumption to be renounced is that "I'll always belong to my parents and believe in their world." Young people want autonomy; yet this autonomy is precarious because young people also want safety and belonging. They possess "condensed energy looking for a direction" but they fear that if they express their true feelings, they won't be loved. They have not as yet internalized the belief that people can love each other despite being different. Any disagreement by a friend has the potential for being seen as a betrayal.

The task identified by Gould for this period is reminiscent of Erikson's concept of identity crisis (see Chapter 3). Those young people who are unable to move away from the myth that "I'll always belong to my parents and believe in their world" are condemned to play out, in their lives, their parents' values, perspectives, and styles of adapting. Failure to shed this false assumption would, for Gould, be equivalent to James Marcia's identity status of foreclosure (see Chapter 3).

Gould's second period occurs at ages 22 to 28, a period Gould tags with the slogan "I'm Nobody's Baby Now." The major false assumption at this time is: "Doing things my parents' way, with will power and perseverance, will bring results. But if I become too frustrated, confused, or tired, or am simply unable to cope, they will step in and show me the right way."

Two issues dominate this period. Even though they may portray themselves as autonomous and self-reliant, people in their twenties must still deal with the strong ties to their parents. They must internalize the realization that "This is it—I'm on my own." They must move toward their own independent views; mastering their own environment becomes vital.

Gould even proposes that many people who marry at this age pick the partner they do because they can't deal adequately with the relationships with their parents. He writes: "Each and every one of us pick partners that, in subtle ways at least, recreate a parent-child relationship that has not yet been mastered" (1978, p. 145). Or, conversely, we may choose a companion who possesses a strong quality we lack; "initially we marry in the effort to achieve wholeness" (1978, p. 113). In summary, Gould concludes that the separateness from our parents that we proudly portray in our twenties is just a fiction.

The second major thrust of the ages 22 to 28 is the rampant optimism. Determination and self-confidence are high; making a million dollars by age 30 is considered attainable. Careers are pursued without much introspection; young adults assume that rewards will come to them automatically "if I do what I'm supposed to do." Even commitments to a relationship are not analyzed deeply; "love will conquer all." These beliefs become false assumptions, ready for rejection, during the next stage.

The third period, salient at ages 28 to 34, Gould titles "Opening Up to What's Inside." Two major false assumptions exist now: first, that life is simple and controllable, and second, that there are "no significant coexisting contradictory forces within me."

Gould portrays the period of the late twenties and early thirties as one of disillusionment and soul searching. Life is seen as much more difficult than it was in one's twenties; self-confidence wavers; the world becomes one that is complicated and unfair. People at this age are more likely to say "Life is a struggle; life is unfair."

Why is this change? One reason is that we feel we are not accomplishing our dreams or even if we have, our life is now on a downhill slide. Dissatisfaction with one's position in the world increases; people at these ages are more likely to say: "I don't have enough money to do what I want."

Second, pressures to play a role become more difficult to fulfill. People become weary of trying to be what others expect them to be; yet they reluctantly persist. They poignantly ask: "Why can't I be accepted for what I am, not for what others (the boss, one's spouse, one's family) expect me to be?" These people, compared to younger ones, are *less* likely to agree that "for me, marriage has been a good thing." According to Gould, divorce increases during this age period, as people can't adjust to each other's developing values.

In Gould's view, a major cause of the incipient distress is parenthood. Dacey (1982), commenting on Gould's perspective, concludes: "As we attempt to explain to children what their values ought to be, we are often forced to see how unsure we are of our own values." Furthermore, the task of instilling values in children conflicts with the parent's emerging need to be accepted for "what I am."

To adapt, people at this age must develop a new view of life and recognize that if they want to satisfy a need or desire, they will have to work on it *directly*. Also, they must come to realize, and accept, how like their parents they are, especially in ways they don't want to be.

Problems and challenges increase during the fourth stage, called by Gould the mid-life decade and applicable to persons ages 34-45. Here the major false assumption is that "there is no evil or death in the world; the sinister has been destroyed." Not only do the unresolved problems of the early thirties create tumult, but the latter is exacerbated by the first emotional awareness that time is shrinking, or even running out, and death will inexorably come. Whatever must be done, must be done now.

Life seems to constrict. There is little time left to shape the behavior of one's adolescent children and even less time to "make it" in one's own career. One must hurry if one's dreams are to be made to come true.

Gould portrays the early forties as an unstable and uncomfortable age. Regrets compound for "my mistakes in raising my children."

On top of everything else, parents may become a problem; elderly parents may turn to their middle-aged offspring for support, thus reversing the roles of dependence and independence. Also the death of one's parents may come quickly, leaving unresolved issues and conflicts.

During mid-life, people have, according to Gould, to "dig deeper" to examine the deepest strata of their own "demonic badness" or worthlessness. The ugly side of our lives can no longer be ignored.

Beyond mid-life, things get better, according to Gould. The ages 43-53 are characterized by the feeling that "the die is cast," that we are whoever we are going to be. "The life of inner directiveness finally prevails" (Gould, 1978, p. 310). People become less competitive and more inner directed. At the same time, they may come to seek sympathy and affection from their spouses in a way that resembles a much earlier dependence on their parents.

Gould has less to say about later middle age and old age. He proposes that as persons reach the ages of 53-60, the negative feelings they experienced in their forties diminish even further. Relationships with their friends, their children, and their parents, if the latter are still alive, become warmer and more mellow. The spouse becomes a valuable companion and less a parent.

THE EMPIRICAL BASIS FOR GOULD'S THEORY

Roger Gould has painted a provocative but depressing picture of development during adulthood. On what basis does he draw his conclusions?

His original data were based on statements made by persons who were outpatients in therapy sessions at the University of California at Los Angeles. Gould had eight medical students listen to the tape recordings of these group therapy sessions and then list the statements about personal feelings that seemed to stand out.

Then other people—not patients—were given questionnaires listing these feelings and were asked to indicate how applicable each statement was to their lives. A total of 524 white, middle-class males and females responded; they ranged in ages from 16 to 60. Gould then determined the number of people in each age category who reported each statement; the age groupings were 16-17, 18-21, 22-28, 29-36, 37-43, 44-50, and 51-60. Men and women were not separated in this data analysis, even though the percentage of subjects who were women was higher in the over-40 groups.

In reporting his results, Gould prepared figures showing the relative incidence of statements by age groups. But his use of rank-ordering creates the illusion of greater differences than may really exist. His failure to do any tests of statistical significance between groups means that we cannot say whether any apparent differences are real ones or not.

Also, it is apparent that these are cross-sectional data; that is, they are drawn from people who were at different ages at the same time. There is no direct evidence that these differences would apply to the *same people* at different times in their own lives. For such a conclusion to be a firm one, it would have to be based on a longitudinal study, one that measures and remeasures the same individuals throughout their lives. Longitudinal methods are, by definition, time consuming and hence are seldom feasible.

An Evaluation of Gould's Approach

In his book, his articles, and his interviews, Gould has a tendency to make extreme pronouncements that he applies to all individuals. Probably it is a myth that life is that simple and binding. A major theme of this book is that no one theory "fits all." Also, posed against the standards for rigorous social science methodology, Gould's procedures fail. Although his observations may be applicable to many of us, their universal validity—recall his "universal time clock"—is not proven on the basis of his data.

I prefer to treat Gould's ideas as hypotheses worth pursuing in later studies. I consider as provocative and plausible his idea that, as we develop during adulthood, we must forsake beliefs that previously were useful to our adaptation. Similarly attractive is his thesis that the person has "an ever-increasing need to win permission from oneself to continue developing" (Gould, 1975, p. 74).

Finally, it is hard to dispute Gould's view that "The direction of change is toward becoming more tolerant of oneself, and more appreciative of the complexity of both the surrounding world and of the mental milieu, but there are many things that can block, slow down, or divert that process" (Gould, 1975, p. 74). Such a broad statement covers everyone, but by the same stroke it lays bare Gould's lack of exploration of individual differences and their determinants.

Plausibility also stems from similarities in Gould's conclusions and those of theorists both previously described (Erikson) and reviewed subsequently (Levinson). Although Gould's theory has more periods in adulthood than does Erikson's, they agree on the dangers of premature identity determination in adolescence and the need for young people to develop independent values. And like Levinson, Gould finds that the early forties are tumultuous ages.

DANIEL LEVINSON AND "THE SEASONS OF A MAN'S LIFE"

Daniel Levinson's theory of changes in development in mid-life, which appeared about the same time as Gould's, reflects differences in theoretical background, methodology, and conclusions (Levinson, Darrow, Klein, Levinson, & McKee, 1978). Unlike Freud, Erikson, and Gould, Daniel Levinson is not a psychiatrist; he was trained in social psychology and participated in the research leading to the publication of the book *The Authoritarian Personality* (Adorno, Frenkel-Brunswik, Levinson, & Sanford, 1950), one of the classic works of social psychology. Levinson candidly acknowledges that his study of adult development was motivated by his desire to understand himself better.

Levinson's Theoretical Orientation

Levinson's major theoretical contribution—an important one— is his ability to combine influences from vastly different perspectives. Among contemporary theorists, he best reflects a synthesis of Eriksonian stage theory, Carl Jung's concept of individuation, and dialectical ideas (the latter to be discussed more thoroughly in Chapter 6). For Levinson, the major task for a man in mid-life is to come to terms with four polarities, or choices in self-image, that face him. We will review these in a subsequent section, after outlining Levinson's conception of stages in adulthood.

The Seasons of a Man's Life

Levinson's initial goal was to blueprint the structure in men's development. (He is currently preparing a book on women's development.) Like previous stage theorists, he pegs his *periods* (a term he prefers to *stage*, for these qualitatively different eras) to ages. For each period, he provides a title for the major task. They are as follows:

  ages 16-24: leaving the family;
  ages 24-28: getting into the adult world (though Levinson, 1985, later preferred the title, Forming a Life Structure);
  ages 29-34: settling down (or, his later term, Developing a Culminating Life Structure);
  ages 35-40 or 42: becoming one's own man (Levinson, 1985, has defined the use of *man* rather than a nonsexist term because the achievement of masculinity—however defined by each man—is central.);

early forties: mid-life transition;
age 45 on: restabilization.

Levinson views adulthood as a set of shifting periods from "structure-building" periods of stability to "structure-changing" periods of transition and back again. Transition periods are important in his theory; each is about three-quarters the duration of a stable period (five years versus seven or eight), and they are the places where change takes place—a reappraisal of past experiences and of shifting to new goals.

Levinson (1979) conceptualizes the resulting changes as structural ones, and, in fact, he presents his theory as one of the formation of life structures, not as a theory of personality development. He is adamant on the latter point; in a letter replying to a critic, he states: "It is not [a study of personality development]. It is a study of the development of individual life structure. . . . We find age-linked periods in life structure development. Periods in adult personality development have not been demonstrated by anyone, and I certainly am not positing them" (p. 727).

"Life structure" is a rather elusive concept (Sears, 1979b, p. 98); for instance, at one point Levinson defines it as the individual's conception of his life at the time. "Where do I invest my energy? What is important? What is missing in my life?" Such questions are relevant to one's life structure.

For Levinson (1985), no life structure is permanent; "I've never seen one last beyond seven or eight years," he has stated. A transition period thus reflects a shift from one life structure to another, requiring that now different aspects of one's life have become central. Transitions do not always demand turmoil or conscious questioning, but everyone goes through them, concludes Levinson (1985). They may include the termination of certain values or self-labels (Levinson's equivalent to Gould's rejection of prior assumptions) and they lead to the initiation of new structures. Parkes (1971) concluded that a psychosocial transition required "the abandonment of one set of assumptions and the development of a fresh set to enable the individual to cope with the new altered life space" (p. 103). In using transitions as a central feature of his theory, Levinson reflects Erikson's conception of a crisis as a transition period marked by personal vulnerability and capacity for change.

Polarities in Mid-Life

As noted earlier, Levinson devotes special analysis to the mid-life transition. He concludes that the early forties comprise a crisis period for many men, leading some of them to adolescentlike periods of doubt and confusion. He reports that 80% of the men he studied experienced a tumultuous period here.

One of the tasks of mid-life is to resolve discrepancies in one's self-image. The dialectical approach, which Levinson uses, conceptualizes adjustments as constantly striving to respond to competing needs. These needs act as end points that tug the individual first toward one, then toward the other. Closure can never be achieved because whichever need is currently unfulfilled is actively seeking satisfaction.

Levinson, like only some of the dialectical theorists, believes that integration of these competing needs or self-images is possible (see Chapter 6 for elaboration). He proposed that four issues (he calls them "polarities") face a man at mid-life. These are:

attachment/separateness
destruction/creation
masculine/feminine
young/old

He writes:

Each of these pairs forms a polarity in the sense that the two terms represent opposing tendencies or conditions. . . . Both sides of each polarity coexist within every self. At mid-life a man feels young in many respects, but he also has a sense of being old. . . . He feels alternately young, old, and 'in-between.' His developmental task is to make sense of this condition of in-between to become Young/Old in a new way, different from that of early childhood. (Levinson, 1978, p. 197)

Each of the polarities provides a perspective on the dilemmas of mid-life:

Attachment/Separateness

We all need to be close to others and yet we need our own identity. In childhood, attachment is vital for survival. In adolescence, we seek separateness, not only from parents but sometimes from society. But in young adulthood, attachment is likely to again tug and pull, not only romantic attachment but the attachment to others in his field of work. In mid-life, a new type of separateness may emerge; the man begins to look inside himself. He may decide to divorce, or may make a stronger commitment to an existing marriage. In the latter sense, Levinson uses "separateness" to refer to an increased concern with one's inner world.

Destruction/Creation

The mid-life transition activates a man's concern with death and destruction. Levinson proposes that here a man recognizes the evil within himself, including his own power to hurt or destroy others or himself. But there is a positive aspect of this recognition of the self-capacity to be destructive. By recognizing his power to tear down things, he begins to realize how truly powerful he can be in creating new and useful forms of life. For example, one aspect of creativity is the ability to sense problems.

Masculine/Feminine

With regard to this polarity, Levinson capitalizes on Carl Jung's distinction between the animus and the anima (see Chapter 2). Jung proposed that each of us possessed both a masculine and feminine part to our personality. The emphasis on expressing only one side costs us greatly, and he believed that a rich adulthood can be achieved only by compensating that part of us that was denied during childhood. For Levinson, mid-life is the period when this deficiency must be reconciled. In defining masculinity, Levinson includes conceptions of oneself as possessing toughness, achievement and ambition, power, and a thinking orientation (as opposed to the feminine feeling orientation). A man must feel secure enough in his masculinity to enjoy his ability to feel, to nurture, to be dependent. Here men can become mentors; they can ease away from competing with others and devote more energy to transmitting their values to younger associates.

Young/Old

We are terribly interested in maintaining our youth, if only to avoid the ultimate consequence of our mortality, our death. At about 40, a man is confronted with evidence of his aging appearance and declining powers, from lines in his face to sags and spreading seemingly everywhere. His eyesight may deteriorate, he may lack stamina or previous physical skills, he may start to forget things. Friends may become ill; his parents may die. Realization that he may die takes on a more personal focus.

How to reconcile the young/old discrepancy? Levinson suggests that each identity possesses some positive aspects; we associate youth with enthusiasm, energy, curiosity, and spontaneity, while we associate the elderly with maturity, wisdom, and tolerance. One resolution is to combine the best of both perspectives in a new young/old identity.

Levinson's Method

The procedure used by Levinson and his colleagues to generate conclusions is a rather atypical one. He chose 40 men, ages 35-45 and carried out what has been called a "briefly longitudinal" study of them. Data collection began in 1968 with in-depth interviews and ended in 1971 with detailed follow-ups. The men were from four diverse occupations—they were biologists, novelists, factory workers, and business executives. Levinson and his staff interviewed and reinterviewed these men about their lives; interviews, spread over several days, accumulated 15-20 hours of responses from each man. They also completed the Thematic Apperception Test and other personality measures. Biographies were prepared for each man. Then Levinson and his staff read and reread all the material, discussed it extensively, and extracted common themes. As Sears (1979b) notes, "In the classical clinical tradition, Levinson uses biographical case material to illustrate the stages of personality development that he sees men as going through" (p. 97). The book resulting from this extensive project is rich in sensitive conclusions, but almost completely lacking in quantified results and statistical tests.

Evaluation of Levinson's Theory

The findings and theory presented by Levinson and his associates are provocative and could be very important, but they suffer from some important problems and limitations.

The theory is impressionistically derived from the data without any expressed criteria for determining what stage the subject was in, whether he encountered the themes and stages as hypothesized, and whether his passage was rough or smooth. Furthermore, our curiosity about the processes by which change comes about is not satisfied (Sears, 1979b, p. 98). *Why* do people change when they do, when equivalent others do not?

In a different area, no statements are provided about the degree of reliability between coders, and thus no indication of the agreement between staff members in the ratings they gave.

There are other major limitations. The data collection stopped at age 45; the interview procedure had a psychoanalytic orientation but the interviews did not go into enough depth to use this theory as an explanation of choices (Sears, 1979b). And, of course, the sample was limited to males.

Perhaps the most serious criticism derives from the discrepancy between findings and conclusions. Levinson's concept of mentoring provides an example. The authors claim that mentoring is crucial in the transition period of "becoming one's own man." Prior to this period, a man felt that no matter what he had accomplished, he was sufficiently on his own. Now he must cut the ties with his mentor; in fact, he must reinterpret the character of the mentor. The mentor, according to Levinson, could be a teacher, a boss, an editor, or an experienced coworker who takes the younger man into confidence, imparts wisdom, sponsors, criticizes, and bestows a blessing. This person is ordinarily 8 to 15 years older than the protègè. The final relinquishing of a mentor should occur during this transition period, between the ages of 35 and 40. Levinson (1977) and his colleagues state that, "One does not have mentors after [the age of] 40" (p. 55). But does one have them *before* the age of 40? As Sears (1979b) notes, late in Levinson's book "we discover that among the 40 men in this study, the mentoring experience rarely occurred in any effective way" (p. 98). The concept appears to be given much more prominence in Levinson's theory than his data so far would seem to warrant. (In a rejoinder, Levinson, 1979, states that half his subjects received little or no mentoring, but that does not mean that good mentoring is unimportant.)

Can other sources of data, via personal documents, clarify this ambiguity? Perhaps. Additional support for lack of mention of mentors comes from a content analysis of psychologists' auto-biographies, carried out by David H. Mack, a University of Kansas undergraduate, and myself. We selected Volume 5 from the collection, *A History of Psychology in Autobiography* (Murchison, 1930, 1932, 1936; Boring et al., 1952; Boring & Lindzey, 1967; Lindzey, 1974). Mack and I selected this series for content analysis because we assumed that if anyone would discuss the impact of a mentor on his own youthful career development, it would be an academic person, and particularly a psychologist. Yet a careful reading of Volume 5 by two independent content analysts reveals virtually no mention of mentoring in any of its 15 autobiographies. Although former teachers, professors, and more advanced colleagues are frequently mentioned, there is almost no detailed indication of a protègè role nor an expression of a close relationship. Gordon Allport's autobiography (1967) probably provides the most detailed and personal description of a mentor; he devotes an entire paragraph to Richard Cabot, a professor of cardiology and social ethics at Harvard in the 1920s. Not only does Allport detail Cabot's contributions to his own development, but he also writes about how he admires Cabot's qualities as a mentor. In contrast to Allport's evocation and to the total neglect by the other autobiographers, Carl Rogers's autobiography (1967) is characterized by a rejection of mentors and a self-concept of a "lone wolf in . . . professional activities" (p. 343) who followed his own course and was not even considered to be a psychologist by his colleagues during the Rochester years (1928-1940). A common theme in Rogers's autobiography is his nature as a rebel—he rejected his parents' anti-intellectual and fundamentalist religious beliefs; he rejected traditional psychotherapeutic assumptions and procedures and, while at the University of Wisconsin, he rejected participation in doctoral training that emphasized "rigorous" examinations and the failing of large proportions of graduate students.

There may be quite plausible reasons why these collections of autobiographies by prominent psychologists fail to mention the mentoring process in detail. The absence may be a function of the setting; it is not necessarily an indication that mentoring did not occur. In fact, the concept of mentoring may be an important one. The lack of a mentor has been proposed by Epstein (1970) as a major obstacle in the professional development of women. Counseling psychologists are beginning to investigate the impact of the concept. (See Chapter 8, for examples.)

EMPIRICAL EVIDENCE FOR THESE STAGE THEORIES

For each of the stage theories described in this chapter we have noted certain logical or methodological limitations. The theorists' own procedures that led to their theoretical contributions are not in keeping with the standards of sophisticated social science methodology. Given these qualms, how much empirical evidence exists for them? Is the "mid-life crisis" truly prevalent in American society? Is there more turmoil for men in their early forties than in, say, their early fifties? Can the theories be applied to women as well as to men?

The ideas reported in this chapter possess a certain degree of plausibility. In our society, specific age ranges have been linked with certain designated tasks; if we had taken the tasks listed in Box 5.1 and asked respondents to indicate appropriate age ranges for each, general agreement would likely not have occurred until recently (Bourque & Back, 1977; Neugarten & Peterson, 1957). (See Box 5.2.)

Particular ages even have special meanings of their own. (See Box 5.3.) Not only have we been accurate gauges of society's expectations, but most of us are responsive to society's pressures to concentrate our energies on these tasks at "the proper time" (Neugarten, Moore, & Lowe, 1965).

Beyond these commonalities, the empirical evidence lends support to the theories in regard to their broadest conclusions. In a review, Whitbourne and Weinstock (1979) note: "There is surprising consistency in the findings of these studies, despite differences in the composition of samples and the methods used to collect information . . . the pattern of the 'average' adult life that these findings portray suggests: a tentativeness and vigor in early adulthood, greater assumption of adult roles and responsibility in an early portion of middle adulthood, followed by a questioning in the latter portion of middlehood" (p. 124).

Some specific studies are illustrative:

(1) Tamir (1980) reported a cross-sectional survey from a large sample of men ages 20-60. Men in their late forties, especially the most highly educated ones, reported more stress and lower self-esteem than men in other age groups, verifying the existence of a "mid-life crisis." These men drank more, were more depressed, and more immobilized than men of any other age group.

BOX 5.2
What's the Right Time?

Two surveys asking the same questions 20 years apart (late 1950s and late 1970s) have shown a dramatic decline in the consensus among middle-class, middle-aged people about what's the right age for various major events and achievements of adult life.

Activity or Event	Appropriate age range	Late 1950s study % who agree		Late 1970s study % who agree	
		Men	Women	Men	Women
best age for a man to marry	20-25	80	90	42	42
best age for a woman to marry	19-24	85	90	44	36
when most people should become grandparents	45-50	84	79	64	57
best age for most people to finish school and go to work	20-22	86	82	36	38
when most men should be settled on a career	24-26	74	64	24	26
when most men hold their top jobs	45-50	71	58	38	31
when most people should be ready to retire	60-65	83	86	66	41
when a man has the most responsibilities	35-50	79	75	49	50
when a man accomplishes most	40-50	82	71	46	41
the prime of life for a man	35-50	86	80	59	66

Activity or Event	Appropriate age range	Late 1950s study % who agree		Late 1970s study % who agree	
		Men	Women	Men	Women
when a woman has the most responsibilities	25-40	93	91	59	53
when a woman accomplishes most	30-45	94	92	57	46

SOURCE: Rosenfeld & Stark, 1987, p. 72.

(2) Lowenthal et al. (1975), comparing men of differing ages who were anticipating a major life transition, found that the preretirement men (average age of 61 years) differed from the middle-aged sample (average age 52 years): They showed a decline on a "masculinity index," placed higher weight on "interpersonal-expressive" goals, claimed less stress from dealing with other people, and were less preoccupied with their jobs or worried about finances. In general, they were more comfortable and relaxed, reflecting Whitbourne and Weinstock's (1979) conclusion from a literature review that the late fifties are a quieter, mellower time of life.

(3) With regard to occupational achievement, outstanding creative contributions are more frequent in the thirties (Lehman, 1953, 1962). Like quality of work, quantity of output varies from one occupation to another, but tends to peak in the forties (Dennis, 1968). (Qualifications to these conclusions—and they are numerous—are evaluated in Chapter 7.) Career drive apparently diminishes in many men after these ages.

Stage Theories and Women's Development

Clearly, these stage theories possess a male bias. They were developed by males, with applicability to males in mind (either explicitly or unconsciously). Gilligan (1980) has noted that women seemingly reflect incomplete and inferior development when judged by developmental standards formulated on, for, and by males. (Chapter 10 elaborates on this point.)

BOX 5.3
The Mystery of Age 40

Why is the age 40 so important in our society? Some 50 years ago a bestselling book by Walter Pitkin told the public that *Life Begins at Forty*, but Jack Benny—and numerous others—refused to acknowledge that they had aged past 39. In a book titled *Forty: The age and the symbol*, anthropologist Stanley Brandes (1985) examines explanations for the obsession with age 40. He reports that the number 40 was important in all three of the ancient Mediterranean religions, and proposes that it traveled with immigrants to the United States to become a permanent "cultural resource." As Wray Herbert (1985, p. 77) observes, this is a "weakly argued" thesis, although it is indisputable that recent popularization of the "mid-life crisis" has given new life to the symbolic meaning of the age 40.

Several differences and omissions emerge. First, there are value differences. In most theories of adult development, autonomy and achievement, rather than attachment and relationships, are the valued developmental milestones. Yet, women, even those in highly professional positions, often define their identities in the context of relationships as well as a context of personal achievement.

Levinson concluded that four tasks fill the agenda in the early adulthood of men: forming a dream, identifying occupation, finding a mentor, and forming a love attachment. Barnett and Baruch (1980), who interviewed women ages 35 to 55 about what had been their expectations for adulthood when they were age 16 or 17, and found that only the last of these four goals was retrospectively relevant to these respondents.

A second difference occurs at mid-life. It may well be that women, in contrast to men, *increase* their desire for autonomy and achievement in middle adulthood (Reinke, 1982). Judith Bardwick (1968) states this as follows:

> The sexes begin adulthood at opposite ends of the psychodynamic continuum; as men are enabled by success in achievement to give up their egocentric preoccupation, and as women succeed within relationships and become more autonomous, both become more interdependent. This implies that men will become more involved

with their internal psychological needs and states and be more sensitive to their dependence upon affirmation within relationships. Women will be better able to engage the world, experiencing themselves as initiators, having gratifications as individuals. (pp. 49-50)

Third, the above theories, never much for recognizing individual differences even in men's lives, fail to account for the vast diversity of lifestyles among women (Reinke, 1982). A woman may not enter the work force until she is 30 or 40, she may work part time, and she seldom has a mentor. It is clear that as a group, women possess more varied combinations of work and family involvement. Typically, three orientations have been distinguished: The homemaker/mother, the "career woman," and the woman who combines both; Bardwick (1980) referred to these, respectively, as the relational and dependent orientation, the egocentric orientation, and the interdependent orientation. Gail Sheehy (1976) added a fourth category: "nurturers who defer achievement" and postpone strenuous career efforts while they marry and start a family. (See Box 5.4.)

Given these differences, how well do the findings on men extend to women's lives? Reinke (1982) reviews several dissertations of relevance. In an early study, W. A. Stewart (1977) tested the validity of Levinson's "age thirty transition" to women by administering a retrospective interview to 11 middle-class women ages 31-39. For those women who had pursued a career beginning in their early twenties, the theory fit; for them, beginning around age 28, an increased sense of urgency to create a marriage and family emerged. The transition usually took four to five years—as Levinson

---

BOX 5.4
Sheehy's Classification of Women's Roles

(1) "care givers," who plan their lives around domestic roles
(2) "nurturers, who defer achievement," that is, they postpone strenuous career efforts while marrying and starting a family
(3) "achievers who defer nurturing," that is, those who postpone motherhood and often marriage in order to complete professional aspirations
(4) "integrators," who try to combine marriage, career, and motherhood

found for men's transitions—and led to drastic changes in some of these women. But for the women who committed to a relationship rather than a career early on, the marriage-family adult life structure remained stable for a longer time, although dissatisfaction with it did begin to appear around age 30. The transition usually took the form of an increase in dissatisfaction with marriage and a desire for a more egalitarian relationship with her husband.

Farmer (1979), in another dissertation concentrating on a small number of women, focused on women in their forties. Most of these had begun adulthood in traditional roles; in mid-life they became more autonomous in their attitudes about themselves and less concerned about gaining the approval of others. Jackson (1975), based on interviews with 25 women in their forties, reported that 64% of them had experienced periods of disruption and change in their late thirties.

A comprehensive survey based on Roger Gould's concepts and using a modified version of his questionnaire was completed by Desjardins (1978), who questioned 10 women at each age from 21 through age 59. However, all the subjects were former homemakers who were now attempting to reenter school or the work force. Desjardins noticed a trend that has been verified in subsequent research; periods of change were more associated with those ages near decade markers (i.e., ages 29, 30, 39, 40) than the middle years, where stability predominated. Women of ages 28 to 32 showed the greatest personal change; the ages 38 to 45 also reflected a major transition period. Of all the women, those at age 40 had the most negative self-concepts. Although this is a cross-sectional study that possesses the previously mentioned limitations of that approach, its systematic surveying of every age point over a 29-year span, among other reasons, qualifies it as an improvement over Gould's original study.

Empirical findings on women's development reflect a shift away from age-based determinants, in keeping with the greater diversity in roles held by women, compared to men. For example, with regard to the shift from traditional female roles to greater assertiveness and career aspirations, the time at which children are "on their own" seems to be a greater determinant than the women's age per se (Rubin, 1979). Similarly, Neugarten (1968) found that women tend to define such terms as "middle age" on the basis of events in their families, or the phase in the families' life cycle.

The most sophisticated recent empirical studies of women's development are two cross-sectional studies that interviewed women of the ages 30 to 60 (Reinke, Holmes, & Harris, 1985; Harris, Ellicott, & Holmes, 1986). All the subjects lived in middle-class neighborhoods in the same medium-sized midwestern city. The subjects in the first study, 60 women who were either 30, 35, 40, or 45, completed a thorough interview, averaging over two hours in length, that sought to detail how and when they had changed during adulthood. For this goal, the women were asked to trace retrospectively their lives since leaving high school and to describe events, thoughts, feelings, plans and goals over the years (Reinke, Holmes, & Harris, 1985). In addition to assessing differences from one age group to others on many specific answers, the research team rated each woman with respect to global life change on the basis of the interview as a whole.

The ages 27 to 30 reflected dramatic change for most of these women. Overall, 80% of the 30-year-olds, 83% of 40-year-olds, and 60% of the 45-year-olds seemed to have undergone a major reorientation in the way they lived their lives or the way they thought about themselves, beginning between the ages 27 and 30. Although change was manifested in different ways by different women, the researchers detected three common phases to the change process:

(1) The initial phase, which usually began between 26 and 30, was characterized by a feeling of *personal disruption*. Specifically, "women perceived themselves as reassessing their lives and seeking some unknown change; they identified life changes and personality changes as commencing at this point; and the incidence of professional counseling (and extra marital affairs) peaked at this period" (Reinke, 1981, p. 2).

(2) The second phase, that usually began between the ages of 28 and 31, generated a *focus on the self and self-development*. At this age, respondents described themselves as having been less oriented to others, seeking something for themselves and setting personal goals (often for the first time). For some of these women, satisfaction with childbearing declined during this period, and separations or divorces became more frequent. Some also reported a new emphasis on physical fitness.

(3) The third period, between the ages of 30 and 35, reflected a *new sense of well-being*. Women stated that "they felt periods of

seeking and introspection were generally over by this time and that they started feeling a great deal of life satisfaction, self-confident about their direction and personal competence, and experienced fewer self-doubts" (Reinke, 1981, p. 2). Remarriages occurred in this period for a few subjects. Preliminary findings from Daniel Levinson's study of women (Levinson, 1985) indicate that for a sample of career women, around age 33 the "age thirty transition" begins to end and women initiate the formation of a "culminating life structure" for early adulthood.

In Reinke, Harris, and Holmes's sample, the late twenties also reflected a peaking of other life events, such as moves across the country, death of family members, and personal illnesses; the incidence of such events declined during the next 15 years. Relationships with their parents seemed to improve when the respondents were in their late twenties and again at about age 40. Although family cycle was a powerful explanation of many of the changes, especially with regard to work, childbearing, and marriage, the preponderance of change at ages 27-30 was independent of family cycle phase.

Why this "age 30 crisis" in women? It is possible that "the age 30 marker has been imbued with societal significance for women" (Reinke, Holmes, & Harris, 1985, p. 1361). In this study, such reevaluation and transition occurred more frequently in women working outside the home at age 26 than in those who were homemakers. (Only 63% of those who experienced changes worked outside the home, whereas only 31% of those who experienced no crisis at these ages worked outside the home). But whether this difference resulted from biological urgency to start a family or increased independence or other factors, we cannot say (Reinke, Holmes, & Harris, 1985).

Although the first of these articles by the same team of investigators finds age *and* family cycle phase both to be related to significant psychosocial changes, the second study—concentrating on women ages 45 to 60—concludes that family cycle phase is more influential at these older ages (Harris, Ellicott, & Holmes, 1986). A total of 64 women, 16 each from age cohorts of 45, 50, 55, and 60, completed a comprehensive interview like the one in the previous study.

Again, a majority of the women (actually, 74%) were rated as having experienced at least one major transition in status and self-

---

BOX 5.5
A Mid-Life Transition

Harris, Ellicott, and Holmes (1986) report the following as an example of one of their interview subjects who experienced a mid-life transition:

> This woman earned an RN degree in her early 20s and then married a man who was beginning a military career. During her 20s and 30s she raised four children and worked part-time, but she never fully developed her own career because of their frequent geographical moves and their family responsibilities. When she was 44, her husband had to retire unexpectedly, and his difficulty adjusting to retirement began to create marital problems. The woman began to feel an increasing need for challenge and stimulation, which was precipitated by the marital problems and her children's departure from home. When she was 45 she revised her occupational goals and subsequently returned to college to pursue a BA degree. The return to school was associated with increasing feelings of self-confidence, self-reliance, and autonomy. At this time, the woman's marital problems escalated, and after briefly considering a separation, she and her husband entered marital counseling. During the next 3 years, they resolved their marital problems and adjusted to their new roles. The woman entered the work force, began building her new career, and entered a period of greater stability and satisfaction. This woman was rated as undergoing a major psychosocial transition between the ages of 44 and 48. (p. 411)

---

concept between the ages of 36 and 60. Harris et al. (1986) used a stringent criterion for a transition; an example is provided in Box 5.5.

Phases of the family cycle contributed to these; 80% of the women experienced at least one major transition during one of the phases of the family cycle. Most frequent changes were during the preschool, launching, and postparental phases, whereas there were fewer transitions during the no-children, school-age, and adolescent phases of the family cycle.

These women, ages 45 to 60 at the time of the interview, did not report any major transition around the age of 40, as men appear to do. Instead, "the women experienced changes somewhat later [during their late forties and fifties]. At that time, the women experienced increases in life and marital satisfaction and positive personality changes such as increased mellowing, patience, assertiveness, and expressivity" (Harris, Ellicott, & Holmes, 1986, p. 415). Another interview study of women ages 45 to 60, by Goodman (1980), generated the same conclusions.

A few empirical studies permit direct comparisons between men and women's development. Lowenthal et al. (1975) interviewed 216 males and females who were facing one of four major life transitions: Graduating from high school, starting married life—these two the researchers called "incremental transitions"—and anticipating one's children leaving the home, or anticipating retirement (two "decremental" transitions). Regardless of the transition, men facing it had more positive self-concepts, as a group, than did the equivalent women. Particularly discrepant were the middle-aged group (men averaging 52 years; women, 48 years). The women of middle age were the most preoccupied with stress of all the groups. Lowenthal et al. noted they possessed many signs of desperation—with themselves, their husbands, and their marriages. In contrast, men of this age cohort had generally positive outlooks. This difference seems to confirm Gail Sheehy's (1976) speculation that men and women are most dissimilar at mid-life. Lowenthal et al. (1975) found that men's and women's lifestyles were, indeed, most discrepant at middle age, with middle-aged women having few activities beyond homemaking and family care, while their husbands were most heavily involved in occupational roles at this time.

6

THE DIALECTICAL APPROACH
AND THE ISSUE OF CHANGE
VERSUS CONSISTENCY IN PERSONALITY

The pattern of personality development through adulthood does not go smoothly. All the conceptions reviewed in Chapters 3, 4, and 5 capitalize on labels like *crises, conflict, transition,* and *turmoil.* But do issues ever get stabilized? Are there points in one's life at which one says, "I've got this major task under control; I can move to something else"?

Erikson's theory, described in Chapter 3, is often portrayed as one that sees choices resolved, as decisions are made at the choice points that demarcate each stage. But it seems to me that Erikson wavers. Although the above interpretation follows from his writings, he also states that conflicts can resurface at a later point. Even the initial issue of trust versus mistrust may be triggered again much later by a set of experiences in adulthood, say, for example, exposure to an unpredictable boss or companion. Even more explicitly does Daniel Levinson's conception capture the flavor of a struggle and a never-complete resolution of developmental issues. Regarding "polarities," Levinson (1978) proposed that they "exist during the entire life cycle. They can never be fully resolved or transcended" (p. 198).

The dialectical approach to personality development brings to the forefront this assumption that no significant issues are ever put to rest throughout adulthood. It views Levinson's stability and crisis periods as mutually dependent, and proposes that it is the mix of the two that makes mature development possible. This chapter examines this conception, both because of its importance but also because of its relevance to an underlying controversy in personality development: Whether one's personality remains consistent or changes during adulthood. This question provides thrust for a review of the relevant empirical literature, in the second half of this chapter.

THE DIALECTICAL APPROACH

The idea of dialectics comes from Plato's analysis of the dialogues of Socrates. In Socrates' questioning of his students, thought was clarified and enriched by challenge, and thus moved toward truth (Smith, 1977). The interplay of ideas, and the resulting challenge, are central concepts in a dialectical approach. Although the term has various meanings throughout the humanities and the social sciences, I consider the approach to include three major points:

(1) the idea of opposing forces, or polarities
(2) the unity of opposites, in the sense that opposites define each other, or lend meaning to each other (Without hate there can be no meaning to love.)
(3) the dynamic relationship between opposites, or their struggle for control, hence necessitating constant change

Dialectical Approaches to Personality Development

How might these abstract ideas be applied to the understanding of personality? In this approach, personality can be described as reflecting opposition within pairs of characteristics, within the individual. Personality development reflects a striving toward fulfillment or achievement of each of these forces, separate from the other. These characteristics can be thought of as needs to be met. They do not reflect simply a presence versus an absence, rather each is an explicit need that has a substantive nature of its own. The tug is between two different poles representing, for example, belongingness and individuality, rather than a state of being awake versus sleepy (Altman, Vinsel, & Brown, 1981).

These contending needs create a state of constant tension in the individual (*tension* like the tension on an extended rubber band, rather than necessarily *tension* in the sense of emotional stress). As one need is effective in pulling the person toward its achievement—that is, as the person devotes more energy to responding to that need—the pull from the other need becomes even more insistent. Thus, in contrast to Erikson, the dialectical approach views *disequilibrium* as a normal state.

Thus, as noted in Chapter 1, in a dialectical view, the characteristic nature of the system is a never-ending struggle. Klaus Riegel, a radical dialectician, believed that developmental tasks are never completed; "At the very moment when completion seems to be achieved, new doubts arise in the individual " (Riegel, 1976, p. 697). In a dialectical analysis, the concept of balance or homeostasis has no permanent applicability, because it is the nature of behavior always to be changing. This approach considers this experience of disequilibrium to be healthy, for it induces change in contrast to a theory that assumes that closure or resolution is possible. A dialectical analysis would propose (to paraphrase Gail Sheehy, 1976) that the whole idea behind the nature of psychosocial development in adulthood is that issues can (and should) never be settled with finality. Furthermore conflict is natural and inevitable and contradictions facilitate development.

Does Synthesis Lead to a Higher Level of Adaptation?

In a dialectical framework, change sometimes is assumed to be a cumulative process. That is, the long-term effects of oppositional forces lead to a synthesis of these in the form of a new structural integration (Altman, Vinsel, & Brown, 1981). For example, the philosopher Hegel spoke of a progression of first, thesis, then antithesis, or opposition, and third, synthesis, or an integrating of these competing forces. Some dialectical theorists consider this integration to be of a higher level or more mature than the forces contributing to it. Recall in Chapter 5 that Levinson, in speaking of the four polarities facing a man at mid-life, described the man's task as, for example, blending his needs for both destructiveness and creation into a higher level of responding. That is, the contradictions within the person may cause the person to feel uncomfortable and motivate him or her to resolve the disequilibrium, leading to a higher level of development.

But as noted in Chapter 1, there is a more pessimistic view held by some dialecticians that the struggle does not lead to assimilation or integration; rather, that the person cycles back and forth, responding to first one need and then another. Levinson, trying to come to terms with the middle-aged man who failed at an attempt at a higher level integration of conflicting identities, speculated that he would form inner contradictions that would be reflected in the flaws of his next life structure.

Typical Dialectical Issues in Adulthood

It is impossible to provide a checklist of "typical dialectical issues of the average American adult," for if we really subscribe to George Kelly's personal construct approach (see Chapter 1), we believe that each of us generates our own labels for these never-ending struggles. But it can be argued that growing up in contemporary society causes many of us to face similar choices. Here are some I have collected from adult-education workshops:

Continuity Versus Change
There is an attraction in continuing to do what you have been doing, because its nice (to a point) for life to be predictable, especially if one has need to be in control. Yet, the need for change also has a pull, not only because consistency can become stagnating, but because change offers novelty and the opportunity for growth. (Another person might offer a similar dialectical struggle, but label it as between order and creativity.)

Achievement Versus Relationships
As we saw in Chapter 5, the workplace exerts a mighty tug upon people, especially those in their twenties, toward achievement. But

men in their forties may feel the need to relinquish this quest for success and supplant it with a sense of sharing, of exploration of feelings, or community with another.

Filling a Role Versus Being an Individual

We are socialized to fill roles, and we know what behaviors are expected of the dutiful son or the solicitous mother. Often we are comfortable playing our designated role, for our predictable behavior makes the recipients of it happy and reassured. By telling us how to behave, the role relieves some of our anxieties. But at the same time, our need for individuality may be clawing for recognition and expression. We may demand to be recognized for our uniqueness, and tugs toward spontaneity and candor may overcome the conforming and superficial nature of rule-dominated behavior.

Immediate Gratification Versus Deferment of Pleasure

This is offered as a dialectical issue not only because it reflects the everyday conflicts of many adults (especially those who need to diet or those who have work assignments with short-term deadlines), but also because it makes the point that Freud's conceptualization of the structure of personality in the young child (see Chapter 2) can be reformulated as a dialectical choice. In fact, Freud has been described as a "reluctant dialectician," in that these systems—in his theory—are in a continuing unresolvable struggle for control.

But these are only examples. A little thought should generate those dialectical issues most appropriate to you or to a particular individual whom you know well.

A Case History Using a Dialectical Analysis

A dialectical analysis may provide a new understanding of development throughout adulthood, if it is applied to the analysis of materials that reflect the person's state of mind at differing points in his or her life. Jenny Masterson, a widow with one son, lived from the late 1860s to 1937. She was no celebrity; in one sense she was just "an average person." Most of her adult life was spent as a telegraph operator. Her husband died one month before her son was born; she was 29 at the time. Between the ages of 58 and 70 Jenny Gove Masterson wrote 301 letters to two young friends, a married couple, who were living in a nearby Eastern college town. The friendship traced back to the time when the husband had been a college roommate of Jenny's son Ross; this was about 10 years before the beginning of the correspondence. The exchange of letters began in March 1926 and continued without interruption—an average of a letter exchanged every two weeks—for eleven and a half years, until Jenny's death in October 1937.

The prominent psychologist of personality, Gordon Allport (1965), collected these letters and after reprinting the contents of most of the letters, he analyzed Jenny's personality development from theoretical perspectives: A psychoanalytic approach (like that of Chapter 2), an existential approach focusing on self-meanings, and a structural-dynamic approach that sought to identify the basic traits descriptive of Jenny's character. Allport carried out his interpretations in the early 1960s, before a dialectical approach had generated much impact on personality development. This is unfortunate because this conception provides a rich and meaningful focus on Jenny's life.

What is missing from the ingredients in the other theoretical interpretations is a procedure for characterizing the dynamic, changing relationship between Jenny and her son, who is certainly the most important person or object in her worldview. But a dialectical analysis provides this; it notes how Jenny's feelings toward Ross shift from rejection to trust and love to distrust and revulsion to, after his death, almost idolization. At an early point in her correspondence with the young couple she expresses the feeling that Ross is lying to her, that he has abandoned her. In March 1926 she wrote: "How impossible it would be for me to ever again believe one word that left his lips" (Allport, 1965, p. 14). At this point she envies his woman friends and calls them "prostitutes."

Later, there is a reconciliation. Ross returns, responds to her, and a mother-son romance of sorts ensues. For her, Ross becomes an object of love. He takes her to dinner, kisses her good night on a rooftop. But subsequently Ross comes to "betray" her again, and she describes her own son as a "contemptible cur." As a final twist, Ross dies at a rather young age, and Jenny's feelings then shift toward acceptance and even veneration of him.

What is the major dialectical issue operating within Jenny? Trust versus distrust of Ross? Of people in general? Financial independence versus dependence on Ross? Each of us, upon reading this collection of letters, might generate a different label. But we would agree that the crisis of their relationship, the absence of equilibrium in it, was central to her personality development during this long span of time.

CONSISTENCY VERSUS CHANGE IN PERSONALITY DEVELOPMENT

For the dialectician, instability is a way of life. But even this perspective recognizes the legitimacy of the quest for stability, at least on a short-term basis. The issue of consistency or changeability has run through all the conceptions so far discussed in this book. As we age, we ask ourselves: Am I the same person I was? If so, it that good or bad? Psychologists of an empirical bent, over the last 50 years, have asked similar questions about people in general. They have not always agreed about the right answers.

The Early Emphasis on Personality Traits

For many years the dominant view in psychology was that one's personality remained the same throughout life; this assumed stability was a result of the emphasis on traits as the building blocks of personality. Traits are usually defined as consistent, generalized qualities of personality that endure over time and that influence behavior. Examples of personality traits include introversion, optimism, hostility, dominance, shyness, and competitiveness.

But the last 25 years have seen a questioning of this belief in consistency; three different theoretical perspectives have given the thrust to the revisionist view. First, a highly influential review, published by psychologist Walter Mischel (1968), concluded that traits showed very little consistency across behaviors; that is, a quality such as honesty, usually considered a trait, could not be generalized across situations. It is important to understand the procedures that tested these ideas; an early example—a series of studies by Hartshorne and May (1928)—will suffice. Children in elementary-school classes were given opportunities to act in dishonest ways in a variety of situations. On one day, the teacher left some coins unattended while a child was in the schoolroom; on another day, each child scored his or her own true/false test so each child had an opportunity to change the score; on other days children were asked questions that tempted them to lie about themselves. Hartshorne and May found very low correlations (an average of .23) between different manifestations of dishonesty; that is, the child who stole money was not likely to be the child who lied; the child who cheated was not necessarily the child who falsified records of his athletic performance. Mischel interpreted these results, along with newer studies testing the generalizability of other traits, to indicate that the situation had a greater influence on the person's behavior than did any internalized personality disposition, a conclusion in keeping with Mischel's Skinnerian or behavioristic orientation.

A second criticism of the importance of trait stability emerged from the rise of humanistic psychology in the 1960s. Spurred by the writings of Carl Rogers, Abraham Maslow, Rollo May, and others, humanistic psychology reflected the philosophical belief in the possibility of change. Not only did it reject a Skinnerian view of people automatically responding to external stimuli, but it also denied the implied predictability of behavior stemming from trait theory's emphasis on stability of personality. In the humanistic viewpoint, people possess a virtual limitless capacity for change. As we have seen in previous chapters, it is now fashionable to believe that change exists—in physical abilities and perceptual skills but also in life-style and religious outlook—and the humanistic perspective has contributed to this perspective.

Stage theory, the topic of Chapters 3 and 5, also contributed to questioning of consistency. The popularity of *Passages* (Sheehy, 1976) implanted the expectations of growth and change in the American consciousness. The "Santa Fe experience"—to be described in Chapter 7— captured the increasing tendency for people in middle age to shift their careers to entirely new and different types of work.

Just one manifestation of stage-related change is Bernice Neugarten's (1968) concept of increased "interiority" with middle age, characterized by greater separation of the person from his or her environment and a decreased complexity or "simplifying" of life.

Certainly we can think of highly publicized persons whose *behavior* has changed dramatically over the years. Box 6.1, describing the changes in Bernadine Dohrn, provides just one example. Similarly in the late 1960s, Jerry Rubin was the personification of protest against the Establishment, a member of the Chicago Seven who protested the police brutality at the 1968 Democratic national convention in Chicago. As psychologist Zick Rubin (1981) has noted, "Jerry Rubin enters the 1970's as a screaming, war-painted Yippie and emerges as a sedate Wall Street (stock) analyst wearing a suit and tie" (p. 18).

Another highly visible change noted by Zick Rubin is that of Richard Alpert, "an ambitious assistant professor of psychology at Harvard, tunes into drugs, heads for India, and returns as Baba Ram Dass, a long-bearded mystic in a flowing white robe who teaches people to 'be here now'" (Rubin, 1981, p. 18).

But do these changes in appearance reflect *personality* change? Zick Rubin (1981) quotes psychologist David McClelland, who was a colleague of Richard Alpert at Harvard and who, two decades later, spent time with Baba Ram Dass; McClelland responded, "Same old Dick—still charming, still as power-oriented as ever" (p. 27).

BOX 6.1
Bernadine Dohrn—Consistent or Changed?

Bernadine Dohrn spent 11 years as a fugitive from justice. Back in the early 1970s, she was virtually a household name; as one of the leaders of the Weatherman faction of the SDS (Students for a Democratic Society), she was wanted for conspiracy to bomb several places throughout the United States. The core of the Weatherman's philosophy was "Kill all the rich people. Break up their cars and apartments. Bring the revolution home, kill your parents, that's where it's really at" (quoted by TRB, 1985, p. 40).

In 1980, Bernadine Dohrn surfaced, surrendering to authorities to face other charges. (The bombing conspiracy charges had been dismissed because of illicit federal surveillance.) Dohrn was given three years probationary sentence. But by 1985, she had passed the New York State bar exam and was employed by the Manhattan office of Sidley & Austin, a Chicago law firm. (She had graduated from the University of Chicago Law School back in 1967.) One of her bosses describes her as "very mature, hardworking, and quiet"; a colleague says, "She acts like a perfectly typical lawyer in a big firm"; another claimed "She's so conservative she's dull" (quoted by TRB, 1985, pp. 4, 41).

Sometimes, dramatic changes in behavior and valued activities may disguise *consistent* values and personality style. Charles Colson was one of the most dedicated staff members in Richard Nixon's White House; he supervised a number of illegal and immoral activities on behalf of President Nixon and was once quoted as saying that he would run down his own grandmother if that was what it took to get President Nixon reelected. After his conviction for Watergate-related crimes and during his prison time, Colson became a born-again Christian. Upon release, he devoted his life to prison reform, and a reading of his recent books (Colson, 1976, 1979) convinces at least this reader of Colson's dedication. But Colson, though "born again," still describes others in "macho" terms; Colson's brothers-in-Christ are invariably "tall," "rugged," "tough," or "jut-jawed."

What Does Consistency of Personality Mean?

The foregoing paragraphs should alert us that *change* can be a broad term and controversies over "personality change" can reflect different meanings. This section examines different conceptions of personality change. Psychologists, when discussing the issue, have at least three meanings:

(1) On a given personality trait, people who are high at say, age 25, are also highest at age 45 or 75. In psychometric terms, this reflects a high test-retest coefficient; it is graphed in Box 6.2. (A longitudinal study would be necessary to generate such data.)

BOX 6.2
An Example of Absolute Consistency

Person	Extroversion Score at Age 20	Extroversion Score at Age 40	Extroversion Score at Age 60
A	55	55	55
B	45	45	45
C	35	35	35
D	25	25	25
E	15	15	15

BOX 6.3
An Example of Relative Consistency

Person	Extroversion Score at Age 20	Extroversion Score at Age 40	Extroversion Score at Age 60
A	55	50	45
B	45	40	35
C	35	30	25
D	25	20	15
E	15	10	5

We may label this *absolute* consistency, because each person maintains the exact score from ages 20 to 40, and 40 to 60. Given the exact consistency in the scores of each individual, it is inevitable that each person maintains his or her position relative to the others. Although this may reflect what some people think of when "consistency of personality" is mentioned, it is a too severe definition of consistency for psychologists of personality.

(2) A second meaning: As different people age, their personalities change in a consistent direction. (See graphic representation in Box 6.3.)

We may label these results as reflecting *relative consistency*. Note that although the patterns in Box 6.2 and Box 6.3 are somewhat different, the correlation coefficients—as a measure of personality consistency—would be the same, 1.00. That is, the method of quantifying the degree of personality consistency is not able to distinguish between absolute consistency and relative consistency.

(3) Now consider a third pattern, graphed in Box 6.4. Like the data in Box 6.3, these results reflect a general decline in extroversion from the ages of 20 to 60. Looking at these results, you may be tempted to conclude that personality is not consistent over time. After all, Person A has dropped from a score of 55 at age 20 to only 25 at age 60. Every one of the five people has a lower extroversion score at age 60 than at age 20. Is this not an indication of *change* in personality?

It is not an indication of change to the consistency theorist; in fact, such advocates would define even this state of affairs as

BOX 6.4
Another Representation of Relative Consistency

Person	Extroversion Score at Age 20	Extroversion Score at Age 40	Extroversion Score at Age 60
A	55	50	25
B	45	32	20
C	35	20	15
D	25	17	10
E	15	10	5

indication of consistency, because each person has maintained his or her relative position from age 20 to age 40 to age 60. Even though each person's level of extroversion has declined and even though some people's scores have declined more than others, at age 60, Person E is still the least extroverted and Person A is still the most extroverted, compared to the others.

Longitudinal Studies of Adolescent and Adult Personality

Psychologists who advocate the consistency of personality and who use correlation to assess the degree of consistency have done a number of longitudinal studies, the results of which verify their expectations. Several of these are reported below.

The Institute of Human Development at Berkeley, California
Jack Block (1971), a psychologist at the Institute of Human Development at the University of California, Berkeley, has studied the consistency of personality for more than 30 years. Several hundred residents of Oakland and Berkeley, California, first measured in the 1930s when they were in junior high school, have been reexamined several times: When they were in their late teens, in their mid-thirties, again in their mid-forties (this latter testing took place in the 1960s). Data collected on them were very extensive— from attitude checklists and interviews to interviews with their parents and teachers, to later interviews with their spouses. Clinical psychologists rated the persons on a variety of personality character-

istics, keeping separate the information from each of the four testing periods listed above. No psychologist rated the materials for the same subject at more than one time period.

The results of this massive study, coordinated by Jack Block (1971), generated a level of consistency within themselves. On virtually every one of the 90 rating scales, there emerged a statistically significant correlation between the subjects' ratings when they were in junior high school and their ratings 30 years later, when they were in their forties. Almost 30% of the 114 personality variables had correlations of .35 or greater from the senior high school testing to age 30 and above. Some correlations were as high as .61. That is, the most self-defeating adolescents tended to be the most self-defeating adults. Cheerful teenagers tended to be cheerful 40-year-olds.

The Baltimore and Boston Studies

Paul Costa and Robert R. McCrae (1976, 1977, 1980, 1985) administered two personality inventories, the 16 PF and the Guilford-Zimmerman Temperament Survey, to a sample of adult males who ranged from the ages of 25 to 82 when they were initially tested. Then these subjects were retested 10 years later.

Very high consistency was found for extroversion; various measures of extroversion, including gregariousness, warmth, and assertiveness, had test-retest correlations of .70 to .84; these are very impressive when one considers the 10-year interval. Anxiety and neuroticism measures also reflected consistency; their correlations were from .58 to .69. Similarly, a tender-mindedness measure showed a correlation of .63, whereas an imaginativeness measure correlated .44. Like Block, Costa and McCrae conclude that neurotic persons are likely to be complainers all their lives. They may complain about different matters, but they persist in complaining.

Also, Costa and McCrae did 6-year and 12-year follow-ups of another group of 200 men, ages 20-76. These produced high correlations leading Costa to claim that "The assertive 19-year-old is the assertive 40-year-old is the assertive 80-year-old" (quoted by Rubin, 1981, p. 20). The average 12-year test-retest coefficient for all scales on the Guilford-Zimmerman inventory was an impressive .73 (Costa, McCrae, & Arenberg, 1980).

These researchers also used retrospective methods to look at changes. They interviewed a sample of adult men, asking them to describe in their own words if and when they had changed in the last 10 years. Costa and McCrae (1978) conclude that a great majority perceived no changes worth mentioning, a conclusion in sharp contrast to those of Levinson and other stage-theory approaches reviewed in Chapter 5. In support of the latter interpretation, Epstein (in a personal communication to Costa and McCrae, May 1979) has argued that old people may retain and report an image of their personalities that they had at younger ages, and thus appear more stable than they really are.

What do these results mean? Let us apply these differing meanings of consistency, presented in Boxes 6.2 through 6.4, and ask if there is any evidence that age has a dampening effect, that is, that individual differences are reduced with increasing age? Not much evidence exists for this. In fact, even with regard to social introversion—certainly the stereotype of elderly life—the increase in reported introversion is only .3 of a standard deviation over 30 years, from ages 50 to 80. Leon, Gillum, Gillum, & Gouze (in press) used 71 men, first retested in 1947 and then retested in 1977. They found significant correlations on all 13 of the MMPI scales. The Baltimore study by Costa and McCrae found *slight* drops over the course of adulthood in people's levels of excitement-seeking activity, hostility, and impulsiveness. No real changes occurred in gregariousness, warmth, assertiveness, depression, or anxiety.

If personality does "stabilize" as the above results imply, how early does it occur? Bachman, O'Malley, and Johnston (1978) tested 1,628 tenth-grade boys and retested them after six years. The general pattern, they felt, was stability, not inconsistency, even though there were increases over the six years in self-esteem, increases in reported drug use, and decreases in aggressive behavior.

Traits Versus States and the Mid-Life Crisis

Consistency theorists such as Jack Block or Costa and McCrae are very dubious that mid-life crises have any permanent effect in the sense of "changing" one's personality. The latter researchers specifically attacked this question in an undergraduate honors thesis, by M. W. Cooper (1977) that they supervised. Cooper developed an inventory of items in order to measure the mid-life crisis (MLC scale); 10 characteristics were included:

   (1) inner turmoil
   (2) inner orientation
   (3) change in time perspective
   (4) sense of failing power
   (5) rise in repressed parts of oneself
   (6) marital dissatisfaction
   (7) job dissatisfaction
   (8) life viewed as tedious, boring
   (9) disharmony with one's children
 (10) a sense of separation from one's parents

As we saw in Chapter 5, Roger Gould portrayed the mid-life crisis as cresting in persons ages 37-43, whereas Daniel Levinson concluded that it occurred between ages 40 and 45. Cooper gave his scale to 233 men ages 35 through 79. Average scores were then computed for different age groups, from the mid-thirties to the mid-fifties; groups spanning 5 years in age and also groups spanning 10 years were composed. Cooper found that there were no age-group differences on the mid-life crisis scale; that is, those men who were 40 to 45 years of age did not, as a group, subscribe to these characteristics to any greater degree than did men in other age groups.

Cooper repeated this procedure with a different group of 315 men, ages 33 to 79. Again, there were no significant differences between age groups. If there is a mid-life crisis, according to Cooper it is not confined to mid-life.

Furthermore, Cooper reports data that lead him to conclude that high scores on the mid-life crisis scale reflect a consistent trait rather than a transitory state, as purported by the stage theorists. By correlating subjects' mid-life-crisis-scale scores with their scores on Eysenck's neuroticism scale, Cooper found a relatively high correlation of .51. Even more impressive was the fact that Cooper had available the scores for these men on a measure of neuroticism that they had completed 10 years before. For different groups, the correlations between the neuroticism score from a decade before and mid-life crisis scores were from .19 to .36, indicating that a long-term tendency toward self-described neuroticism was related to reporting of crisis-related responses.

CONSISTENCY AMONG "THE BEST AND THE BRIGHTEST"

One of the major longitudinal studies of personality change in adulthood was done for another purpose, to identify those characteristics that caused some of the freshmen men at Harvard University to excel over their peers. Despite the limitation that its sample was restricted to Harvard freshmen—and only an elite sample of those—the variety of materials it collected about these men and the fact that it systematically followed them up for 30 years makes it worthy of extended review in this chapter.

Originally called the Grant study of adult development, it was initiated in 1937 through the financial support of William Grant, a variety-store millionaire and philanthropist. Grant and the director of the Harvard University health service agreed to carry out a study that would select a small but healthy sample of several consecutive college classes for intensive medical and psychological study. They used men from the Harvard freshman classes of 1939 through 1944; originally, 268 young men were selected, although 10 of these dropped out of the study during college, mostly because of the wishes of their parents.

The directors of the project were fascinated by what Freud had called "the psychopathology of everyday life"; that is, problems are always with us and good mental health resides in the ways of reacting to problems, not an absence of problems. The quality of one's adjustment becomes most visible only when one faces difficult problems. Some adaptations are better than others, and the original purpose of the project was to identify the ways of adaptation to problems used by the most capable young men. Specifically, the researchers wished to identify the defense mechanisms, or ways of adaptation, used by these young men, to determine which were most effective, and to see how consistent they were. The directors of the study selected those freshmen who were superior in physical and mental health and ability. Preference was given to ambitious, success-oriented persons, rather than rebels or easygoing types.

These young men completed 20 hours of tests—physical, mental, and psychological. They were even given measures of body type and they provided urine samples. Each had eight interviews with a psychiatrist. While they were still freshmen, an interviewer visited their parents (wherever they lived) and completed a family history, including information about child rearing.

Furthermore, from the time of their graduation from Harvard college until 1955, these men answered questionnaires annually about their employment, family situation, hobbies, sports interests, vacations, political views, and drinking practices. From 1955 on, these questionnaires were administered in alternate years. During the years 1950 to 1952, when these men were in their thirties, an anthropologist intensively interviewed each of them, and they were readministered a projective test of personality, the Thematic Apperception Test. At that time, the research staff even classified their children's adjustment to life.

George Vaillant, a professor of psychiatry at Harvard Medical School, joined this long-term project in 1967 and personally interviewed a sample of 94 men from the original group, between 1967 and 1969 (the men were then in their late forties). These men included best-selling novelists, members of the U.S. President's cabinet, newspaper editors, teachers and professors, and judges; clearly they were among "the best and the brightest." In 1969, in their late forties, their average income was $30,000, 95% had been married (though 15% were divorced), most were extremely satisfied with their occupations, but 40% had received psychological counseling at some point in their lives.

Vaillant's (1977) book about the study identifies what he considers four distinct levels of development in an individual's life, and he proposes that there are specific kinds of defense mechanisms, or types of adjustment, typical of each level. (See Box 6.5.)

Central to the topic of this chapter is Vaillant's procedure in constructing an Adult Adjustment Scale that rated 32 different behaviors with respect to their relative maturity. (This rating scale is reprinted in Box 6.6.) Then, using a separate set of coders, Vaillant classified the types of defense mechanisms used by the men in his subsample. Comparing the 30 "best outcomes" and the 30 "worst outcomes" among these men, based on the ratings they received on the Adult Adjustment Scale, Vaillant found the two groups differed drastically with regard to the types of defense mechanisms they employed. For example, 45% of the "best outcome" men used mature defense mechanisms, whereas less than 20% of the "worst outcome" men did. In contrast, 25% of the "worst outcome" men

---

BOX 6.5
Vaillant's Defense Mechanisms

Mature

    (1) suppression
    (2) sublimation
    (3) altruism
    (4) humor
    (5) anticipation

Neurotic

    (6) displacement
    (7) intellectualization
    (8) depression
    (9) reaction Formation
  (10) dissociation

Immature

  (11) acting out
  (12) passive aggression
  (13) hypochondriasis
  (14) fantasy
  (15) projection

Psychotic

  (16) denial
  (17) delusional projection
  (18) distortion

SOURCE: Vaillant, 1977.

---

employed either immature or psychotic defenses, whereas only 5% of the "best outcome" men did. And clearly the use of immature or psychotic defenses was related to future behavioral problems. For example, one third of the men who used the most immature defense mechanisms between the ages of 20 and 45 developed chronic physical illnesses or died during the next decade. Seven of these Vaillant called "perpetual boys." Like earnest Boy Scouts they worked hard at their jobs and required little in the way of counseling for psychological adjustment problems. But they never worked through the Eriksonian life tasks. At middle age, they were still tied to their mothers; only two of the seven ever married. They were downwardly mobile, and had the worst career record in the study.

The Grant study provides strong evidence that adjustment in late adolescence is predictive of "success level" at mid-life, even among this highly selected group of subjects. But such a conclusion rests on a subjective foundation, in that Vaillant's definition of many assessments and terms—such as *successful working, successful*

BOX 6.6
Rating Scales Used by Vaillant

I. ADULT ADJUSTMENT SCALE (a rating from 0 to 32)

Taking the entire twenty-five-year period (from college graduation to 1967) into account, one point was assigned for each of the following thirty-two items that was true. A score of less than 7 defined the Best Outcomes; a score of 14 or more defined the Worst Outcomes.

I. Career
   a. Failure to receive steady promotion or increasing responsibility, if possible, every five years since graduation.
   b. Not listed in *Who's Who in America* or *American Men of Science*.
   c. Earned income is less than $40,000 (unless in teaching, clergy, or responsible public service or quasi-charitable work).
   d. Earned income is less than $20,000 (1967 dollars)
   e. Occupation does not clearly surpass father's (income, responsibility, occupational status).
   *g. Has not actively participated over the years in extracurricular public service activities.
   h. However prestigious in the eyes of others, his job either is not one that he really wants for himself, or over the years it has failed to match his realistic ambitions.

Rater agreement for each item was eighty-five to one hundred percent, except for items marked with an asterisk, where agreement was seventy-five to eighty-five percent.

II. Social Health
   a. Failed to achieve ten years or more of marriage (without separation) or failed to express overt satisfaction with that marriage on two or more occasions after the first year. (Eventual divorce did not affect this item.)
   b. Divorced, separated, or single. (Exclude widowers.)
   c. Never wanted to have or adopt children. (Ignore this item if he is single due to external cause—e.g., Catholic clergy.)
   d. One-third or more of children are markedly underperforming scholastically, delinquent, or getting psychiatric care. [Subsequent data analysis showed that this question would have been useful in 1975, but in 1967, when it was asked, it correlated with nothing.]

e. Maintained no contact with surviving family of origin, except by duty or necessity.

f. Regularly stated that he has less than usual interest in or fewer than average number of close friends. (Subjective evidence.)

*g. Not regularly a member of at least one social club and evidence from less than two occasions that he has more than one close friend. (Objective evidence.)

h. No regular pastime or athletic activity that involves others (family members do not count).

N.B. Items a, b, c, f, g, and h were used to separate the Friendly from the Lonely men.

III. Psychological Health

a. For more than half of years described, did not use full allotted vacation time or spent it at home doing chores or on dutiful visits to relatives.

b. Explicit statement that subject had missed something by being too calm, unruffled, controlled, or unemotional (at two points in time). [Like Item II-d, this item was not significantly correlated with overall adjustment.]

*c. Failure to express satisfaction with job on three or more occasions and once in the past three years.

d. Expressed explicit dissatisfaction with job at three points in time and once in past three years, or had changed occupational field once or job three times since age thirty without evidence of concomitant improvement in personal satisfaction or success.

e. Evidence of detrimental (interferes with health, work, or personal relations at home) use of alcohol, or use of sedative or stimulant drugs weekly for more than three years, or more than six ounces of hard liquor a day for three years, or use of tranquilizers for more than a year.

f. Ever hospitalized because of mental breakdown, alcohol misuse, or "physical" illness without evidence of somatic pathology.

g. Evidence on more than two occasions that he is chronically depressed, dissatisfied with the course of his life, or evidence that he is consistently labeled by himself or others as being emotionally ill.

h. Has sought psychiatric help for more than ten visits.

IV. Physical Health

a. One hospitalization or serious accident since college [Item not significantly correlated with overall adjustment.]

b. More than two operations and/or serious accidents since college (battle wounds excluded). [Item not significantly correlated with overall adjustment.]

c. Two hospitalizations since college (excluding those due to surgery, trauma, or physical checkup).

d. Own estimate of general health since college expressed in less than the most favorable terms on more than one-fourth of occasions.

e. On the average misses two or more workdays a year due to illness.

f. On the average misses five or more workdays a year due to illness.

g. Afflicted with chronic illness (requiring medical care) that significantly limits activity *or* more than a month of work lost consecutively due to illness.

SOURCE: Reprinted from Vaillant, 1977, Appendix C, pp. 389-390.

living, or *adaptation*—reflect his own value judgments. He states that adaptation implies success (1977, p. 361) and even acknowledges that healthy success in the study was sometimes confused with materialism (1977, p. 365). He concludes that "a man's capacity to remain happily married over time" (1977, p. 320) is the best indicator of mental health. Even the original selection of subjects has been criticized for being "preselected for their conformity to a perception of the normal and the admirable" (Wolff, 1978, p. 97).

Despite its limitations, the Grant study is so thorough in its processing of information accumulated over a 30-year period that Vaillant's conclusions are worth reporting. He believes that the results provide strong support for Erikson's theory of eight stages of psychosocial development. For example, he notes that a few subjects had very unhappy childhoods; those subjects, failing to have developed a sense of trust in the world about them, were unable to form many friendships in adulthood, nor to develop a playful or humorous attitude toward life. As Dacey (1982, p. 86) notes in commenting on Vaillant's work, "Although childhood variables had considerably less impact on the later lives of men in the study than psychologists have led us to believe, Vaillant did find a relationship between a seriously unhappy childhood and later difficulties in life."

But Vaillant also proposes the addition of two other stages. He advocates that for men, at least, a new stage that he titled "career consolidation" arises between the stages of intimacy and generativity. In keeping with Gould's and Levinson's observations, he finds that his subjects, between the ages of 25 and 35, were oriented to their careers, worked very hard, and showed unquestioning conformity to work values.

Mentors were usually rejected during this age period. Vaillant (1977, p. 218) reports that many of the men had described mentors at age 19 but had forgotten them by age 47. More of the successful than unsuccessful men had mentors. Thus, the Harvard men's reactions give support to Levinson's proposition that there is a period in which "becoming one's own man" is important.

The second additional stage, Vaillant believes, occurs after the generativity crisis, in the late forties and early fifties. Calling this "keeping the meaning versus rigidity," Vaillant argues that those who "keep the meaning" develop an acceptance of the weaknesses of their fellow human beings. These men wish to maintain and protect their culture even while recognizing that it is imperfect. They are more resigned to the inevitability of the future, more contented. In contrast, those who become increasingly rigid also become more and more alienated from their fellow men.

While generating new stages on the basis of his data, Vaillant also fails to find support for some of the central developments in previous theories. For example, little support emerged for the contention of Levinson that fear of one's own death becomes predominant during the generativity stage. Vaillant also saw few examples of *crises*; although change did often occur, mostly it was relatively slow and steady. He notes that for most of the men, fear of the death of their marriage partners was far greater than fear of their own death.

RETHINKING CONSISTENCY

If we play by their rules, the consistency theorists can make an impressive claim about the stability of personality throughout adulthood. But their "rules" include their own definitions of consistency, especially the use of correlation coefficients to assess degree of consistency. And even critics acknowledge that certain aspects of personality are relatively stable, including emotional style, introversion/extroversion, anxiety level, and depression. Similarly, interviews with older people directed at identifying their coping styles have noted that these are typically continuations of style used throughout their adulthood (Reichard, Livson, & Peterson, 1962). But one critic, Orville Brim, is more interested in other aspects of personality, such as people's values, their self-esteem, and their sense of control over their own lives. He concludes that "These are the elements of character that undergo the most important changes over the course of life" (quoted by Z. Rubin, 1981, p. 24). Likewise, Daniel Levinson is also critical of stability measures, claiming that these are not what adulthood is really about. The emergence from a mid-life crisis, proposes Levinson, leaves one a different person from before.

A different type of reaction to claims of consistency uses a statistical analysis, asking how much consistency is accounted for by a correlation. Assume that over a long interval, say 10 years, there occurs a correlation of, say, .70 between relative positions of individuals on two administrations of the same personality measure. Such a finding is typical of those reviewed earlier in this chapter, and such correlations are usually interpreted as reflecting high degrees of consistency over time. But to determine how much variance is accounted for by a correlation coefficient (i.e., how much of the variation in scores on one measure is determined by variations on the other measure), we must square the correlation coefficient. The square of .70 is .49; so only about half of the variation is common. Even when a correlation coefficient of .70 has been obtained, a lot of change has occurred. People can change their relative positions on the two measures rather extensively and still contribute to such a "high" correlation.

Similarly, another kind of methodology chosen to study consistency—the retrospective approach—may lead us to "see" more consistency than was actually there. Most of us want to believe that we are consistent; conversely, "unpredictability" is not a desirable personal characteristic in our society.

Are there ways of resolving the apparent conflict between consistency and the stage theorists' views of abrupt upheaval and transitions during adulthood? Yes, several perspectives would argue that both can seemingly operate within the same person.

Norma Haan, another researcher at the University of California at Berkeley, concludes that well-adjusted individuals do adjust their personalities and values to reflect changes throughout the life cycle. Haan (cited in Casady, 1975) compared the personalities of well-adjusted young and middle-aged adults to those of older persons. She detected that both groups had very similar sets of traits, but they tended to rely on different traits more heavily at specific ages of life. The young and middle-aged adults valued intellectual traits and pursuits, and wanted to see themselves as dependable, productive, likable, and straightforward. The older persons, in their sixties and seventies, emphasized other traits in themselves, such as their capacity for intimacy and close interpersonal relations. They were more protective of others and placed high value on cheerfulness, gregariousness, and a sense of humor. They cared less for manifesting intellectual skills.

A dialectic approach is also relevant to the dilemma posed here. Consistency versus change can, in and of itself, be viewed as a dialectical issue. Advocates of consistency would describe as a tug a "powerful drive to maintain the sense of one's identity, a sense of one's continuity that allays fear of changing too fast or being changed against one's will by outside forces" (Rubin, 1981, p. 24). But at the same time, most of us feel the pull of a desire to be "a purposeful, striving organism with a desire to be more than [we are] now" (Rubin, 1981, p. 24). An attraction of the dialectical approach is that it provides a formulation by which consistency and change can each be characteristics of the same individuals. It is regrettable that this issue often becomes an ideological debate, because reasonable advocates of each side agree that there exist constraints on their conclusions. Paul Costa has been quoted as saying: "The assertive 19-year-old is the assertive 40-year-old is the assertive 80-year-old unless *something happens to change it*" (Rubin, 1981, p. 26). And Orville Brim has stated that people's personalities will keep changing throughout the course of life *unless they get stuck*. Both are essential; a stable personality is necessary to develop a sense of identity, but the potential for growth is the hallmark of humanity.

7

OCCUPATIONAL CHANGES IN ADULTHOOD

The first half of this book has portrayed various conceptions of personality development and psychosocial development during adulthood. Subsequent chapters apply these concepts to important aspects of adult life: careers, intimate relations and marriage, sexual attitudes and behavior, sex roles, political and religious values, and adaptation to aging. For each of these topics, my emphasis is on developmental concerns, or the changing nature of the phenomenon across the 50 more years of adulthood. The chapter-length coverage of each of these aspects also permits further investigation of the validity and applicability of the theories presented in the earlier chapters.

In the case of occupational choice, one of the most respected theories of career development—that by Donald Super (1966, 1986)—follows the individual's career through the entire period of adolescence and adulthood. Super emphasizes changes in self-concept and their inevitable impacts on choice and change of career. Conveniently for the structure of this book, Super employs a stage theory of occupational development (although he has been faulted by some for failing to incorporate recent concepts and methods from life-span developmental psychology; see, for example, Vondracek, Lerner, & Schulenberg, 1986). The first stage, occurring between the ages of 15 and 25, is characterized by exploration and trial, with consideration of several avenues, either systematically or in a trial-and-error fashion. The second stage, called the establishment phase, occurs between the ages of 25 and 45, and involves the implementation of a career choice and stabilization within an occupation. In keeping with Gould's concepts described in Chapter 5 of this book, the individual expects that hard work—even, for some, the extreme of "apple polishing"—will provide recognition and advancement, and the young worker may seek additional technical training to facilitate progress up the occupational ladder. Emphasis here is on conformity to the life style of "superiors" in the organization, and a rather stable career pattern. The maintenance stage, applicable according to Super at ages 45 to 55, involves continuity of vocational behavior along established lines, although a reevaluation phase may occur here, too. An outcome is a sense of becoming resigned to one's failure to reach the anticipated level of achievement.

By use of *maintenance* to label this stage Super does not necessarily mean that development is constant (Whitbourne & Weinstock, 1979). There is even a dialectical flavor to Super's (1957) treatment of this stage; he writes that "Perfect equilibrium is never reached, that vocational adjustment is a continuous process throughout the whole of life and that even the maintenance stage is not, as the name may be thought to imply, a period of undiluted enjoyment of the fruits of labor. Instead, the labor continues, although perhaps somewhat less arduously because its pattern is by now well established" (p. 149). At age 55 begins a deceleration stage or "disengagement," that prepares the worker for retirement. The last stage is the retirement period around age 65; the worker may experience a severe discontinuity in both work role and self-concept (see Chapter 11 for elaboration).

It should be apparent to you that Super's vocational-development theory contains many of the same qualities of the general stage theories of Chapters 3 and 5, even to its specifying of precise (and too confining) age limits for each stage. And the theory also suffers the limitation of previous ones in its implicit male bias; theories built on the experience of men assume a career pattern that is linear and uninterrupted (Perun & Bielby, 1981). For women, it is common for the combination of work and family responsibilities to produce an interrupted career pattern.

THE PLACE OF WORK IN ONE'S ADULT IDENTITY

For young people who have completed their schooling and are now ready to enter the world of work on a full-time and "permanent" basis, change has characterized their lives up to this point. Although they realize that their jobs may be one of the most lasting features of their adult life, they may not be prepared for such an enduring commitment. Undergraduate students have, on occasion, confided to me that the idea of working in the same job for 40 years is utterly incomprehensible to them. And well it might; even the professional literature in occupational psychology has virtually a gap (Hall, 1986) with regard to research on maintenance of one's career during mid-life.

Yet they realize that one's identity as a worker is central. Soon after we meet someone, we are likely to ask: "What kind of work do you do?" We ask this not only because we assume that we will know more about the person from the answer, but because we, too, value our work identity. When given a "Twenty Statements" test that asks the person to provide responses to the question "Who Am I?," most adults mention their occupation among the initial five self-labels.

Yet our feelings toward our own work identity may reflect a love-hate relationship. Sarason (1977, pp. 13-14) notes that the question, "How do you like your job?" triggers different and sometimes ambivalent feelings about our work. At a superficial level, our initial response is usually "Well of course I like it." But at a deeper level we may question what we are doing. Our work identity, like our self-identity, may go through periods of relative turmoil and then relative stability. And with younger adults of the "baby-boomer" generation, Hall and Richter's (1985) study indicates that a new set of values affects the attitudes toward work held by this cohort. Baby boomers place high priority on the balance between work life and family life, partly because the preponderance of two-career families has forced them to.

Society places expectations on us to enjoy our work, especially if our occupation is a prestigious, well-paying one. As more and more people move into high-level professions, they are all expected to experience satisfaction and fulfillment in their work. But what if they don't? What if they burn out or lose interest? Sarason (1977) observes:

> To express dissatisfaction or boredom with or a waning interest in one's work—particularly if one's work is judged by society as fascinating and important, as in the case of many professions—is no easy matter. To face up to such dissatisfaction is literally to question what one is and to have to justify continuing as one has. It is no less difficult, upsetting, and propelling than to come to the realization that one no longer wishes to live with one's spouse. Our experience suggests that to talk candidly about one's relationship to one's work is as difficult as talking about one's sex life. We define ourselves, and are defined by others, by what we do: our work. To question this definition produces internal conflict, in part precisely because we know that we have come to see ourselves quite differently from others. (p. 57)

This is a provocative statement from one of the most experienced observers of career change in adulthood. Perhaps you think it is too extreme, in its statement of the difficulty we have in expressing dissatisfaction with our jobs. Many of us recall the Johnny Paycheck song, "Take This Job and Shove It." But note that Sarason is especially referring to jobs that outsiders see as "fascinating and important." Society may tolerate—or even expect—ditch diggers or garbage collectors to grouse about their working conditions. But for heart surgeons or architects to vacillate about their career identity creates questions and chagrin, partly because we reason, "If they are not satisfied in their high-paying, important positions, how can we be satisfied with our mediocre jobs?"

Sarason's claim that it is just as hard to talk frankly about one's job dissatisfactions as it is to reveal one's sex life may also strike the reader as too extreme. But Sarason (1977) observes that "Our society has made it far easier to change marriage partners than to change careers (partially or drastically) but the dynamics behind both types of changes are similar if not identical" (p. 71).

Ideally, one's personality and one's choice of an occupation should be congruent. John Holland's (1963, 1973) widely cited theory of career development sees choice of a career as a three-stage process in which self-knowledge and knowledge of the world of work have matured to a point that an intelligent and congruent career choice could be made. In Holland's view, our vocational interests are an extension of our personalities. One cause of job dissatisfaction is a lack of a good match between the person's work orientation and the rewards generated by his or her occupation. Work orientations have been classified into intrinsic and extrinsic orientations. Intrinsic aspects of a job include the nature of the job task, the degree to which it is challenging and fulfilling, its opportunity for personal growth, and its proper level of difficulty. In contrast, an extrinsic orientation reflects the wage level, the working conditions (how clean, how comfortable), and the job security. For some workers, intrinsic factors are more important, whereas for others, extrinsic aspects take precedence. And even for the same worker, there may be a shift from intrinsic to extrinsic motivations over the span of adulthood.

Occupations differ in the kinds of rewards they provide. Sometimes it is not feasible to establish a match between the person's needs and what the occupation offers, but the worker may continue in the job for many years despite this lack of congruence. The position may have initially offered challenge or excitement, but then inertia sets in, as the work becomes routine.

A dialectical analysis (see Chapter 6) is helpful in understanding persons who, in mid-life, shift positions. Why would a person give up a well-paying, prestigious position? We often stereotype such people as perpetually dissatisfied and emotionally unstable. But research evidence (Krantz, 1977) suggests that people who change jobs in the middle of adulthood are no more maladjusted than the rest of us. Changes are often a response to dialectical tugs—toward intrinsic rewards rather than earlier extrinsic rewards, for example. They often reflect rational attempts to move from what have become unsatisfactory occupational situations. Krantz (1977) concludes: "The fundamental difference between those of us 'normals' who stay in the trajectory of our lives and careers and those who choose to change that direction is the solution chosen, not in the problems themselves" (p. 167).

SPECIAL PROBLEMS OF THE PROFESSIONAL PERSON

Before further analysis of career change during mid-life, we need to devote extended attention to the special problems of those persons in professional or executive positions who lose their interest in their work. In one sense, society's assumption is correct; people in positions that pay more and carry more perquisites are more satisfied with their jobs. Few, if any, physicians want to change jobs with pipe fitters or bricklayers. But the exceptional case illustrates the dialectical thrust of the phenomenon. John Coleman (1974), while an economist and college president, decided to break the lockstep and vary the rhythm of his life by spending his sabbatical leave working anonymously in menial jobs. For two months he dug trenches and laid pipe in Georgia, and then worked for $2.50 an hour as a garbage collector in College Park, Maryland. (Some years later Coleman resigned his position as president of a charitable foundation and took over the ownership and management of a country inn in Chester, Vermont.)

Not many people at Coleman's level of eminence would emulate his actions. But some, at least, would acknowledge that, for them, professional work generates its own types of discontent. Why? Sarason (1977) offers three reasons:

Lack of Control Over One's Work Schedule

For most people in the professions, the work has intrinsic rewards (as well as extrinsic ones). A surfeit of riches abounds in that there is always too much work to do. As the person becomes more proficient and more recognized, more opportunities beckon. Accomplished family physicians soon have so many patients that they are working exhausting hours. The entrepreneur sees more and more markets develop, but each requires a finite portion of his or her time and energy. The renowned scholar gets so many invitations to write chapters and give speeches that each loses its appeal and becomes an ordeal. Outsiders may suggest the solution is "Just say no" to requests that cause an expansion of services or an exhaustion of energies. But many professional persons credit their success to their willingness to work harder than their colleagues or to their unique collection of skills and abilities, and it is hard for them to decline opportunities that provide recognition or offer challenges. The proficient physician may feel an obligation to his or her community; the scholar may fear that saying "no" is the first indication of a dying interest in his or her search for truth. Although they long for a manageable work schedule, their very nature makes this unattainable.

Conflict Between One's Self-Concept and One's Reputation in the Community

A second source of dissatisfaction for professional persons is the discrepancy they feel between the level of esteem accorded them by their clients, or society in general, and their own self-concepts. A heart surgeon may be idolized by patients who see the physician as a miracle worker who has saved them from death, but the physician's own reaction may be, "I didn't do a very good job with that patient; I was too slow, I made mistakes." One physician has confided, "The more my patients treat me as a god, the more I feel like a hypocrite." Similarly, students may respect and commend a professor for the sophistication and erudition of her lectures, even as the professor castigates herself for failing to review the most recent sources. Although the discrepancy between clients' views of us and our own self-concepts may be a source of discomfort at any job level, Sarason seems accurate in identifying it as a particular problem in occupations that (a) run the risk of public adulation, and (b) include an expertise beyond the common knowledge of the layperson.

Lack of Challenge

A third source of dissatisfaction stems from our professional activities that were previously challenging but are so no longer. It's difficult for professional people to talk about declining motivation, because their work is often seen by clients, family, and friends as an endlessly fascinating and rewarding line of endeavor (Sarason, 1977). To reflect such concerns is to raise questions in the minds of others about one's competence or emotional stability. Sarason (1977) concludes:

> If an individual is by conventional criteria doing well (e.g., he is gaining recognition, his income is increasing, he is respected for his knowledge and expertise, he has a comfortable home, travels, etc.), we unreflectively assume that his feelings about his work are isomorphic, so to speak, with these 'objective' indices. (p. 114)

BOX 7.1
Reactions to Professional Job Burnout

What happens when job dissatisfaction in a professional person disconfirms society's evaluation of the person? Robert F. was 42 and superintendent of schools in a Midwestern suburban community that contained a university. A Ph.D. from a leading university, he had been a classroom teacher and a principal. His salary as a school superintendent in the mid 1970s was $42,000. He resigned in the middle of the school year; his work had lost its satisfaction.

When friends heard that he had resigned, they first assumed that he had accepted a "better" superintendency. When he told them that he had no other job, they thought he was being coy or secretive. On further thought, many speculated that he was in trouble, or ill, or in an unhappy marriage. After a couple of weeks, a number of his friends finally accepted his affirmation of job dissatisfaction, and some expressed their admiration and envy for his action.

SOURCE: Sarason, 1977, p. 112.

As in "Richard Cory," the poem in which the highly successful, well-respected millionaire commits suicide, we ask why? See Box 7.1 for one example of society's reaction.

For many a professional person, dissatisfactions like those in the above paragraphs accrue over the years, so that by the late thirties or early forties, they have forced the person into a painful reexamination of his or her work identity. "For the professional person mid-life is, like the beginning of adolescence, experienced as an eruption of internal stirrings which had best not be articulated" (Sarason, 1977, p. 105).

But isn't this true of everyone? The stage theorists described in Chapter 5 would certainly propose so. Sarason (1977) argues that it is more so for the professional person who "came to his career with greater expectations that he was embarking on a quest in which all his capacities and curiosities would be exploited, the vibrant sense of challenge, growth, and achievement sustained, and his sense of personal worth and importance strengthened; the material rewards he would obtain would be as icing on a delicious cake" (p. 106).

THE "ONE LIFE, ONE CAREER" IMPERATIVE

One cause for the consternation when a person changes vocations in mid-life is the implicit assumption in our society of "one life, one career," or as Sarason (1977) colorfully expresses it, society views the developmental task of the young individual as deciding "from a smorgasbord of possibilities the one vocational dish he will feed on over the course of his life" (p. 123). The early choice of a career is expected in our society. Children early on are quizzed, "What do you want to be when you grow up?" Not usually tolerated are answers such as, "Well, I'd like to be a marine biologist for about 10 years, then I'd like to design houses, and then be a farmer." Colleges require their undergraduates to declare a major field, leading them toward seemingly irrevocable career commitments. Sometimes, the decision to go to graduate school or law school is primarily motivated by a desire to delay deciding on a career.

Frequency and Causes of Occupational Change

Despite these pressures, many people do change jobs during adulthood. Sommers and Eck (1977) report that 30% of the work force and 10% of technicians and professional people experienced a career change in a five-year period. Osherson (1980) estimates that five million citizens of the United States change their occupation in a given year.

Why does this happen? Three different explanations have been suggested. The "counter-culture hypothesis" concludes that dissatisfaction with the present social system has led individuals to leave the mainstream of society. The rapid growth of communes in the early 1970s supported this claim; many members of communes were former professional persons, executives, and managers who "dropped out of the rat race" that they felt was corporate life (Roberts, 1971). They sought participation in a different type of social system, one that did not possess the values of competitiveness, materialism, regimentation, depersonalization, and status distinctions they found present in the white-collar world. Krantz (1977), in his observation of the "Santa Fe experience" (to be described in the next section), also concludes that the predominant motive was the rejection of a previous life-style. As one mid-life career changer told Moffitt (1986) "Yes maybe there's a little drop in the standard of living, but there's a big jump in the quality of life" (p. 47).

A second explanation—sometimes labeled the "developmental hypothesis"—pictures the career shift as a manifestation of a personal crisis. A man may experience such a crisis at mid-life when he realizes that he is not accomplishing his lifelong goals, or, in Levinson's terms, not attaining his "dream." Osherson (1980) has portrayed the crisis as one of *loss*, of coming to terms with the lost self, or the discrepancy between who you are and who you expected to be. Sarason (1977) has used the example of the Frenchman, Paul Gauguin, who left his banking career to go the South Seas to paint. For such persons, the urgency of acting—the "now or never" aspect—is a driving force to radical change. A 45-year-old man who had abandoned his high-paying job without any definite plans for another told an interviewer that he had liked his work; "I was actually enjoying myself more than I had in years. It was just that if I was ever going to try something different, I had to do it now" (Moffitt, 1986, p. 47).

The remaining explanation places focus on sociological rather than intrapersonal causes for occupational change. In periods of rapid social, economic, and technological change, such as we currently are experiencing, careers become obsolete, or at least need upgrading. Typists become word processors; bookkeepers become computer operators. Shifts in the skills needed by society lead to shifts in jobs. The cost of living has demanded that more wives and mothers work outside the home; by the same token, a second salary in the family may make more feasible a career change that requires a period of retraining or further education, and hence temporarily no income.

Empirical Studies of Men who Change Careers

Two empirical studies of men who changed careers in mid-life have been completed by psychologists (Krantz, 1977; Osherson, 1980). Although neither has a large number of subjects—one interviewed 30 men, the other 20—their conclusions are similar, and each provides detailed examples of the reasons for the changes.

David Krantz interviewed 30 men, all of whom moved to Santa Fe, New Mexico, and changed jobs. All were well-educated, with at least a bachelor's degree; many had postgraduate education. Aged 32 to 56 at the time of Krantz's interview, each man had at least five years experience before his change. And many of the shifts were quite radical; a New York City banker became a waiter in a ski resort, a Broadway set designer became a bartender, an advertising agency head switched to the director of a small art gallery, a social worker became a construction worker, an eminent TV producer became a bus driver, and a stockbroker shifted to an ice cream store owner.

Despite the diverse occupations chosen, Krantz found many common themes in the reasons for the changes. For these men, the change extended beyond just that of their occupation. "For all the people interviewed, the decision to change careers involved far more than simply giving up the immediate activities involved in the work setting" (Krantz, 1977, p. 172). For some, the choice involved rejecting an unacceptable future reality, such as living in an urban environment, where he felt alienated and unsafe, or an eroding family structure because of work demands or a long commute. The shift also symbolized a freedom from the restraints of their previous jobs. These men were searching for control over their own lives. Furthermore, they had reevaluated and redefined the significance of work as a definition of their lives. For some, work has remained central; for others, less so. For the latter, their identities are now less defined by their jobs, material possessions, or family background. An editor and publisher, Phillip Moffitt (1986), after interviewing people who had shifted careers concluded: "What I think is starting to occur is not a phenomenon of failure, but of success. . . . These are people with the strong self-image necessary to maintain an identity without the prop of a career or professional label: Doctor, Lawyer, Businessman" (p. 47). One of these men told Krantz (1977): "People in Santa Fe do not stand on formality or judge you by material signs of success. You're accepted for what you are and not what you've accomplished" (p. 183). Moving to Santa Fe—a city that has come to symbolize this transformation—was also symbolic to these men; the change in physical location was an important step in removing constraints. Traveling in a sense causes us to be different people, or at least it varies what have become habitual ways of acting.

In the second empirical study, Osherson (1980) analyzed the life histories of 20 men, each of whom, as a result of a mid-life crisis, left established professional careers to become creative artists or craftsmen. Initially they were research scientists, executives, business managers, lawyers, and professors; of the 20, 18 had gone to graduate school. All had spent at least three years, after their training, in a professional career; they were between the ages of 35 and 50 when interviewed. All were now—and had been for from 3 to 10 years—either an actor, a potter, or a visual artist.

On the basis of his interviews, Osherson concludes that these men were seeking to recapture a part of their selfhood that had been lost. He uses Levinson's analysis of shifts toward feminine (i.e., artistic) values during mid-life. The focus on a values substitution also explains a recently increasing trend for men in their middle years to enter seminaries to study for the ministry. In the 12 years between 1975 and 1987, the average age of seminarians increased from 25 to 31, and older persons (i.e., over age 30) now comprise 44% of the 52,000 seminary students in the United States (Associated Press, 1987). Interviews with these people reflect a generalized feeling that their previous life had its good points but "it didn't deal with values and the solid issues of people's lives" (Associated Press, 1987, p. 8A).

Like Krantz's subjects, the men in Osherson's sample reflected changes beyond simply their occupational identities. Nine of the 13 marriages dissolved during this period.

Is a Crisis Necessary to Bring About Change?

To what extent do the changes described in the previous section result from a crisis? Does the second of the three explanations under Frequency and Causes of Occupational Change reflect a general trend? Lawrence (1980) selected 10 persons who had changed jobs between the ages of 35 and 55 in an effort to determine if a drastic upheaval in their lives had been associated with their occupational change. Five of these subjects were men; five were women. Among their job shifts were: librarian to writer, small business owner to career counselor, professor of physics to musician, and clerical worker to custodian. Lawrence had hypothesized that a mid-life career change is the outcome of the resolution of a mid-life crisis but she observed a crisis pattern in only 3 of her 10 subjects. In one of these the crisis was externally generated; the owner of a family business suffered unanticipated difficulties with the Internal Revenue Service, forcing him to sell his business and look for new work. A second was both internal and external; a clerical worker, without any family ties, faced the loss of a person she had been in love with for 18 years. She became a custodian, but still remained single. The third example, the most internally caused crisis, was a Jesuit priest who, affected by the death of his brother, was forced to examine his inability to express his feelings. He resigned from the priesthood, married, and became a college administrator. So, for each of these three, a personal change preceded the career change.

But for the other seven it was hard to detect any precipitating crisis; the personal change associated with the career change took place throughout the career-change process. Some of them planned a change for a long time. Even though outsiders may have characterized their job shifts as sudden or dramatic, the career changers perceived a continuity in their lives. Lawrence (1980) notes: "Although these subjects made externally identifiable career changes, it is clear that in all ten cases, a direct relationship existed internally between the kind of work they did and enjoyed in their first career and what they chose to do in the second" (p. 44). From the inside the shift was not spontaneous; rather, they saw it as evolutionary over a period of time. Box 7.2 presents one example.

BOX 7.2
An Example of Evolutionary Career Change

Mrs. Lloyd, who shifted from a public-school librarian to a writer, told an interviewer:

I guess I feel that I didn't make a mid-life change. Well, I'm sort of always changing, and it isn't that I never settled into any one thing. Its . . . well, I have a friend who describes me . . . 'You would reach out and pull in strands, a strand from here and a strand from there, and you're always weaving a new pattern, and when that new pattern suits you, then you adopt it.' And I think that's sort of true about me. It's kind of real. It's not . . . like I ever made a big mid-life change.

The study of middle-aged men who shift careers for the ministry also concludes that the change did not usually stem from an identifiable crisis. Ellis Larsen, who has completed a survey of these men, is quoted as stating, "Most of the men had sensed a calling to the ministry early in life, but for some reason, weren't able to follow it then" (Associated Press, 1987, p. 8A).

OCCUPATIONAL DEVELOPMENT IN WOMEN

Previous sections of this chapter noted that the frequently cited theories of occupational choice systematically fail to account for women's development. Leona Tyler (1977) has pungently expressed the state of theorizing: "Much of what we know about the stages through which an individual passes as he [sic] prepares to find his [sic] place in the world of work might appropriately be labeled 'The Vocational Development of Middle Class Males'" (p. 40).

A provocative review by Perun and Bielby (1981) makes three distinctions between women's occupational development and men's: (1) The determinants are different; (2) The trajectory of the work cycle or career pattern is less predictable in women; and (3) The process of synchronizing work and family responsibilities throughout adulthood may be more difficult for women than for men. As a result, women may be in more conflict at some occupational stages about priorities in their life structure. For example, the late twenties are considered a primary time for career building in men; for women these are also primary childbearing years. For men, mid-life is a time of reevaluation and possible change; women at mid-life may be returning to a career or even initially establishing one. Therefore reassessment for them may be entirely different.

As we saw in Chapter 5, women may be classified into several types of groupings, based on their emphasis on one role or another. Rossi (1965), for example, classified women into *pioneer* or *traditional* categories based on the types of careers they pursued. Traditional women chose those occupational fields consistent with generalized conceptions of women's roles; they were more traditional in their own orientations, but not necessarily less likely to be employed. Pioneer women entered fields that were predominantly male. They tended to have more commitment to a career than did traditional women, and their career patterns tended to be stable and uninterrupted.

Super (1957), in a laudable attempt to adapt his career-development theory for the situation faced by women, identified seven career patterns, or routes taken by women through their working lives. These were:

(1) stable homemaking and marriage shortly after completion of schooling, with no work experience outside the home;
(2) conventional career pattern; that is, women who worked briefly after graduation until marriage and did not return to work outside the home;
(3) stable working outside the home, with consistent continuous work;
(4) double-track or consistent work and homemaking responsibilities;
(5) interrupted career pattern with working, not working, then working with return to the same or different job;
(6) unstable career pattern with several working, nonworking alternations with no particular recurrent pattern and little consistency; and
(7) A multiple trial pattern of successive unrelated jobs.

Whenever the empirical evaluation of women's occupational development is contemplated, the use of a longitudinal methodology is especially necessary, because of the career interruption that many women experience. For example, Mulvey (1963) followed up a high school graduating class 20 to 27 years later. She concluded that a major determinant of the subjects' life satisfaction was the degree to which the woman chose her career pattern. The women who were most dissatisfied were those whose career patterns were controlled by either financial or other factors and not by their personal choices.

CHANGES IN CREATIVITY DURING ADULTHOOD

Some consistent themes occur in the previous sections; these even extend back to the stage theories of Chapter 5. Changes take place in the mid-life of some men, leading to less commitment to their vocations, or a shift to another type of career. The driving force to succeed, characteristic of the twenties and early thirties, diminishes, or is replaced by other motives.

Are there other bodies of literature that support these conclusions? What about creativity? How does creativity proceed across the life span? Do achievements in a career peak at a particular age? Do people get more creative as they get older? If not, what inhibits creativity with increasing age? And if it is the case that mental productivity declines with increasing age, is the explanation decreasing intelligence, lessened creativity, motivational changes, or something else? We will find various answers in the following section, although a provocative statement by an eminent psychologist can serve as a stimulus. Donald Hebb (1978), in an account of his own intellectual abilities written when he was 74 reported: "Today, I have none of that drive, that engrossing, dominating need to fiddle with and manipulate ideas and data in psychology.... The real change, I conclude, is a lowered ability to think; the loss of interest in psychological projects is secondary to that" (p. 23).

Defining Creativity

Although recognized as an important characteristic, creativity has been difficult for psychologists to isolate and define. A number of operational definitions have been provided, and a variegated set of tests to measure creativity are available. And although these generally agree that creative acts generate products that are original, unusual, appropriate, and yet simple and straightforward, these tests differ greatly in the way they measure creativity.

The Remote Associates Test, developed by Sarnoff Mednick (1963), presents the subject with sets of three words, with instructions to generate a fourth word that is associated with each of the three. For example, if one were presented with *cookies, sixteen,* and *heart,* a word that might be associated with each is *sweet.* As Dacey (1982) notes, this procedure reflects Mednick's belief that creativity is a process by which ideas already in the mind are associated in unusual, original, or useful combinations. What makes creative people distinctive, in this view, is that they persist in exploring more and more associations in their minds.

Mednick goes on to propose that "familiarity breeds rigidity," or the more we know about a subject, the less likely we are to be creative about it. Certain procedures or principles become so entrenched that we no longer question, or seek new associations. If this is the case, it may explain why theoretical physicists and master chess players are said to have reached the period of their peak performance by the age of 36. For example, Elo's (1965) longitudinal study of master chess players concluded that at age 63, almost 30 years beyond their peak, they were performing at a level like that back when they were only 20—but not as well as they did in their late thirties.

A different conception of creativity sees it as a task of restructuring. Rather than methodically exploring one association after another, creative people, in this view, deal with whole problems and restructure them in their entirety. Michael Wertheimer (cited by Dacey, 1982), for example, proposes that in creative activity one develops an overview of the entire structure and only then is there a manipulation of parts. A creative musician gets a half-formed idea of a finished piece of music and then works backward to complete the idea. This analysis conforms with the comments of Ludwig van Beethoven about his ability to hold the theme for a symphony in his mind for years, as he worked out the parts and the notes for particular instruments.

This conception of creativity is more tolerant of opportunities for creative work with increasing age. The person in his or her fifties or sixties or seventies, with greater knowledge and possibly a greater number of perspectives, might better be able to produce creative solutions. The composer Franz Joseph Haydn illustrated this view, in that some of his most brilliant compositions were done toward the end of his long career. Haydn lived for 77 years; at age 63, in the year 1795, he composed his trumpet concerto, still considered the premiere trumpet concerto in the world, and in his late sixties and early seventies he composed his famous oratorios, *The Creation* and *The Seasons*.

It is quite possible that each of these contrasting conceptions of creativity is correct; in certain settings, for certain tasks, a different approach may be appropriate. "Creativity" in scientific research or crime detection may involve constant manipulation of jigsawlike pieces of information, until the right combination emerges. "Creativity" in painting or musical composition may involve developing a "big picture" and then relating aspects within it to each other. We need to keep these distinctions in mind as we review the empirical findings on creativity and age; unfortunately, there has been little research on age changes in creativity (Kausler, 1982).

Surveys of Creativity in Adulthood

The seemingly straightforward question: At what ages do people make their most creative contributions? is not easily answered. Lehman (1953), in an early review, used biographical information about several thousand highly productive individuals born after the year 1774. He concluded that creative output increases fairly rapidly up to one's late thirties or early forties; then there is a gradual decline that leads to a considerable decrease in middle age. He found that 80% of the high-quality productions were made by people younger than age 50. Scientists were their most productive between the ages of 30 and 39, but writers and historians—in contrast to the general trend—were most productive between their mid-forties and mid-fifties. But note the emphasis here is on the quantity of work and fails to take into account the *quality* of creative work. Jaques (1965) points to many artists and musicians whose work in their forties became more careful and painstaking, more "sculpted," hence their rate of productivity decreases as the quality improves. Yet Manniche and Falk (1957), determining the age at which Nobel Prize winners did the work for which they received the prize, found that mostly the late twenties or thirties were the determinants.

Conclusions about the early peak for creative or ground-breaking works were not without criticism (Botwinick, 1967). Dennis (1958, 1966) faulted Lehman's study because it included so many individuals who died before they reached old age. To avoid including subjects with different longevities, Dennis analyzed the biographies of 738 creative persons, all of whom lived to age 79 or beyond. His conclusions were different from Lehman's; for example, the peak period for scholars and scientists (except mathematicians) was the forties to the sixties, with some still producing in their seventies. (These groups had little creative output in their twenties.) Artists had a somewhat different pattern, with a peak period in their forties, but they were almost as productive in their sixties and seventies as they were in their twenties.

Dennis interpreted the difference in the patterns as a result of scientists needing a longer period of training and greater experience accumulating and interpreting data. Also, artists operated as individuals, whereas scientists often worked in groups. If, as in Beard's (1874) view, creativity is composed of two essential elements—enthusiasm and experience—the greater experience needed by the scientists would account for the "delay" in the scientists reaching their creative peak. But, in a careful study of productivity and creativity in 10 eminent psychologists, Dean Simonton (1985) found that the ratio of their creative works to all their products did not systematically change with age. That is, the quality of their work in later years was just as highly regarded as that of their early or middle years.

Previous studies focused on persons with demonstrable creativity or giftedness. Jaquish and Ripple (1980), at Cornell University, took a different approach. Drawing samples of children, adolescents, young adults, middle-aged adults, and elderly, they administered to the subjects a measure of creativity that assessed three aspects of divergent thinking (fluency, frequency, and originality). After comparing average scores for the different age groups, they concluded that persons ages 40 to 60 did significantly better than did those persons in the 18-25 and 26-39 age groups. For those people in the oldest age group (ages 61 to 84), creativity scores were significantly lower than those of any of the younger age groups, but the difference was greater with respect to quantity of creative products than for quality. For the middle-aged and elderly groups, those participants with more favorable self-concepts were more creative (rs of .41 and .43).

This latter relationship is especially important because of the vast individual differences with respect to creativity in old age. Pablo Casals played the cello brilliantly at the age of 95 and P. G. Wodehouse published one of his best novels at the age of 90. At the age of 84, the philosopher Mortimer Adler published his fifteenth book in the last 10 years. When abilities continue to be used, they do not decline as quickly or at all (Butler, 1967). The motto "Use it or lose it" seems to apply to creativity, too. But it would simplify matters too much if we left the topic of creativity with the possible implication that ability differences are the only important determinants. As these examples of creativity in older ages reflect, creative productions are the result of heightened motivation, also. The apparent decline in creativity may reflect in the aspiration levels of older adults; there may be less urge to accomplish new things or to make one's mark anew (Pruyser, 1987). Similarly, as Renner, Alpaugh, and Birren (1978) argue, an environmental-press explanation may fit. That is, the environment of many older people may discourage creative or divergent thinking; creativity may not diminish with age as much as the demand for it does (Kausler, 1982).

AGE DIFFERENCES IN LEARNING AND MEMORY

Perhaps the changing orientation to work during adulthood is a manifestation of declining mental abilities. The elderly—if not the middle aged—are stereotyped by our society as becoming more forgetful and less adaptable (Schaie, 1983). Do people in middle adulthood begin to display memory changes that affect their job performance?

This is a difficult question to answer, because research on age differences in learning and memory has emphasized differences between young adults and the elderly. Little has been done on understanding the memory processes *throughout* the adult life span. Furthermore, different theories of learning and memory have used different procedures and materials, thus making a direct comparison of results impossible (Walsh, 1983). However, reviews (Elias, Elias, & Elias, 1977; Dacey, 1982; Walsh, 1983) produce these generalizations:

(1) The long-term memory abilities of older adults differ little from those of young adults. But from middle age on, the content of long-term memory becomes selective, with focus more on reminiscences from their youth and early adulthood than from more recent times (Goleman, 1987; Rubin, 1986). Psychologist David C. Rubin concludes, "It seems to be that reminiscence flows more freely about the period in life that comes to define you: the time of your first date, marriage, job, child" (quoted by Goleman, 1987, p. 17).

(2) With respect to short-term memory (for example, the ability to memorize a phone number or a ZIP code), differences between the elderly and young adults may be partially owing to lessened

motivation to remember by the elderly. But once the amount of material to be remembered extends beyond the capacity of the short-term memory store, older persons are able to recall less than younger adults (Walsh, 1983, p. 165).

(3) The most serious deficiency of the elderly is in regard to self-generated ways to *organize* material to be learned or remembered.

(4) When the elderly are provided an organizational structure to use for memorizing information, they perform just about as well as young adults (Hultsch, 1969, 1971, 1974). Similarly, older adults show "little disadvantage compared to the young in remembering sentences and discourse materials" (Walsh, 1983, p. 174).

If we extrapolate these results to persons at middle adulthood, we may conclude with some confidence that memory deficits do not usually account for any differences in career commitment that may surface during the ages of 40 to the late fifties. A greater effect may come from self-fulfilling prophecies stemming from messages that tell middle-aged people that once we are past our thirties, life is a continuous decline.

AGE DIFFERENCES IN INTELLIGENCE

Might changes in level of mental ability during adulthood account for the changes discussed earlier in this chapter? Does intelligence decline as one gets older? Certainly opinions abound about such declines. Dacey (1982, p. 125) quotes Mark Twain in his 1884 book *Puddin'head Wilson*: "It was a very curious thing. When I was about 13, my father's intelligence started to drop. His mental ability continued to decline until I reached 21, when these abilities miraculously began to improve." But "young people project more negatives on later years than reality suggests is correct" states James Birren, former director of the Andrus Gerontology Center at the University of Southern California (quoted in Gunderson, 1987, p. 6D).

Dacey's (1982) approach to answering the questions in the above paragraph is, I believe, a very helpful one. He contrasts three different responses: Yes, intelligence does decline with age; No, it does not; and Yes, it declines in some ways but no, in other ways it does not. Each viewpoint is reviewed below.

David Wechsler (1958), author of one of the most widely used intelligence tests, believed that most cognitive abilities peak between the ages of 18 and 25, and then decline. This "occurs in all mental measures of ability including those employed in tests of intelligence," he proposed (p. 135). Wechsler's conclusions were based on extensive research data, but they were all cross-sectional data, in which older people (often with less education and fewer cultural opportunities) were compared to younger adults (Schaie, 1983, p. 138). Longitudinal studies of changes in IQ scores tend to lead to the opposite conclusion, that intelligence does not decline with age. For example, Terman's study of gifted children, which began in 1931, retested its subjects in 1941, in 1956, and 1969. In the last testing, when the subjects were around 40 years old, their IQ scores had increased an average of 10 points from what they had been at age 30 (Kangas & Bradway, 1971).

Also, in a fortuitous happenstance, psychologist William Owens (1953; 1959) found test scores 30 years later for 363 people who had enrolled in Ohio State University in 1919. He was able to locate and retest 127 of them; at the time of retesting they were around the age of 47. All but one of 127 showed an increase in IQ over this 30-year interval. In 1966, when these people were 61 years old, 97 of them were retested again and none of their scores had changed significantly. These are impressive results, not only because they reflect a stability during adulthood, but also because they further support a conclusion that Wechsler's results were affected by the educational differences in his subjects of differing ages; that is, that age and cohort were confounded and that "education may be one of the prime causes of such cohort effects" (Denney, 1982, p. 812). In fact, Botwinick (1978, p. 224) offers a general conclusion that "Longitudinal studies tend to reflect less decline than cross-sectional studies and they often show decline starting later in life."

But one's IQ score is a reflection of many different mental abilities; intelligence is no longer viewed as a unitary concept. A potentially fruitful analysis of changes with age makes a distinction between two types, fluid and crystallized intelligence. Horn and Cattell (1967) use the term crystallized intelligence to refer to those skills that we acquire through education and exposure to our culture. As Schaie (1983) notes, "Crystallized abilities depend upon the acquisition of certain kinds of information and skills transmitted by the culture that are not available to the individual simply by virtue of his characteristics as a human being" (p. 139). One's vocabulary level, level of information, and mechanical knowledge are examples of crystallized intelligence. Horn and Cattell conclude that level of crystallized intelligence does not normally decline over the period of adulthood; in fact, it increases, at least from the ages of 20 to 60.

The other type of mental ability, labeled fluid intelligence, does decline with age. Fluid intelligence covers those abilities that are related to the physiological characteristics of the organism and hence are culture-free, including reaction time, spatial visualization, memory span, and verbal reasoning. For example, what letter comes next in the series SUXBGM? There is a sort of paradox here; our knowledge of words maintains itself or even improves, but our ability to use words in reasoning diminishes. Horn claims that the

---

BOX 7.3
Language Loss in Later Adulthood

Susan Kemper (1987), a cognitive psychologist at the University of Kansas, has studied the language development of healthy people ages 50 to 90. One skill she has investigated she calls word-finding, or the ability to express a word—a person's name, a place, a term—when you want to. This is an example of the short-term memory; while long-term memory of older people continues to be quite effective, short-term memory storage seems to diminish.

Of relevance to the distinction between fluid and crystallized intelligence is Kemper's research on the age differences in the ability to process information expressed in complex sentences. Kemper finds the most common difficulty occurs when a long subordinate clause precedes a main clause. Normally, when you hear such a clause, you must wait until hearing the main clause before processing it; the main clause gives the context. Consider the sentence: "Because Bill left the party without his coat, John was upset." The wait for the main clause appears to require a processing step that deteriorates with increasing age (Howell, 1987). Kemper believes that this decline does not usually emerge until the late sixties and early seventies (if at all) and then becomes stronger in the late seventies and early eighties.

decline in such reasoning is equal to about five IQ points from the ages 25 to 40, and about five points for every 10 years of living beyond the age of 40. He speculates that perhaps it accelerates with advanced age. An example is provided in Box 7.3.

One of the problems in evaluating the question of changes in intelligence during adulthood comes from the operational definition of intelligence based on performance on standardized IQ tests. Often such tests contain speeded components; that is, one's scores are determined by how quickly one answers. It is on these speeded types of measures that the greatest decline occurs with age; in contrast, "on abilities where speed is not of primary importance, there is very little change in intellectual function for an individual throughout adulthood" (Schaie, 1983, pp. 144- 145). The definition of "intelligence" given by the typical man or woman on the street is usually broader, including such aspects as varied as "street smarts" and "wisdom."

The latter quality, especially, may grow throughout adulthood, even though it is not directly assessed by intelligence tests.

Wisdom appears to blend qualities of cognition, emotion, and intuition (Clayton & Birren, 1980). It is associated with maturity and age, although it is not seen as acquired by chronological age alone. Recall that "wisdom" is the ideal accomplishment of Erikson's last stage of psychosocial development.

Furthermore, older persons show more cautiousness than do younger adults (Botwinick, 1978). As Schaie (1983) observes, "Young people in most test situations tend to make many more errors of commission than omission, but the reverse is true for the elderly.... Cautiousness may often be adaptive, but in this instance it may make the elderly appear less able than they actually are" (p. 147).

8

SEX ROLES AND ANDROGYNY

Late in 1987, Secretary of Transportation Elizabeth Dole resigned her powerful cabinet position in order to assist her husband, Senator Robert Dole, in his campaign for nomination by the Republican party as its presidential candidate. Critics asked why she was pressured to resign to avoid a conflict of interest when male candidates who themselves hold public offices did not (Cohen, 1987).

Shortly thereafter, another possible presidential candidate (this time for the Democratic party), Representative Patricia Schroeder, made a tearful announcement that she would not be a candidate. Her behavior elicited a breadth "of often complicated feelings"; "some women were angry, others embarrassed. Many were sympathetic, and several were disturbed by what appears to be a double-standard on tears" (Weinraub, 1987, p. 12).

These examples reflect the power of sex-role stereotypes (or gender-role stereotypes) in our society. Each sex is evaluated differently, based on the pervasiveness of sex-role norms, or beliefs about appropriate behavior for women and men.

MASCULINITY, FEMININITY, AND ANDROGYNY

Society often has avoided a basic distinction. We are aware of the distinction between male and female, and generally we can agree about the differences between the concepts of masculinity and femininity (see below). But society has assumed that being male means possessing masculinity and being female means possessing femininity, and many people in contemporary life have conformed to these expectations; in fact, they have been trained to do so. (Gender schema theory, one attempt to explain how this happens, is described in Box 8.1.)

But for several decades psychologists have been dissatisfied with the lumping together of maleness and masculinity, or with the inexorable yoking of femaleness and femininity. Psychologists have recently undertaken the construction of personality scales of masculinity and femininity that presumably could be found among

---

BOX 8.1
Gender Schema Theory

How do we develop stereotypes about sex roles or gender roles? Sandra Bem (1981, 1982, 1983, 1984) has proposed gender schema theory, which reflects partially a cognitive developmental framework, along with social learning theory and cultural factors (Basow, 1986). Gender-schema processing is considered a readiness on the part of children to encode and organize information according to how the culture defines sex roles. For example, a child may observe that boys usually are described as "strong" or "brave," while girls are more often described as "nice" or "sweet." As Basow (1986) notes, cultural stereotypes become self-fulfilling prophecies because the child learns not only that the sexes differ but, more importantly, certain attributes are associated more with one sex than the other.

The extreme degree to which our society classifies behaviors and objects into "masculine" versus "feminine" only intensifies the development of a gender schema in children.

males *and* females. That is, they have assumed that, psychologically, some men and some women may be more similar to each other than different from each other. They believe that an emphasis on these psychological qualities can contribute something extra in our effort to understand behavior.

Constantinople (1973) has reviewed the early research on this issue. She notes that although the early investigators differed in some of the details of their measurement procedures, they consistently made two assumptions: (a) that masculinity and femininity represent two opposite poles on a scale and (b) that the dimension of masculinity/femininity is unidimensional, rather than being a complex conglomerate of characteristics. But a change in perspective has taken place more recently, as investigators examining male/female differences began to argue that masculinity and femininity are quite separable sets of characteristics and that both men and women can possess varying degrees of each set (Bakan, 1966; Block, 1973; Carlson, 1971).

These theory-derived conclusions generated a number of important measurement developments, in which researchers devised scales to measure femininity and masculinity separately (Bem, 1974; Berzins, Welling, & Wetter, 1975; Heilbrun, 1976; Spence, Helmreich, & Stapp, 1974). The assumption underlying each of these investigations is that one set of characteristics can be considered masculine (or *agentic*, in Bakan's terms) and another set can be considered feminine (or *communal*). Usually the masculine scales contain terms such as *independent, competitive,* and *self-confident,* whereas the femininity scales contain words such as *kind, gentle,* and *warm.* Although males as a group score higher on the masculinity scale and females as a group score higher on the femininity scale, the two scales are unrelated (Bem, 1974; Spence & Helmreich, 1978). In other words, a particular individual might score high on both scales, low on both, or high on one and low on the other. Statistically, this means that the correlation between the two scales approaches zero. In more descriptive terms, it means that both females and males can be either high or low in either femininity or masculinity; in contrast to the assumption of earlier investigators, the presence of one set of characteristics does not imply the absence of the other.

Psychological Androgyny

To categorize people who possess these varying combinations of characteristics, investigators have borrowed the term *androgyny* (originally used by the ancient Greeks to refer to individuals who combined the physical characteristics of both sexes). In its use here, the term refers to a combination of *psychological* characteristics. A person who scored above the median on both the femininity scale *and* the masculinity scale would be classified as androgynous. If the person scored above the median on only one of the scales, he or she would be labeled as masculine sex-typed or feminine sex-typed, depending on which scale was high. Those persons scoring below the median on both scales have been labeled *undifferentiated*.

Using this method of categorization, Spence and Helmreich (1978) examined the masculinity and femininity scores of different groups of people. Among a typical college-student sample, approximately one-third of the males were masculine sex-typed and one-third of the females were feminine sex-typed. One-fourth to one-third of the students scored as androgynous; the remaining students were either undifferentiated or were sex-typed in atypical ways (masculine-sex-typed females and feminine-sex-typed males).

Although it is relatively easy to place people in one of these four categories, considerable disagreement exists over what these categories mean. For Sandra Bem (1974), whose work on this topic was the first to be widely recognized, the androgynous person is an ideal toward which we should strive. By combining positive masculine and feminine characteristics, the androgynous person, in Bem's opinion, can function effectively in a wide variety of situations that call for either masculine or feminine behavior. She believes that sex-typed persons, in contrast, are more limited, because they are able to operate effectively in some situations but not in others. Other investigators take a more cautious approach, arguing that the personality characteristics of masculinity or femininity may or may not relate to what we typically consider sex-role behaviors. For example, the personality characteristics of femininity may not be entirely related to homemaking skills; rather, running a home may be related to both masculine and feminine (or agentic and communal) characteristics (Spence & Helmreich, 1978). Still other critics have argued that the notion of androgyny is a phenomenon that is peculiar to the United States, where individuality is valued and interdependency is scorned (Sampson, 1977). According to this view, traditional sex roles and characteristics may be functional in most societies and at most times—or, at a minimum, the advantages of the androgynous personality remain to be demonstrated.

Completely contradictory to this view is one by Rebecca and Hefner (1982), claiming that androgyny does not go far enough. In an article titled "The Future of Sex Roles," they write:

> Although the work on androgyny is a major advance in our view of sex roles, we still do not know if this abstract concept captures all the different ways that people behave in real life. We do not know how a person becomes androgynous, if androgyny has a distinct place in the development of sex roles, or if, indeed, androgyny is itself an end point. The sweeping societal changes in roles for women and men that are already occurring remind us that we must not be content with any one concept of the nature of people. This is why we have thought out a developmental model of sex-role transcendence which tries to capture the emerging possibilities—possibilities that might be quite different from the way of life that we now know. Transcendence means to go beyond what we know. In the area of sex roles it means to go beyond the rigid definitions of masculinity and femininity so that these terms lose their meaning. (p. 161)

Rebecca and Hefner (1982) in their article mean by transcendence an atmosphere in which choices are no longer traced even to the concepts of masculinity and femininity. Apparently their criticism of androgyny is that it is defined as a combination of sex-related traits. They state:

> Transcendence, then, involves several levels of change. It has to do with going completely beyond (transcending) present gender specific behavior, personality, and expectations. This is something quite different from a mere time-sharing of masculine and feminine characteristics in the same person, nor is it a mere freeing of both females and males to be both masculine and feminine. It requires the invention of new ways of being that are not merely fusions of what we already know. . . . A woman will be nurturant not because it is feminine but because she needs or wants to be nurturant. (p. 162)

As we can see, the notion of androgyny has accumulated its share of controversy since it was introduced into the psychological literature. Theoretical controversy has been accompanied by abundant research, and we are continually learning more about what it means to be androgynous. It is important to remember, however, that in regard to an operational definition, androgyny is just a convenient label for a combination of high scores on both masculinity (instrumental) and femininity (expressive) scales. Looking at the scales separately, we find that they are related to different kinds of behavior. People who score high on the masculinity scale generally have higher self-esteem. They are also more likely to have high achievement needs, to be dominant, and to be aggressive, compared with people who score low on masculinity (Taylor & Hall, 1982). High scores on the femininity scale are related to different kinds of behavior. For example, high femininity is related to the ability to show empathy, sociability, and skill in decoding nonverbal communications (Spence & Helmreich, 1978; Taylor & Hall, 1982).

The androgynous person, by definition, has both these kinds of skills, and in many situations this combination may be advantageous. In conversations, for example, both instrumental and expressive skills may be useful. Being instrumental may allow you to initiate discussion and introduce new topics; being expressive may allow you to relate to the other person and interpret his or her mood. Research has shown that androgynous people are more comfortable in conversational settings (Ickes, 1981). In one set of studies, male and female subjects representing various combinations of masculinity and femininity scores met each other in a waiting room (Ickes & Barnes, 1977, 1978). Their conversations were recorded on videotape and analyzed, and each member was also asked how much he or she had enjoyed the conversation. The results may contradict some common assumptions. The lowest levels of interaction and lowest levels of reported enjoyment were found among pairs in which the male was traditionally masculine sex-typed (high in masculinity and low in femininity) and the female was feminine sex-typed (high in femininity and low in masculinity). In contrast, when both persons were androgynous, levels of interaction and mutual enjoyment were high. These results support the hypothesis that the possession of both instrumental and expressive skills leads to more rewarding encounters.

SEX ROLES IN YOUNG ADULTHOOD

The extended analysis of masculinity, femininity, and their relationships in the previous section provides a foundation for a developmental analysis of the impact of sex roles during adulthood. At different periods during the adult years, these sex roles carry different manifestations.

As Dacey (1982) observes, young adult men and women share many goals in common. In Chapter 3, Erikson's task of establishing intimacy was described, and Chapter 5 advanced Gould's claim that the twenties were the ages when young people had to relinquish their connection with their parents. At the same time, young adulthood is often considered to be the period in which male/female differences are their greatest (Dacey, 1982). This section concentrates on different issues for women (role conflict) and for men (fear of femininity) during the young adult period.

Role Conflict

In this book, roles have been defined as expectations for behavior; thus, role conflict is defined as any situation in which incompatible expectations are placed upon a person because of his or her membership in a position. Role conflict creates tension because it almost inevitably forces the person to violate someone's expectations. In a useful review, Sales (1978) proposes that, compared to men, women are more likely to experience role conflict, especially in the workplace. They have special limitations placed upon them because of the pervasiveness of the feminine sex role in our society. That is, a woman can either ignore the role demands coming from an expectation of being feminine and choose to behave "just like a man" on the job, or she can moderate her assertiveness and display the aspects of her personality that she values (or knows are effective in winning over her coworkers).

Sales writes:

When competing roles are added to a women's role repertoire, the potential for role conflict mounts. A husband socialized in traditional ways may expect his wife to be supportive, respectful of his work obligations, and admiring of his competence. . . . A women who is herself a job-holder may not nurture her husband's ego as well as a wife whose only contact with the work world is through her husband. Since she is contributing economically to the marriage, she expects more participation in decision making and household tasks. It is hard for a woman who is independent and assertive at work to become the compliant wife on her return home. (p. 159)

Role Overload

Somewhat different, but overlapping with role conflict, is the problem of role overload; the latter places a burden on individuals through the expectations of fulfilling too many roles, or of spending more time than available in fulfilling each of the roles. The emphasis here is on time demands, and resultingly, role overload is a common plight of young women who attempt to be "superwomen" by combining work, marriage, and family roles. All these demand extensive time; Sales (1978) writes:

Role overload can be resolved by withdrawing from some roles or by renegotiating expectations with role partners. Husbands may be asked to share in household tasks, children may if old enough be asked to assume more responsibilities, alternative child care or housekeeping services may be devised, or bosses may be told that their demands are excessive. Although these solutions are often difficult to implement, they are the only ways of effectively eliminating role overload. (p. 160)

Role Discontinuity

A third difficulty facing young women is role discontinuity, or the stressful response to the sharp shifts in the pattern of sex roles over time. Sales (1978) suggests that women are much more likely to experience role discontinuity than are men. The pattern is most diverse for women with children: They typically work until the first child is born; then they reduce or abandon work in preschool years. Perhaps they work part time while their children are in school, and they may be full time in their forties. These shifting role demands require continued adjustments for many women. Other women may experience problems because they are unable to acknowledge a status change; for example, when a new parent still feels constrained to fulfill all of her social obligations.

Sales (1978) and Dacey (1982) suggest the following as ways that role transitions may be eased for the person:

(1) the person may develop the ability to adopt to changing social expectations;
(2) the person may use available social supports to ease role entrance;
(3) people may informally seek information about new roles from others; and
(4) the stress is lessened if other valued roles are part of the person's repertoire.

GENDER-ROLE CONFLICT IN YOUNG MEN

Young men in our society face another type of conflict. The heavy-handed nature of being socialized to become a man can create oppressive effects. We are aware of the deleterious effects of sexism on women's opportunities but men are also oppressed by rigid socialization processes that limit their potential to be fully functional human beings (Pleck, 1981, 1982).

Many men have been socialized to behave in sexist ways; they have difficulty in developing and integrating new male roles that are compatible with nonsexist behavior. Yet sex-role strain occurs; it is, in fact, the result when rigid gender roles restrict people's abilities to actualize their human potential. Garnets and Pleck (1979) operationally define sex-role strain "as a discrepancy between the real self and that part of the ideal self-concept that is culturally associated with gender" (p. 278).

Rigid gender roles lead, in some men, to what has been labeled *fear of femininity*, by James M. O'Neil (O'Neil, Helms, Gable, David, & Wrightsman, 1986). Fear of femininity is defined as a strong concern that oneself possesses (or is seen as possessing) feminine values, attitudes, and behaviors, and that these will reflect negatively upon oneself (O'Neil et al., 1986). That is, a man may fear that people will see him as stereotypically, negatively feminine—weak, submissive, and dependent. O'Neil has proposed that six components of fear of femininity are functional:

(a) Restricted emotionality, or difficulty in expressing one's own feelings, or denying others their rights to emotional expressiveness, especially with regard to such feelings as tenderness or vulnerability.

(b) Homophobia or having fears of homosexuals or fears of being homosexual, including possessing beliefs, myths, and stereotypes about gay people.

(c) Socialized control, power, and competition, or the desire to regulate, to restrain, or to have others or situations under one's command, striving against others with the purpose of winning or gaining something.

(d) Restricted sexual and affectionate behavior, or having limited ways of expressing one's sexual needs and affections to others.

(e) Obsession with achievement and success, or having a persistent preoccupation with work, accomplishment, and eminence as means of substantiating and demonstrating one's value.

(f) Health care problems, or having difficulties maintaining positive health care in respect to diet, exercise, relaxation, stress, and a healthy life style.

O'Neil proposed that fear of femininity is strongest in young adulthood, and then begins to diminish. O'Neil and Fishman (1986) propose that men redefine their career and gender role identities over the life cycle, and especially experience gender role conflict during periods of career transition.

SEX ROLES IN MIDDLE ADULTHOOD

As Chapters 5 and 6 have described, something different happens during middle adulthood. Now that the children are gone, the man can let the anima aspect of his personality emerge, as well as the animus (see Chapter 2). Meanwhile, the woman may be preparing to reenter the job world, or increase her commitment to it. A role reversal begins to occur in each sex.

The Empty Nest Syndrome

As the preceding paragraph states, many women face an almost complete loss of one role while in their forties, as children reach adulthood and leave home to establish independent lives. Role discontinuity can be severe for the woman whose prime focus has been on nurturance and provision of child care for 20 years.

But more women react positively to the empty nest. Women whose children have left are more satisfied, less self-pitying, and less easily hurt than women whose children are still at home (Lowenthal et al., 1975). They generally show fewer depressive symptoms when their children are on their own (Radloff, 1975). Also, women's feelings about marriage show marked improvement once children have left home.

But role discontinuity may be increased by the onset of menopause at about the same time; these women may now feel useless, old, barren, and unneeded. Such feelings are strikingly similar to those experienced by some men at retirement.

The negative impact of menopause should not be exaggerated, however. Women react to menopause in differing ways. Only 4% thought that menopause was the worst thing about middle age, but 50% thought menopause caused a negative change in their appearance. About one-third reported negative changes in their physical and emotional health, and two-thirds did not think it affected their sexual relationships.

Sex Roles in Later Adulthood

In later adulthood two developments are important. One, called the cross-over phenomenon, is an accentuation of the role reversal begun by some couples in middle adulthood. Neugarten (1968) describes it as follows: "Women as they age seem to become more tolerant of their own aggressive, egocentric impulses, whereas men, as they age, (become more tolerant) of their own nurturative and affiliative impulses" (p. 71).

Sales (1978) adds the following:

Women play a more dominant role in marital decision making than they did in earlier periods. Referred to as *peak wife-dominance*, both husbands and wives often consider the wife the dominant partner.... This pattern, which is a dramatic reversal of the earlier marital power structure, is further evidence of the increased assertiveness that women show in middle age. They no longer feel as dependent on their husbands for approval, have greater self-direction, and can engage in active effort to gain their desired objectives. For many traditional women, the mid-life crisis seems to culminate in their final unleashing from earlier sex-role personality constraints. They may be aided in their transition by the corresponding decline in their husband's need to play his marital role according to social prescriptions. Both partners, newly comfortable with expressing their personal rather than their sexual imperatives, may reshape their marriage into a more rewarding form. (pp. 183-184)

This leads to the second phenomenon, a movement toward "normal unisexuality" (Dacey, 1982). That is, the differences between men and women, so many of which seemed to be based on sexuality, are no longer as important. Older men and women seem to have more in common with each other.

In later adulthood, other issues may develop that lead once again to different reactions by the two sexes. For example, Chapter 11 describes the reaction of men and women to the loss of their spouses.

9

SEXUAL RELATIONSHIPS AND MARRIAGE

Is there life after marriage? Chapter 7 described the effort to escape the pervasiveness of the "one-career imperative" in contemporary society. An equivalent issue is the commitment to a lifetime marriage. Newspapers and magazines tell us of the increasing percentage of marriages that end in divorce. A dialectical analysis is useful here: at times, commitment to a marriage may be comfortable and reassuring; at other times, this commitment may be threatening. Perhaps this is one of the explanations for the fact that despite the centrality of "long-term marriage" as a value in our society, the median length of a marriage in the United States, as of 1986, was only slightly over seven years (Kantrowitz, 1987).

How do married couples respond? What changes take place during a long-term marriage? How does the sexual aspect of a relationship change over the course of 20, 30, or 50 years? These are some the questions faced in a chapter that attempts to provide a developmental analysis of sexual behavior and marriage.

ESTABLISHING A SEXUAL RELATIONSHIP

Some 50 years ago, most American couples had their first sexual intimacy on their wedding night; today fewer than one of every five couples postpone sexual intercourse until their marriage. Hence, as a background for analyzing the sexual aspect of a marriage relationship, it is necessary to review the findings on the extent of premarital sexual behavior.

Obtaining accurate data on sexual activity outside of marriage is, of course, difficult to do, because of reluctance on the part of some respondents to reveal personal information. Furthermore, many of the studies on this topic used as their subjects "captive samples" of college students, who may not accurately represent the entire population of young unmarried people. We face a dilemma; we need to report these findings, because they are better than no information; still, we need to be careful not to generalize specific incidence rates too widely.

Standing back from the figures for specific studies of sexual experience of college students—studies done at different times over the last 30 years—we detect several trends. The percentage of unmarried young people who report sexual experience has increased dramatically, from about 40% to 75% of men and from about 25% to 67% of women. The major change came in the 1960s and early 1970s, along with a spirit of questioning everything and adventurousness. In general, percentage of respondents reporting being sexually active increased in those studies that were done up to around 1983; since then, there has been little or no increase. Increased concern over the effects of sexual promiscuity, including the incidence of AIDS, has contributed to the stabilizing of the premarital sexual incidence rate.

The values that are salient in our society shift from decade to decade and year to year; Chapter 10 describes the impact of these shifting values on a number of topics. These shifts, some of which are predictable, some of which result from unanticipated conditions, reinforce the utility of a dialectical approach to the analysis of sexual relationships. One way of conceptualizing these values in provided by the sociologist Isador Rubin (1965); Box 9.1 describes these six differing value positions regarding the purposes of sexual

BOX 9.1
Rubin's List of Six Values Positions
Regarding Sexual Behavior

(1) Traditional asceticism: The sole purpose of sexual behavior is procreation and it should strictly be limited to marriage. Thus sexual activity is a necessary evil, and young people who are instilled with this traditional value often have difficulty expressing their sexual nature.

(2) Enlightened asceticism: Sexual activity needs to be carefully monitored and controlled. Although it is not considered evil as such, and people are encouraged to express their needs and feelings, sexual activity should be exercised only under carefully delimited conditions.

(3) Humanistic liberalism: This "relativistic" position proposes that an evaluation of sexual activity should be based on the relationship of the people who are engaging in it. One viewpoint that fits this category is that of "situation ethics"; this liberal position endorses any type of sexual activity as long as it is justified by the consequences.

(4) Humanistic radicalism: After careful education, any type of sexual activity is accepted. There is no blanket rejection of any type of behavior as long as no physical or emotional harm results.

(5) Fun morality: The view here is that the main reason for sex is to have fun. There should be no limits on frequency or type, as long as no one is physically abused.

(6) Sexual anarchy: An extreme position that advocates no restrictions on any type of sexual behavior.

activity. A quick examination of this list will lead to an awareness that each value is advocated by certain segments of our society, and from time to time, different values are the norm in our society.

Given the shift in percentage of young people who have engaged in sexual intercourse prior to marriage, it may be concluded that movement has been away from the traditional asceticism described in Box 9.1 toward the next couple of values. This change in the norm has implications for sexual morale during marriage, and it is that topic to which we next turn.

SEXUAL MORALE IN MARRIAGE

Several years ago the columnist Ann Landers asked her female readers to respond to the question: "Would you be content to be held close and treated tenderly, and forget about 'the act'?" More than 90,000 women responded, and 72% of these said yes. Of those, 40% were under the age of 40. Publication of these results led to a variety of responses in the mass media, mostly with reactions of consternation and surprise. Sex therapist Ruth Westheimer even called it "dangerous" because it was misleading. Although 90,000 respondents is an impressive number, we cannot conclude that 72% of women in general are satisfied only with close feelings of genuine intimacy without sexual intercourse.

Unfortunately a tendency exists to equate sexual morale with frequency of intercourse. Things are more complicated than that.

There is evidence that sexual morale is high early in a marriage despite whatever difficulties are encountered. Intercourse occurs frequently in the early months of marriage and decreases in frequency over the length of the marriage. It has been estimated (Broderick, 1982) that the average frequency of sexual intercourse per month is as follows:

> during the first six months of a marriage: 12 per month
> marriage of 2 years: 8 per month
> marriage of 5 years: 7 per month
> marriage of 10 years: 6 per month
> marriage of 25 years: 4 per month
> marriage of 30 years: 3 per month

The inexorable linear quality of the above figures, and especially the "decline" in frequency, should not be overinterpreted and most certainly should not be used as a norm table by someone who wants to "keep score." These figures are based on large numbers of couples, but there are problems in concluding from them that a particular couple shows a decline in the morale of its marriage. For example, divorce rates peak after the third or fourth year of marriage; also it is during this general period that pregnancy is more likely to occur. The decrease in frequency of intercourse during pregnancy (especially in the third trimester) is found in many cultures, not only in the United States, but in Thailand, Czechoslovakia, and other countries.

The occurrence of pregnancy is one example of the conclusion that frequency of intercourse is not the only indication of sexual satisfaction (Broderick, 1982). Women who have a positive attitude toward their pregnancy tend to improve or at least maintain the quality of their sexual relationships with their husbands, whereas those with negative attitudes experience a decrease in sexual satisfaction. Several explanations may be proposed for this:

(1) *Stimulus generalization:* This term refers to the reaction of the woman who loses enthusiasm for everything associated with an unwanted or unpleasant pregnancy, including the activity that brought it about.

(2) Negative manifestations of the pregnancy (fatigue, nausea, sleeplessness) seem to be more frequent when the woman's attitude toward the pregnancy is unfavorable.

(3) The quality of the couple's affection for each other prior to pregnancy predicts the pregnant woman's degree of satisfaction (Broderick, 1982).

But most pregnant women apparently succeed in maintaining a level of sexual activity that closely reflects their desires. And even though their interest in sexual intercourse declines in the third trimester of pregnancy, their interest in being held does not diminish.

Sexual-intercourse incidence rates based on length of the marriage neglect the awareness of sexual needs in older women. The ground-breaking surveys of sexual behavior by Alfred Kinsey and his colleagues in the late 1940s and early 1950s concluded that women reached their peak of sexual functioning in their middle years. But Kinsey's surveys almost overlooked the study of older persons. In his study of women (Kinsey, Pomeroy, Martin, & Gebhard, 1953), only 56 women over the age of 60 were included in his sample of respondents. One of the problems is a sexual double standard: older men are considered "more sexual" whereas older women are not. This is ironic, given that most older men do experience some decline in the physiological aspects of sexual intercourse, whereas women are more able to maintain sexual responsiveness at older ages.

Although there is a gradual diminishment of sexual response in males over the adult life cycle, a substantial percentage of men continue to function even into advanced old age. Masters and Johnson's (1966) study of sexual physiological responses found that men in their sixties took two or three times longer to respond to direct sexual stimulation, and other studies have found that younger males (ages 19-30) responded six times quicker than older groups (ages 48-65).

Five studies of sexual potency in aging males (summarized by Broderick, 1982) found that for men in their early sixties, from 60% to 82% (in different studies) maintained their sexual potency; in men in their late sixties, these percentages were from 50% to 75%. Somewhere between 25% and 45% of men in their late seventies were still sexually potent.

As noted before, women's orgasmic capacity seems unaffected by aging. Older women may need extra lubrication but their orgasmic capacity remains the same or better. Masters and Johnson (1966) reported that women often experienced increased erotic feelings after menopause, perhaps because they were relieved of fear of pregnancy and its responsibilities. However, this distinction may be a function of the "pre-pill" generation—women who were of childbearing age before this type of birth control was available (Broderick, 1982).

All reports agree that the frequency of sexual intercourse drops off strongly in old age. Pearlman (1972) reports that only 20% of elderly men have sexual intercourse two or more times a month. But it is hard to know how much the diminished rate is a function of biology, of health, of relationships or of expectations. It may not be an exaggeration to claim that society disapproves of sex among the elderly. We stereotype sex as an activity of youth. Attitude surveys show that people assume the elderly are uninterested in sex. This is an extension of college students' mistaken beliefs about the frequency of their parents' sexual activity. Pocs and Godow (1977) asked college students to estimate their parents' frequency of sexual activity. On the average, students estimated their parents had sexual intercourse less than half as often as indicated by surveys of sexual incidence rates in couples of their parents' age. Some 6% of the students refused even to answer questions about their parents' behavior. Responded one: "Whoever thinks about their parents' sexual relations, except perverts?" One-fourth of the students estimated that their parents never had sex or had it less than once a year.

SEXUAL RELATIONSHIPS IN "SUCCESSFUL" MARRIAGES

A substantial correlation exists between satisfaction with frequency of intercourse and overall marital satisfaction; that is, couples who are happy in the relationship engage in about as much sexual behavior as they like. But again, such a correlation reflects a general trend, and there remain vast differences and discrepancies. One of the most revealing of the studies that illustrate this diversity is that by Cuber and Harroff (1965), who interviewed 100 married couples (ages 35 to 55) who were "successful" in the ways that most people measure success. Every couple had been married for at least 10 years and were still married at the time of the interview; in fact, none of these couples claimed that they ever seriously had considered divorce or separation. They were "socially conspicuous," because of the nature of their work in business, government, the military, medicine, education, or the arts. The husband was at the top of his profession or business organization. But despite these similarities the sociologists found vast differences in the sexual relationships among these "successful" couples, leading them to classify the couples in five types.

About one-sixth of the couples had a "vital" relationship; sexual intercourse was frequent and mutually rewarding. Communication between the two people flourished; they shared life experiences and each considers the other indispensable; an activity is uninteresting if the spouse is not a part of it. Romance lived in a continuing vibrant relationship.

Cuber and Harroff (1965) classified a few of the couples into a *total relationship* category, really an extension of the vital relationship. The difference is that in the "total relationship" the points of "vital meshing" between partners are more numerous; "in some cases all of the important life foci are vitally shared" (p. 58). The authors, however, report that this kind of relationship is rare.

In contrast, another one-sixth of the couples the authors called "the conflict-habituated." They constantly quarreled; they deliberately hurt each other emotionally. Sexual behavior between them was only one of several battlefields. Sometimes they were involved with lovers outside the marriage. Cuber and Harroff (1965) note that the intermittent conflict was rarely concealed from their children, even though the parents claimed otherwise. They observe: "There is a subtle valence in these conflict-habituated relationships. It is easily missed in casual observation. So central is the necessity from channeling conflict and bridling hostility that these considerations come to preoccupy much of the interaction" (p. 46).

In between these two groups, the sociologists distinguished two other types. About one-third of the marriage relationships they labeled "devitalized." These couples had previously had a vital relationship but had lost that quality. The zest was gone; one called her marriage "dull." They both missed and resented the former vitality, and thus had become quite apathetic about marriage itself. These couples did not share many interests and activities, and didn't spend much time with each other. Sex was quite often perfunctory or absent; occasional discrete affairs were tolerated. In many of these couples there were certain aspects of their relationship— their children, their house—which they shared and found satisfying; hence the social scientists did not classify them as extreme as the *conflict-habituated*.

The fourth group, comprising about one-third of the couples, was labeled the "passive-congenial" type. These couples had settled into a comfortable, loyal relationship; as a matter of fact, they were happy with their less intense relationship. Many of these couples had put more of their energy into other activities than their marriages. They took each other for granted but saw this a virtue rather than a vice; they had not expected the intensity of the courtship phase to continue and so were not embittered when it did not. They express little conflict with each other, although "some admit that they tiptoe rather gingerly over and around a residue of subtle resentments and frustrations" (Cuber & Harroff, 1965, p. 51).

DIVORCE, REMARRIAGE, AND SEXUAL RELATIONSHIPS

Of those who become divorced, approximately 80% remarry. Some 50 years ago, only one of every three divorced persons remarried, partly because of the stigma of divorce (Dacey, 1982). In

1952, the fact that U.S. presidential candidate Adlai Stevenson was divorced was a significant factor in many voters' reactions to him; in 1980, there was hardly any public notice over the fact that presidential candidate Ronald Reagan was divorced and remarried.

Among women born between 1945 and 1949, 17% of their first marriages had ended in divorce by age 30, and one-third of all marriages today involve at least one party who has been married before. For divorced people who remarry, women wait an average of 3.4 years, whereas men wait a little less, 3.1 years (Schmid, 1987).

No substantial research exists comparing the sexual adjustment of remarried persons with that of once-married couples of the same ages. But Pietropinto and Simenauer (1979) reported that more than half of the remarried respondents to their survey said that their sex life was now excellent and 21% reported having sex at least five times a week, as opposed to 15% of first-married people.

SEXUAL BEHAVIOR OUTSIDE OF MARRIAGE

We are all aware of the vast variety of sexual relationships outside of marriage; differences exist with regard to the sex of the partner, the permanence of the relationship, the commitment to it, and many other aspects. Three major types exist: homosexual relationships, heterosexual relationships between two people unmarried but living together, and extramarital relationships. Each will be briefly described below, with emphasis on whatever knowledge is available on the developmental nature of the relationship

Homosexual Relationships

Bell and Weinberg's (1978) study, conducted by the Kinsey Institute at Indiana University, is perhaps the most useful in providing a classification of the lifestyles of homosexual men and women. They generated five categories that described 70% of the persons in their San Francisco sample:

(1) The "closed-couple" relationship: These couples reflected intimacy, exclusivity, and continuity. About 15% of the male pairs and a higher percentage of the women were in this type of sexual relationship.

(2) "Open-couple" relationship: These pairs lived together but their relationship did not preclude other sexual partners even though jealousy was a pervasive problem when such liaisons existed. This type of relationship reflected characteristic behavior of 25% of the men.

(3) "Functional" relationships: This type of homosexual person had many sexual partners and few commitments or regrets.

(4) "Dysfunctional" homosexual lifestyle: This type of person had few partners or sexual activity, but was tortured by self-doubt and guilt.

(5) The asexual lifestyle: The person who is less active than those in previous categories.

Reports of the sexual behavior of homosexual men published as recently as 10 years ago (see for example, Lief, 1978) emphasized a characteristic promiscuity, with frequent encounters with strangers. With the rise in the incidence of AIDS, such patterns are changing, and doubtless such typologies as even the carefully done one by Bell and Weinberg are no longer correct with regard to percentages of people in particular categories.

Prior to the advent of fears about AIDS, female homosexual life styles, more often than the men's, emphasized a long-term, committed relationship with a single partner. Lesbians reported less sexual activity than either heterosexual couples or male couples (Blumstein & Schwartz, 1983).

Unmarried, Heterosexual Relationships

The decade of the 1970s saw an eightfold increase in the number of cohabiting couples in the United States under age 25; among those ages 25-44, it increased sixfold (Cherlin, 1979). For the first half of the decade of the 1980s this trend continued; 1985 was the first year in more than a decade that the number of unmarried couples living together was less than the year before (Schmid, 1985). Even with the slight decrease, there were still 1,983,000 cohabiting couples in the United States (Kelley, 1985). Even surveys now a decade old (Pietropinto & Simenauer, 1979) reported that 14% of married couples had lived together prior to marriage, and of those married for a second time (or more), 35% had cohabited.

As Dacey (1982) notes, cohabitation is not usually a permanent substitute for marriage. Either the living-together relationship ends after a while—Dacey estimates a year or less—or the couple decides to get married. Cherlin (1979), after observing the progress of cohabitation in Sweden, France, and the United States, views it as an emerging first stage of marriage. Surveys of premarriage records in one county in Oregon concluded that 53% of the couples who took out marriage licenses were living together prior to marriage (Jacob, 1986).

Extramarital Relationships

Extramarital relationships are a staple of television soap operas, trashy and not-so-trashy fiction, and the lifestyles of some of "the rich and famous." Kinsey's studies, published in 1948 and 1953, reported that 50% of the males and 25% of the females in these samples had had at least one such experience. (But Kinsey's samples were not representative samples; they were composed entirely of volunteers.) Other estimates of incidence of extramarital relationships are sometimes lower, but the sex difference remained distinct, until more recent reports.

The most up-to-date estimates show a smaller discrepancy between the sexes with the women's rate of extramarital relationships having increased, whereas the reported rate for men has stayed about the same. In fact, a Yale University survey of 25,000 respondents (Stewart, 1985) found that women in their thirties are just as likely as men of that age range to participate in a sexual affair.

Other sex differences exist. Men are more likely to engage in an initial sexual affair during the first five years of marriage, whereas for women this decision is more common after 15 or 20 years of marriage.

Despite the strong disapproval voiced about infidelity, many married people feel that they can be tempted into it. Only 39% of the population view themselves as totally beyond temptation (28% of husbands and 49% of wives).

Why, then, does infidelity exist? Dissatisfaction with the marriage itself is given as the most frequent reason. But we need to recognize that an extramarital affair can be generated by a variety of causes. Cuber and Harroff's (1965) typology of five types of marriage described earlier in the chapter, is helpful here. They concluded that:

Infidelity . . . occurs in most of the five types, the total relationship being the exception. But it occurs for quite different reasons. In the conflict-habituated it seems frequently to be only another outlet for hostility. The call girl and the woman picked up in a bar are more than just available women; they are symbols of resentment of the wife. This is not always so, but reported to us often enough to be worth noting. Infidelity among the passive-congenial, on the other hand, is typically in line with the stereotype of the middle-aged man who 'strays out of sheer boredom with the uneventful, deadly prose' of his private life. And the devitalized man or woman frequently is trying for an hour or a year to recapture the lost mood. But the vital are sometimes adulterous, too; some are simply emancipated—almost bohemian. To some of them sexual aggrandizement is an accepted fact of life. Frequently the infidelity is condoned by the partner and in some instances even provides an indirect (through empathy) kind of gratification. The act of infidelity in such cases is not construed as disloyalty or as a threat to continuity, but rather as a kind of basic human right which the loved one ought to be permitted to have— and which the other perhaps wants for himself (or herself). (p. 62)

A second important reason is the premarital sexual frequency of the person. The greater number of sexual partners the person had before marriage, the more likely he or she is to be extramaritally active sexually.

MARRIAGE—A LASTING INSTITUTION?

Despite the pattern of other types of sexual relationships described in the last few sections, and despite the numerous criticisms of marriage, it is still considered a significant event that changes the lives of both its participants. Even in the late 1960s and early 1970s, when young Americans were scrutinizing every conventional value, about 80% of the weddings in the United States included a religious ceremony. And despite the increase in unmarried people (staying single or living together) among those 35 or older, the percentage who were unmarried dropped during the 1970s (for men, from about 7% to 6%, and for women from about 6% to 5%).

Is marriage an institution that is universally valued? In one sense, not as much as it used to be, but in another sense, it remains as strong as before. In 1957 a survey of representative U.S. adults (Veroff & Feld, 1971) found that 80% of them believed that only sick or immoral people would not want to marry, but in 1976 a repetition of this study (Douvan, 1979) reported that only 25% felt that not marrying was wrong. Similarly, the percentage of women who hope to get married has decreased, and the median age at marriage increased more than two years (to 25.7 for men and 23.8 for women) from 1970 to 1985 (Schmid, 1987).

Some observers (for example, McFarlane, 1987) are concerned about implications of this delay to marry, one being that it reflects a fear of making a binding pledge to someone else. Jonda McFarlane (1987) writes, "Those who fear the commitment of marriage, who avoid the trouble and the responsibility in the name of more time, more money or more pleasure, cheat only themselves. Those who wait until they reach all their other goals before presenting themselves to a deserving mate often find their success empty" (p. 8). This is one viewpoint, but society's values, manifested in the choices of young and marriageable people, reflect a dialectical shift from one tug to another. I expect that at some point in the future the average age at marriage will shift downward again.

But as we saw earlier in this chapter, the vast majority of those

---

BOX 9.2
What Is the Divorce Rate, Anyway?

Often the mass media tell us that 50% of marriages in the United States end in divorce. This is a misleading statement. It appears to be based—inappropriately—on a document back in 1984 from the U.S. National Center on Health Statistics, which reported that there were 2,400,000 new marriages and 1,200,000 divorces during that year. Yes, if we divide 1,200,000 by 2,400,000 we get 50%, but it is misleading to conclude from that that half of marriages terminate through divorce or dissolution. Those 1,200,000 divorces are composed of marriages that began perhaps years or decades before. Louis Harris of the Harris Poll estimates that the divorce rate is much lower, that about 13% of marriages end in divorce. In any single year, he concluded, only about 2% of existing marriages break up (Associated Press, 1987).

who end a first marriage in divorce remarry—five-sixths of the men and three-fourths of the women. As noted earlier, in recent years, more than 30% of people who marry have been married at least once before. From one-half to two-thirds of these remarriages last until one of the married partners dies. And remarried people are substantially happier than separated or divorced people. Each year in the U.S. the number of new marriages increases (Schmid, 1987) and marriage is an institution that doubtless will continue as the foundation for intimate relationships, despite the trend toward increased cohabitation and significant divorce rates. (See Box 9.2 for clarification.) Especially, then, it is appropriate to examine how a marital relationship develops, the topic of the next section.

THE DEVELOPMENT OF THE MARITAL RELATIONSHIP

Social scientists have sought to specify a sequence of developments that lead to marriage.

Social psychologist George Levinger (1979) has presented a descriptive analysis of marital relationships based on the combination of attractions and barriers that are present. Some of the attractions that he identifies are material rewards, such as family income; others are either symbolic, such as status, or affectional, such as companionship and sexual enjoyment. Barriers are conceived of as the potential costs of divorcing, such as financial expenses, feelings toward children, and religious constraints. Finally, Levinger suggests that people also weigh the alternative attractions, such as the value of independence or a preferred companion or sexual partner. This framework is helpful in a general way in identifying some of the factors that may come into play when individuals decide whether to maintain or discontinue a relationship. We can predict that when the attractions of the present relationship decrease, the barriers to escape from the relationship diminish, and the strength of the alternative attractions increase, then, at that point, an individual would choose to get out of the relationship.

A comprehensive list, developed by Adams (1979), is reprinted in Box 9.3; no list can deal with every consideration and eventuality, however. Just as "the progress of true love is never smooth," so too

---

BOX 9.3
The Sequence of Developments Leading to Marriage

---

(1) attraction to marriage itself—a conscious, expressed desire to marry
(2) propinquity—geographical closeness, availability
(3) early attraction, based on such surface behaviors of the partner as:
  (a) gregariousness
  (b) poise
  (c) similar interests and abilities
  (d) physical appearance and attractiveness
  (e) similarity to one's ideal image
(4) perpetuation of attraction, aided by
  (a) reactions by others, including being labeled as a couple
  (b) disclosure: opening oneself up to each other
  (c) pair rapport, being comfortable in each other's presence
(5) commitment and intimacy; establishing a bond
(6) deeper attraction, enhanced by:
  (a) value consensus or coorientation, providing validation of each other's viewpoints
  (b) feelings of competence reinforced
  (c) perception of other similarities in the partner, such as:
    (1) attractiveness
    (2) levels of emotional maturity
    (3) affective expressiveness
    (4) self-esteem
    (5) race, ethnic group, or religion, if important
    (6) birth-order matching
    (7) deciding that this is "right for me" or "the best I can get"
    (8) marriage

SOURCE: Adapted from Adams, 1979.

---

must every conceptualization fall short by the nature of its purported simplicity and rationality.

Attraction Versus Attachment

The development of a close relationship takes time. Those qualities that contribute to the early stages, such as physical attraction, may not be related to important factors at the later stages, such as attachment. Research findings conclude that what brings a couple together "almost inevitably" recedes into the background as the relationship matures (Goleman, 1985, p. B-5). Lillian Troll (1982) has sagely written:

> An examination of long-term relationships—parent/child, sibling, old friend, and long-married couple relationships—suggests that there may be an inverse relationship between attraction and attachment. In the beginning of a relationship, attraction is high, because part of the impetus is novelty and discovery. But attachment is low, because bonds are not yet cemented. . . . In the course of repeated interaction, however, novelty is gone and attraction reduced—but attachment may have become very strong. The two members of the dyad have become part of each other; they have achieved a joint identity. A breakup at this time may never be completely overcome. (p. 294)

As marriage continues, intense communication and self-disclosure may decrease, while loyalty, investment, and commitment to the relationship may increase.

Recent thinking about love and the developmental nature of an intimate relationship reflects these trends.

For example, in the early stage of a relationship, spouses are particularly likely to make attributions about the causes for the partner's behavior (Holtzworth-Munroe & Jacobson, 1985). As the marriage progresses, these attributions decline in frequency and importance unless conflict predominates in the interactions between the partners (Baucom, 1987). Robert Sternberg (1986) has proposed that love has three major elements—intimacy, passion, and commitment—and that these three elements develop at different rates in the course of a relationship. *Intimacy* represents the warmth and closeness in a relationship. It develops gradually over the course of a relationship, continuing to grow (although at a progressively slower rate) as the partners share experiences and feelings. *Passion* represents the more intense aspect of relationship; passion typically develops very quickly but then drops off as the partners become accustomed to each other. Los Angeles psychologist Berta Davis (quoted by Gindick, 1985), calls this phase "a wondrous sense of specialness," that a couple experiences at the beginning of their relationship but is doomed to be short-lived. *Commitment* can be of two types. A short-term commitment involves the decision that one loves another person; a long-term commitment involves willingness to maintain that love and to make the relationship succeed. This aspect of love typically develops slowly at first, and then speeds up as the rewards and costs of the relationship become clear.

Psychologist Ellen McGrath (quoted by Gindick, 1985, p. B-5) sees commitment as a more genuine aspect than passion: "It's based on knowing who you are. You're appreciative of them [the partner] because they care for you even knowing who you are. And they are that way about you. It's a more real stage. It's more comfortable. If people base a relationship on (commitment), a relationship has a better chance of succeeding."

SATISFACTION WITH ONE'S MARRIAGE

The previous section emphasizes that a long-term marriage is a frequently changing phenomenon, with different needs and costs surfacing at different times in the relationship. "Satisfaction" with one's marriage thus needs to be viewed in dialectical terms, with shifts in its degrees and emphases.

The overall concept of "marriage satisfaction" has been an elusive one for other reasons, too. Generally, two criteria have been applied to define a satisfactory marriage: Stability and happiness. In fact, these two have been associated; in our society, many people assume that a long-term marriage must be a happy one. But happiness and stability are not the same thing; as we saw earlier in the chapter, many marriages may reflect "success" in lasting over 15 years and leading to economic wealth and social prominence, and yet be devoid of sexual compatibility.

Happiness in one's marriage is also related to one's expectations. Highly educated persons have higher expectations, including the expectations of self-actualization and romantic love through marriage. The less educated may have fewer options and hence lowered expectations.

Sex Differences

In general, husbands tend to find their marriages more satisfactory than do wives.

A survey by a newspaper of 2,330 men found that most of them (actually, 77%) who were in their first marriages would marry their wives again, if given a chance (Cruver, 1986). (Slightly over 80% of the remarried men would again marry their current wives.) In contrast, a survey in *Women's Day* magazine reported that only half of the 3,009 women surveyed would remarry their husbands. (For women in second marriages, the figure increased to 63%.) Even more extreme in its expression of wives' dissatisfaction is the recent survey by Shere Hite (1987), who concluded that 98% of the women in her sample want to make "basic changes" in their love relationships. But Hite's analysis is based on the 4,500 women out of 100,000 who responded to a mail questionnaire. This 4.5% return rate is much too low to conclude that the sample is representative.

When asked to list "what you *don't* like about your marriage," 45% of the men listed nothing, whereas only 25% of the women responded that way. A husband's dissatisfaction does not seem to increase over the length of the marriage as much as a wife's does. Women's affiliative needs are often satisfied just by getting married and being married. But their reactions change. Of women married less than two years, 52% were very satisfied and none were dissatisfied. But of women married 20 years or more, only 6% were very satisfied and 21% were very dissatisfied.

In fact, men generally say they are satisfied with their marriages if their overall lives are going well, but women who are unhappy with their marriages are unhappy in other aspects of their lives. A "figure-versus-ground" contrast seems to exist here; marriage is more often secondary to a man's self-esteem, compared to its primary role for the woman.

There is an irony here. Jessie Bernard (1973) observes that even though marriage is a condition desired more by women than by men, it is much more beneficial to men. For example, married women have worse mental health than either single women or married men. Single women have many fewer psychological-distress symptoms than do married women.

Age Differences

Stage theories and dialectical approaches to adult development receive support from an analysis of age differences in marital satisfaction. As you would expect, honeymooning couples are the groups most satisfied with their marriages. But the next most satisfied is the elderly, followed by those in the "launching phase" (when children are leaving home). Least satisfied with their marriages are parents whose youngest children have just entered school, and parents of teenagers. Satisfaction figures for men were: married 10 years or less, 74%; married 10-20 years, 70%; married more than 20 years, 81% (Cruver, 1986). Sexual aspects of the marriage become less important determinants of satisfaction later in life (Pineo, 1961).

FRIENDS AND SPOUSES

A significant example of the evolving nature of the marital relationship is the couple's choice of and definition of "friends." Each partner in a new marriage has her or his own friends, but there is a gradual shift toward "couple friends" (Troll, 1982). Traditionally, such new pairs of friends have been more often recruited by the man, through his work (Babchuk & Bates, 1963); despite the fact that most newly married women also have jobs outside the home, male dominance still prevails here.

Probably one of the reasons for this is the sex difference in choice of friends. Men focus on similarity; "he's like me," or "we like the same things so we get along." Men choose friends who fulfill certain functions; "my poker-playing buddies," "my tennis partner," "my friend who advises me on my taxes." Women more often chose friends with whom they can develop a relationship in which reciprocity and mutuality are salient; their friends are more likely to be "all-purpose" friends who provide support and sharing rather than fulfilling a specific need or function (Candy 1977, cited by Troll, 1982).

In younger couples, each partner tends to name friends of his or her own sex and age (Hess, 1972). But in couples married 50 years, both of the factors were less important (Parron, 1979, cited by Troll, 1982). In these couples, there was considerable overlap in the friends of the husband and the wife.

THE LONGITUDINAL STUDY OF MARRIED COUPLES

Previous sections of this chapter have implied the presence of a pattern of changes in the marital relationship over time. The most effective methodology for determining what changes have taken place is a longitudinal one. This section describes two studies of married couples, using a longitudinal method.

The project directed by Ted L. Huston (Huston, Robins, Atkinson, & McHale, 1987) concentrated on the early part of a marriage. A total of 168 couples were interviewed a series of times at three periods during their first two and a half years of marriage. Husbands and wives were interviewed separately.

The focus of the interviews by Huston and his colleagues was on the tasks and activities recently carried out by each member of the married couple; in essence, it was a behavioral self-report. Although the goal of the researchers was a comprehensive description of activities and relationship shared by the couple, our focus here is on the changes in the affective quality of the interaction during this period. Huston et al. report: "Both the parent and nonparent groups declined considerably in the frequency with which they expressed affection or otherwise behaved in ways that brought pleasure to the partner. . . . We found that couples declined substantially on each of the positive behaviors . . . except 'talking together about the day's events'" (Huston et al., 1987, p. 64). However, there was no significant increase in negative behaviors over this time period.

The second longitudinal study was a much more extended one. Maas and Kuypers (1974) followed the development of some of the couples who were parents of the children in the Berkeley (California) Growth Study. (Other results of this important project were described in Chapter 6, on the issue of consistency of personality.) A total of 142 parents were reinterviewed when they were between the ages of 60 and 82; 95 of these were women and 47 were men. All 47 of the fathers had remained married for more than 40 years to the mother of the child who was the subject in the original longitudinal study. Their wives were included in the sample of 95 women (most of the other women in the sample were widowed). Maas and Kuypers decided to classify the men and women separately, based on their present life-styles. Four types of life-style emerged from the men, two-thirds of whom were retired. (However, whether the man worked or did not still work was not a salient determinant of his classification into a particular life-style category.) A description of each type follows.

Family-Centered Fathers (N = 19)

Central to these men's lives were matters of marriage, parenting, and grandparenting. Most of their satisfactions came from the marital relationships and their grandchildren. In contrast to the other three types of men, they see their children and grandchildren frequently. They are also active in clubs and other formal groups, but are little involved in church. They are moderately satisfied with life and report that they rarely or never think of death.

In viewing their past lives, they report that stability is the key. Overall, 90% of them followed a single career line, and have kept the same friends over the years.

Hobbyist Fathers (N = 11)

Leisure-time activities and interests are at the core of the lives of these men. They engage in more recreational activities than do the men in the other groupings; interestingly, most of these activities are done alone. They report more interests than they had in their forties, but we get the sense that these activities are "out there" and serve as function for these persons, rather than being an integral part of their lives. This instrumental orientation can be detected with regard to these men's relationships with their wives, too; many of them report being able to count on their wives "to do things" for them.

A withdrawn life-style characterizes these men. They are loners; they do not see their grandchildren very often. Yet they frequently attend church; 45% do weekly, compared to only 5% to 12% of the men in the other types. And they are the group who report the greatest satisfaction with their life-style and their home life.

Remotely Sociable Fathers (N = 9)

These men have a low level of involvement as marriage partners. They do not communicate with their wives very much and report being dissatisfied with their marriages. They stay busy and report having lots of "friends"—in fact they visit with other men more frequently than any other group. But their gregariousness appears to be superficial; they are not very involved in these relationships.

With respect to their relationships with their children and grandchildren, they are the opposite of the family-centered fathers described in the first category; they see the relationships with their own children as not close at present, as becoming increasingly remote with age, and lacking in affection or function. But they are optimistic about "how the world is going today" and few have made plans for death, such as preparing a will or purchasing a burial plot.

The men in this group tended to come from upper-class backgrounds; they were satisfied with their early life and experienced occupational and social success back then.

Unwell-Disengaged Fathers (N = 8)

These men have a compliant-submissive relationship with their wives; in these marriages one or the other spouse makes all the important life decisions. But as a group, they feel they cannot count on their wives to "do for" them.

Basically, these men have withdrawn from the world. Theirs are the highest ratings on "life dissatisfaction" and their marriages seem to be changing for the worse. They engage in few recreational activities; don't interact much with their grandchildren; and have little energy. Throughout their lives they reported poor health and less stamina; in fact, they have been preoccupied with health concerns their whole lives. Their life-style seems to be a consistent one rather than a result of some recent experiences or changes; they report that even when their children were young, they were distant from them.

For the 95 women in Maas and Kuypers's (1974) study, six discriminable patterns emerged; several of these were quite different from the men's. They were the following:

Husband-Centered Wives (N = 23)

For these women, the center of their daily living was their husbands; they do most activities with them, and they have little involvement in other activities. They don't see their siblings, children, or grandchildren very much; in this respect they differ from the family-centered fathers in the first category. They are very satisfied with their home life and life-style; they are in relatively good health.

Visiting Mothers (N = 16)

These women are characterized by high energy and social activity. They are highly involved as hostesses or guests, as parents, or group members. Social life is the core of their life-style, especially informal social interaction. They possess a large social network of relatives and friends; also the church is important to them (80%—by far, the highest percentage of any type—belong to a church).

These women have a relatively large number of children and grandchildren; they appear to have a good relationship with them, and don't obtrusively try to control their children.

Even though the husbands of 14 of these 16 women are still alive, the marital arena is not the central focus of their life-style. Perhaps one reason—but it could be an effect rather than a cause—is that more than half of the husbands still work (a relatively high percentage, compared to the other types).

Uncentered Mothers (N = 21)

The central nature of the daily life-style of these women is hard to characterize but it is essentially negative. They have few recreational interests, few club memberships, few close friends or confidants, and few activities of any type done with other persons. They do see their children and grandchildren often but report they are not as involved with them as the women in other groups are. They are dissatisfied with their present financial situations and with their health.

Overall, 17 of the 21 women in this group (81%) no longer have a marital partner. Apparently the death of their husbands was a shattering event for many of these women, as they had had a family-centered life. They had more children than the women in the other groups.

Furthermore, they live under the most disadvantageous conditions; they are the oldest group (almost three-fourths are in their seventies or older); they are in poor health; and the majority live alone.

Employed, or Work-Centered Mothers (N = 12)

Most of these women live alone, too, and 9 of 12 are no longer married. But they are highly involved as workers and very satisfied with their work situations. (One-half work part time and one-half work full time.) They are very satisfied with their health status, have many different hobbies and recreational pursuits, and visit others frequently. One-third of them report seeing at least one of their children every week. They tend to be younger than most of the other types, and free of physical disabilities and complaints. This group has shown the most change over time; in their thirties and forties they were the lowest in energy level, but in their elderly years they are characterized by high levels of energy.

Disabled-Disengaging Mothers (N = 12)

Women in this category resemble the husband-centered wives (first category) except that they register no satisfaction in marriage. In fact, they are not very satisfied with any aspect of their lives. They are disengaging or withdrawn from their former involvement in life, and have no close friends. Relationships with their children are strained. Almost half of them have husbands who still work, and they participate in activities with their husbands, but do not enjoy them. Like the unwell-disengaged fathers, these women had health problems in their early adult years, and they continue to be highly involved with a sick role in life. The majority have several physical disabilities.

Group-Centered Mothers (N = 11)

The life-styles of these women extend beyond their families into the areas of clubs and other formal groups, plus church and politics. They attend group meetings frequently, perform leadership roles in these groups, and are very satisfied with their group activities. Although most of them are married, the marital role is not the most important aspect of their lives, nor is being a homemaker. As parents they tend to be somewhat dominant; they give their children advice but little else. They possess the highest educational level and come from well-to-do families. They are in good health, are optimistic, and see things changing for the better. A certain remoteness and formality is typical of these women; they enjoy intimacy at a distance.

Is there any evidence that members of aging couples, married more than four decades, pattern their life-styles in ways that seem responsive or reciprocal to their partners' own emerging life-styles? Maas and Kuypers conclude not; they seem to develop quite independently. For example, of the 47 intact couples in their long-term longitudinal study, 19 of the men were "family-centered" but only five of these had wives who were "husband-centered." An equal number of the "husband-centered" wives had husbands whose hobbies and leisure-time activities were central to their lives. Maas and Kuypers note that for both men and women, the family-centered or husband-centered type is only moderate in life satisfaction. The moral of their study, for these researchers, is that those of each sex who are most satisfied with their lives are those whose lives are focused beyond—but don't exclude—their families.

These longitudinal studies are worthwhile beginnings, but they provide us little in the way of variables that distinguish between successful long-term marriages and ones that fail or continue to exist in name only. Family therapists point to the following as some of the factors that seem to make a difference:

(1) Problem-solving skills, especially willingness and ability to negotiate. A study of couples married 30 to 40 years, compared with couples who divorced at mid-life, done by Maggie Hayes (cited by Elias, 1984), found differences in communication and conflict patterns. When asked if their partner was easy to talk to, 83% of the persons in the still-married couples agreed, whereas only 27% of the divorced did so. The way of handling feelings of anger toward the partner is a crucial variable here; the successful marriages seem successful in deflecting negative feelings and keeping them from escalating (Goleman, 1984).

(2) A sense of optimism about their future, plus a view of potential crises as positive challenges.

(3) A sharing of basic values and goals, and of at least some activities and interests.

(4) A feeling that the two partners love each other in roughly equal degrees (Goleman, 1984).

(5) A need for intimacy. Dan McAdams, in his program of research on intimacy needs, finds people with these needs as having a preoccupation with themes of harmony, responsibility, and commitment. They also possess "positive passivity"; they are adept at listening and letting a relationship grow naturally without manipulating it.

In a nationwide study of 1,200 men and women, McAdams and Bryant (1985) found that those with stronger intimacy needs had a better sense of well-being, were happier, and felt more secure. Using the body of data on former Harvard freshmen analyzed by

Vaillant (1972) and described in Chapter 6, McAdams judged the relative needs for intimacy in these men when they were 30 years of age, using TAT-type stories they generated, and compared these with their marital adjustment 15-20 years later. The higher their need for intimacy at age 30, the more they enjoyed their marriages and their work (Goleman, 1986).

The research of Robert Sternberg, cited earlier, also concludes that intimacy becomes more crucial, particularly for women, as successful relationships endure (Goleman, 1985).

10

CHANGES IN VALUES AND ATTITUDES

The 40, 50, or more years that comprise adulthood for most of us include an incomprehensible collection of experiences. Many of these reflect our relationships with others, and these human relationships invariably involve conflict (Langdale, 1986). It is conceivable that these happenings change our views of the world, our basic values, and our judgments of what is important in life. But do they do so in any systematic way? Is it possible to say that during adulthood people generally change in a consistent fashion? Do they become more conservative, or less, more trusting—or less? Do the determinants of what people consider as moral behavior uniformly change? Do they become more restrictive in their political attitudes or social behavior? This chapter examines these issues. In doing so, it operates from a foundation of stage theories, that would hypothesize that changes in values inevitably occur at certain age periods during adulthood, but the chapter also uses a dialectical framework where appropriate.

VALUES

The concept of a *value* has several distinct meanings (Rokeach 1968). I will refer to a value as a standard for decision making, a guide in choosing what is important or how to behave. Following the use of the term by Rokeach (1968), we may think of values as "abstract ideals, positive or negative, not tied to any specific attitude, object, or situation, representing a person's beliefs about ideal modes of conduct and ideal terminal goals" (Rokeach, 1968, p. 124). We are aware of at least some of our values, but others may operate at an unconscious or unaware level, but both types are reflected in the choices we make. Everyday choices—whether to go to a football game or an art museum, choosing a colorful, "outrageous" piece of clothing over an acceptable but "dull" one, telling a friend a "white lie" or telling that friend the brutal truth—show in our behavior which values determine our actions. The very fact that daily life involves hundreds of unexamined choices implies that each of us may have many competing values demanding their advocacy at any one time. The concept of a *value system* is useful here, reflecting a hierarchical organization or rank-ordering of values in terms of their importance to each of us.

Values differ from attitudes in several respects. An attitude has an object; we possess attitudes toward specific topics, including everything from the Soviet Union to mandatory drug testing to foreign cars. Values are broader in focus; often our attitudes toward specific objects, processes, or people may be derived from our values.

The measurement of values by psychologists has been a topic with isolated periods of fertile growth, but long periods during which the topic was ignored. In the 1930s the operationalizing of values received a boost from the construction of an instrument titled the Allport-Vernon Study of Values (Allport & Vernon, 1931). Six values, based on Spranger's *Types of Men* (1928), were measured: theoretical, economic (or functional), aesthetic, social, political, and religious. The study of values became a popular measuring instrument, and was revised in 1951. Often, a widely used instrument can, unintentionally, color or shift the predominant theoretical definition of a construct; the wide usage of the Study of Values is an example. It conceived of values as personal goals or interests rather than as moral imperatives, being influenced by Spranger's contention that there were "types of men" who reflected different dominant interests (Robinson & Shaver, 1969).

But for the period of the 1950s and early 1960s, the measurement of values was largely ignored by psychologists; Robinson and Shaver (1969) offer two reasons: "The first has to do with psychologists' desire to define their discipline as a part of the larger enterprise of scientific research, with its emphasis on rigorous objective methods. Patterning themselves after physicists, differentiating themselves from philosophers, many psychologists consider(ed) value judgments to be outside the boundaries of an empirical discipline. They seem to have confused making value judgments, which is incompatible with scientific objectivity, with studying objectively *how other people make them*—a phenomenon as amenable to psychological study, in principle, as other forms of human learning and choice. . . . The second major problem, once the psychological study of values is accepted as legitimate, is to find a fruitful conceptual or theoretical framework from which to initiate research" (pp. 406-407, italics in original). The latter problem was referred to earlier in this chapter. Research on the measurement of values received a spurt in 1968 with the publication of Milton Rokeach's Value Survey. (See Box 10.1.) Rokeach distinguished between terminal and instrumental values—ends versus means— with respect to their place as guiding principles.

As the above paragraphs imply, there are many types of values.

BOX 10.1
Rokeach's Terminal Values

---

  (1) a comfortable life
  (2) a meaningful life
  (3) a world at peace
  (4) equality
  (5) freedom
  (6) maturity
  (7) national security
  (8) respect for others
  (9) respect from others
(10) salvation
(11) true friendship
(12) wisdom

This chapter focuses on three types: moral values, religious values, and political ones. For each of these, after an initial description of the most useful conceptualizations, the section will describe whatever available evidence exists about changes during adulthood.

MORALITY AND MORAL VALUES

What determines our choices of right and wrong? Are there moral concepts of good and bad that people use to resolve conflicts? Do people agree as to the standards for moral action? During adulthood, do conceptions of morality change? Moral values reflect one type of value that has benefited from sophisticated psychological conceptualizations that are highly developmental in their orientation.

Kohlberg's Theory of Moral Development

With respect to the adult years, the most extended example of the developmental view is the theory of moral judgment developed by the late Harvard psychologist Lawrence Kohlberg (1958, 1963, 1980, 1981), who theorized that six stages of moral development may account for the changes in perspective on issues like justice, equality, and reciprocity experienced by people as they move from childhood through adolescence to adulthood. Kohlberg's theory reflects the general characteristics of stage theories described in Chapter 3; in his theory, each stage is a step in an invariant hierarchical cognitive scheme; furthermore, each of these stages reflects a different organization of the way in which people "perceive the sociomoral world and reason about it" (Walker, 1986, p. 110). Additionally, Kohlberg proposes that not all people will reach the maturity of moral development reflected in the sixth and final stage. As they move from the first stage onward, they may become stuck at any one stage and use that as a filter through which they resolve moral dilemmas for the rest of their lives. But for those who progress through the stages, they pass from one level to a second and then a third level, at each level changing their basis for resolving moral dilemmas. Additionally, like at least some stage theorists—especially Erikson—Kohlberg believes that certain types of moral reasoning are more desirable than others; specifically, he proposes that each later stage is ethically superior to the ones before.

Kohlberg and his colleagues defined moral thinking as primarily based on a concept of justice, or just resolution of dilemmas about conflicting rights. Kohlberg (1971) wrote: "A just solution to a moral dilemma is a solution acceptable to all parties, considering each as free and equal, and assuming none of them knew which role they would occupy in the situation" (p. 213). As noted by Cohen (1980), such a definition echoes the theory of justice advocated by John Rawls (1971), who capitalized on this minimal risk strategy. He saw the progression toward justice evolving in six steps. The three levels and the two stages within each level are the following:

Preconventional level. Young children are responsive to culturally determined rules and labels such as *good* and *bad,* or *right* and *wrong.* But children interpret these labels in light of the *physical or emotional consequences* of their actions; that is, an action that leads to being punished must, therefore, be bad, whereas those that lead to receiving favors, or otherwise getting rewarded must have been good. Also, young children, at this level of what might be called *subnormal moral development,* interpret good or bad in light of the physical power of those who announce and enforce the rules and labels; that is, at this level, "might makes right." Young children, operating within this preconventional orientation, begin by responding at Stage 1, but as they grow older, the vast majority of them move to Stage 2 responses.

The first stage in Kohlberg's theory reflects a *punishment and obedience orientation.* To the child behaving at this stage, the consequences of an action determine the goodness or badness of the action; nothing else matters. If a child does something and does not get caught or punished for it—such as taking cookies from the cookie jar—the child concludes that the act must not have been wrong. Fear of authority is thus central to behaving "morally" at this stage.

The second stage is, in Kohlberg's terminology, the *instrumental-relativist orientation,* or *hedonistic orientation.* At this stage, what the child labels as *right* actions consists of those behaviors that satisfy one's own needs and occasionally the needs of others. Children whose behavior reflects this stage of moral development are still considered "preconventional" in their orientation because their actions are still primarily motivated by selfishness. Although acts might on first appearance seem to be unselfish—for example, a boy helps his grandmother cross a busy street—they are done by the child in an expectation that he will benefit in the long run. Human relations are viewed in the language of the marketplace: "You scratch my back and I'll scratch yours."

Although this orientation emerges in rather young children according to Kohlberg's scheme of development—perhaps at ages 4 to 6—many adults in our society may still reflect this outlook. Furthermore, parents often encourage "moral" behavior in their children by appealing to the youngster's selfish interests: "You should help your grandmother across the street because that'll cause her to give you a nice present on your birthday."

Conventional level. According to Kohlberg, "morality," for most Americans, means either obeying the laws and rules, or behaving in a way that people expect of you. For the person operating at this conventional level, a shift occurs, the self-centered orientation of the preconventional stages is supplanted by one that reflects an awareness of the rights, feelings, and concerns of others. That is, at this typical level of moral development, the fulfilling of the expectations of one's family, religious group, or nation is seen as a valuable in its own right, regardless of the immediate consequences to the person. The orientation is not only one of conformity to the social order, but of loyalty to it. Emphasis is on actively maintaining, supporting, and justifying the social order and identifying with the persons or groups in it.

The *interpersonal concordance* or *good-boy/nice-girl orientation* is the third stage of development in Kohlberg's theory and is typically reached during high school (Candee, 1980). Moral behavior, in the view of the person at Stage 3, is that which pleases, helps, or is approved of by others; maintaining the quality of interpersonal relationships is at the forefront. Intentions are important in defining morality here; the notion that someone "means well" becomes important for the first time, and one earns approval for being "nice."

The other stage (Stage 4) at this conventional level is, in Kohlberg's terminology, called the *law-and-order orientation.* Here the emphasis is on obeying laws and rules and maintaining the social order. Moral behavior thus consists of doing one's duty, showing that one respects authority, and perpetuating the given social order *because it is* the given social order (Kohlberg, 1963). Many adults never progress beyond this conventional level of moral development (Kuhn, Langer, Kohlberg, & Haan, 1977).

The postconventional or principled level. At the third and highest level of morality in Kohlberg's conceptualization the person further internalizes the standards for determining morality. The person makes an effort to define moral values and codes of conduct apart from the authoritativeness of the groups or persons advocating these principles and apart from the person's own identification with these groups. The code of conduct reflects the emergence of a set of principles that may or may not agree with the proscriptions, rules, and laws of the groups of which the person is a member.

Kohlberg sees this as a development of adulthood. He wrote: "with regard to adult moral stages, biography and common experience indicate dramatic or qualitative changes in adulthood in moral ideology. . . . The conclusion is that there are indeed adult stages. Stage 5 and typically Stage 6 thinking is an adult development, typically not reached until the late twenties or later" (1973, pp. 188-190). He estimated that 10% to 20% of adults reflect this principled level of moral development (Kohlberg, 1980).

Different explanations exist for the impetus for changes into post conventional morality. Kohlberg (1973) posited environmental or situational factors, that is, factors outside the person. For example, when young people leave the sheltered environment of their homes for one (especially college, though a marriage or a life in a bigger city might suffice) in which their traditional values and principles are challenged by other persons. But others have emphasized that internal factors, especially continued development of one's personality, might account for the shifts. For example, Lifton (1986) writes: "Specifically, two dimensions within an individual's total personality structure form necessary though not sufficient conditions for moral maturity. The first is a cognitive dimension, that is, being a rational, logical, unemotional individual. The second is an interpersonal dimension, that is, being concerned with persons other than oneself. As these two dimensions more and more come to characterize an individual's personality, so will his or her level of moral development increase in sophistication" (pp. 58-59).

Returning to an explication of the specific stages, the *social contract* or *legalistic* orientation falls in this highest level of moral maturity and is the fifth stage of development. The persons operating at this stage realize that their internalized standards of right and wrong are at variance with the laws or norms of society. These might include, for example, beliefs that nuclear war or execution of murderers are immoral. The person at Stage 5, while objecting to the death penalty on grounds that it violates the principle of maintaining human life, still recognizes that the death penalty is the law of the land, or at least of that state. The essence of the Stage 5 orientation is the attempt by the person to change the laws or rules through democratic means. The Stage 5 person says, in effect, "I believe the death penalty is wrong in principle, but I accept that it is the law and that the law is a representation of consensus views. Therefore I will lobby to change the law; I may write letters to the newspapers, I may circulate petitions; I may campaign for political candidates who promise to abolish the death penalty." Those persons behaving at Stage 5 feel a distance from society's consensus values but they realize that they must exist in society and work within it to change it. This fifth stage resembles the "official" morality of democratic governments and the U.S. Constitution.

The orientation of *universal ethical principles* is the sixth stage of Kohlberg's scheme. At this highest stage, what is morally right is not defined by the laws and rules of the social order but by one's own conscience, in accordance with self-determined ethical principles. Rather than being concrete moral rules, these principles are broad and abstract; they might include universal principles of justice, principles of reciprocity and equality of human rights, and respect for the dignity of every human being. For example, one's position regarding the acceptability of abortion on demand may reflect one's principles about the sanctity of human life or, conversely, about the rights of individuals to control their own bodies. Kohlberg has found that post conventional morality (both Stage 5 and Stage 6) "is probably attainable only in adulthood and requires some experience in moral responsibility and independent choice" (Kohlberg, 1973, p. 500). An example of a person reflecting Stage 6 morality—a 60-year-old woman—is provided in Box 10.2. Kohlberg (1981) cited Socrates, Jesus Christ, Abraham Lincoln, and Martin Luther King as persons reflecting Stage 6 morality in their behavior.

BOX 10.2
An Example of Stage 6 Behavior

Jean Gump is a 60-year-old woman now serving a six-year sentence in the Federal Reformatory for Women in Alderson, West Virginia. Her crime: an assault on a Minuteman II missile silo, near Butler, Missouri, on Good Friday, 1986. She and four other protesters attacked the missile silos with sledgehammers and human blood. The attack was largely symbolic; no serious damage was done. But the action reflected Jean Gump's values; "I believe our government is involved in illegal activities that have no end; I have said 'no' to the government and their policies," she said (quoted in Uhlenhuth, 1987, p. E-1). Mrs. Gump has had a long history of working for the peace movement through what she calls "legitimate channels," including the organization of nuclear-freeze movements. But the attack on the missile silos reflected a decision to take a more radical strategy. "I have a responsibility to not only speak the truth, but to live the truth," she stated (quoted in Uhlenhuth, 1987, p. E-2).

The effect of her action on her husband's values is an example of Kohlberg's claim that growth in moral development comes as a result of our values being challenged by those of a person operating at a higher level of morality (see, for example, Candee, 1980, p. 180, and Schochet, 1980, pp. 211-212). Her husband, about the same age as Mrs. Gump, had looked forward to the relaxed life of a retiree. But her activities led to some soul-searching on her husband's part: "Her example began to redirect my energies," Joe Gump has said, though his evolution toward protest was slower (Uhlenhuth, 1987, p. E-2). Joe Gump joined her in protest; at this writing he is awaiting trial for the charge of damaging federal property.

Kohlberg has boldly claimed that "All individuals in all cultures go through the same order or sequence of gross stages of development, though varying in rate and terminal point of development" (p. 175). Although some have referred to this claim as an "academic conceit" (Reid & Yanarella, 1980, p. 117), the empirical studies that examine the moral-judgment levels of children, adolescents, and adults provide some general support for Kohlberg's theory, as do the infrequent studies that assess children's moral-judgment levels and retest them 5, 10, or 20 years later (Kohlberg, 1958, 1963, 1981).

Proposing a Different View of Morality: A Woman's View

As noted earlier, Kohlberg measured the development of morality through ethical dilemmas that assumed that justice was the primary criterion. (These were considered dilemmas because no solution existed that did not carry some negative costs.) Other conceptions of morality were ignored (Langdale, 1986); Peters (1971) wrote: "How do children come to care? This seems to be the most important question in moral education, but no clear answer to it can be found in Kohlberg's writings" (p. 262). Kohlberg based his theory on the responses of boys and men; in doing so, he did little to discourage others from assuming that this conception also characterized girls' and women's development. More pointedly, Kohlberg expressed his belief that fewer women achieve the higher stages of moral development in his theory because their allegiance to their children precludes their developing abstract moral principles centered upon the concept of justice. Hence, we may conclude that a more-than-implicit developmental inferiority for women exists in Kohlberg's theory. (It even extends backward to Piaget's 1932 observations of boys and girls on the playground.) Carol Gilligan (1982), a former student of Kohlberg's and later a colleague of his at the Graduate School of Education at Harvard University, has objected to the male-oriented focus of his theory and its failure to be relevant to the socialization and experience of women. She has written about the "unfair paradox . . . that the very traits that have traditionally defined the 'goodness' of women are those that mark them as deficient in moral development" (Gilligan, 1982, p. 18); that is, that classify women as Stage 3 in Kohlberg's system.

Furthermore, Gilligan has developed a systematic conception of women's development that, although resembling Kohlberg's in structure, differs radically from it in content. One way in which it is structurally similar is that at an early level, persons of both sexes share an inability to distinguish the perspective of others from one's own perspective. It is also structurally similar in that Gilligan proposes that women pass through three levels, and that these levels, like the men's in Kohlberg's, move from self-centeredness to an other-oriented to an autonomous conception.

The differences in the two approaches are more important than their similarities. Although Kohlberg's approach has a rules orientation, with emphasis on abstract concepts and especially the concept of justice, Gilligan proposes that women possess a responsibility orientation with emphasis on sensitivity to others and the concept of care. For women, development is understood within a context of relationships, and connected with other people. In contrast to men, whose identity is defined through their separation from others, for girls and women identity is defined through attachment (Gilligan, 1982, p. 8). And for women, the moral dilemma results not from competing *rights*, as is the case for men, but from competing *responsibilities*. Thus, in Gilligan's words, for women it "requires for resolution a mode of thinking that is contextual and narrative rather than formal and abstract" (Gilligan, 1982, p. 19).

Like Kohlberg, Gilligan bases her theory on subjects' responses to moral dilemmas. But although Kohlberg posed his subjects some hypothetical dilemmas involving fictitious persons, Gilligan listened to the "voices" of women in the real world; she interviewed 29 females (ages 15 to 33) who were facing a real-life decision themselves, whether or not to abort a pregnancy. Some of these were unmarried, and some were still students in high school; others were married but for one reason or another were unsure that they wanted to carry the fetus to full term. (Although Gilligan is to be commended for using real-life dilemmas, research indicates that the decision to abort is influenced by other factors, too; see Box 10.3.)

Based on these detailed interviews and follow-up interviews a year later, Gilligan concluded that women may progress through three levels of moral development, but the focus is on *care* rather than *justice*. In all women, she concluded, the conflict is between obligations and responsibilities to oneself and to others. Their initial level of orientation, like Kohlberg's preconventional morality, is entirely selfish. The self is the sole object of concern in what Gilligan labels the *orientation to individual survival*. When asked what one "should" do, the only thought is what one "would" do for oneself.

BOX 10.3
Abortion Decisions and Moral Development Stages

Smetana (1981) studied the reasoning of women about their decisions whether to abort a pregnancy, much as Gilligan did. She compared 48 unmarried young women who were pregnant (in an unplanned way) with a control group of 22 women who had never been pregnant. Each subject was interviewed and also completed Kohlberg's measure of moral-development stage. Clear differences emerged in regard to how the pregnant women interpreted abortion; one-fourth of these women viewed it as a moral issue (that is, considerations of life and justice were central). But about one-third saw it as a personal issue beyond the moral domain; that is, emphasis on values of autonomous choice and control of one's own body were salient.

The remaining 40% saw the decision as reflecting both moral and personal considerations. Of most interest is the relationship between this and their eventual decisions; 93% of the women who viewed abortion only as a moral issue continued their pregnancies, whereas 94% of those who saw both aspects as relevant were more evenly divided in their decisions. No differences in Kohlberg's moral-stage level existed between those who saw abortion as a personal decision and those who perceived it as a moral issue.

If there is any sense of *obligation*—seen by Gilligan as central to women's development—it is an obligation only to oneself. There is no awareness of conflict.

But some of these women move from selfishness to a sense of responsibility and a different interpretation of *obligation*. Like Kohlberg, Gilligan sees moral growth resulting from an awareness within the person of conflicting conceptions of morality. The young woman may become aware of conflicts within herself; for example, she may wish to establish a connection with another person (that is, to have the baby and begin married life); yet she may also value her freedom and independence. The criterion for moral judgment changes and "should" and "would" begin to conflict. What one wants isn't always right.

This realization leads to Level 2, the conventional level of morality, called by Gilligan *goodness as self-sacrifice*. Morality here is defined as meeting the expectations of others and submitting to the norms of society. Primarily, concern is over not hurting others, and meeting the needs of others.

In considering whether to abort a fetus, a woman must, in Gilligan's (1982) piquant phrase, "confront the seemingly impossible task of choosing the victim" (p. 80). If she is an unmarried high school student who decides to have the baby, the victim may be herself—expelled from school, subjected to ridicule by her peers, abandoned by her boyfriend, ostracized by her parents. Or if she is a self-employed woman with little income, deciding to have the child may make the baby an instant victim of limited funds, little maternal support, and an impoverished future. For the woman at Level 2, the possible reactions by other people are salient. What will my parents think? Will my boyfriend reject me? Will another child place a burden on our family resources and cause my husband to blame me? At this level, the "right" way the dilemma is resolved is to decide in a way that hurts the others the least. But the stakes are high for the woman herself; her own needs are sacrificed in the decision, and she may soon struggle to free herself from the powerlessness of her own dependence.

And yet some women initiate their movement beyond Level 2. They begin to scrutinize the logic of self-sacrifice; the word "selfish" comes back in, but at a higher level of analysis. The woman begins to ask: "is it selfish or responsible—moral or immoral—to include her own needs within the compass of her care and concern" (Gilligan, 1977, p. 498). She becomes aware of both "what other people think" *and* her own inner judgment. The new goal is to be honest to oneself, so the virtue of *truth* replaces that of *goodness*, as a determinant of morality. In the words of the nineteenth century feminist, Elizabeth Cady Stanton, "self development is a higher duty than self sacrifice." This third level, then, is called by Gilligan the *morality of nonviolence*. The basic injunction is one against hurting, and this becomes a principle governing all moral judgment and action, in its condemnation of exploitation and hurt.

For example, in the film *Kramer Versus Kramer*, the wife and mother realizes that she is not being true to herself in her present condition, and at the risk of repudiating the norms of society and its views of her obligations and responsibilities, she abdicates her family role, that has been dominated by "goodness" and self-sacrifice. She has come to realize that to be responsible for oneself, it is first necessary to acknowledge what one is doing. She seeks to understand herself, and when she has completed that quest, she is ready and willing to carry out her responsibilities, at a level of morality. With it, comes a realization that self and other are interdependent.

In summary, for Kohlberg and for men, the moral imperative is "to use rules in order to respect the rights of others and thus to protect from interference the rights to life and self-fulfillment" (Gilligan, 1982, p. 100). The choice, hence, is between competing *rights*, with a perspective colored by *rules*. In Gilligan's view, for women the moral imperative is to alleviate the troubles of the world. The choice is between competing *responsibilities*; for example, a woman would, as a victim of injustice, be much more concerned with compensation for suffering than with having that suffering "justified." If someone agrees to repair your roof and you pay in advance, and if the job is not done as promised, the masculine orientation is to seek justice via a court of law, whereas the feminine conception focuses on the violation of a trusting relationship between the parties.

For women, the right to property—or even the right to life—is not weighed in the abstract, in terms of its logical priority—as the law sees it—but "in terms of the actual consequences that the violation of these rights will have in the terms of the people involved" (Gilligan, 1982, p. 95).

Let us consider a couple of examples, to illustrate the differences. Throughout history mankind (and the term is used deliberately) has been willing to make sacrifices for an ideal. But often fellow human beings have involuntarily been part of the sacrifice. Mahatma Gandhi stands as a superlative example of Kohlberg's Stage 6, because he operated out of a concern for universal human rights. All the major decisions in his life reflected these internalized principles. Yet Gandhi also superimposed his own values on his wife and children; Gilligan concludes that he "sacrificed people to the truth." "I was," said Gandhi, "a cruelly kind husband. I regarded myself as [my wife's] teacher and so harassed her out of my blind love for her" (quoted by Erikson, 1969, p. 233). Gandhi, in the guise of love, imposed his truth on others "without awareness of a regard for the extent to which he thereby did violence to their integrity" (Gilligan, 1982, p. 104).

The male perspective would emphasize the right to achieve a life of fulfillment to others, but a female perspective would combine this with the mutuality of respect and care for one's loved ones.

Several Biblical stories are also illustrative. The patriarch Abraham prepared to sacrifice the life of his son to demonstrate the integrity and supremacy of his faith. And in the Book of Judges, Chapter 11, we are told of Jephthah, who led the forces of Gilead in battle against the Ammonites. Jephthah made a rash promise to the Lord; if he was granted a victory over the Ammonites, he would offer as a burnt offering to the Lord "whatsoever cometh forth of the doors of my house to meet me" (Judges 11:31, King James Version). Jephthah doubtless assumed that this would be a sheep or a goat, but when he returned as victor, his daughter rushed out of the house to greet him, dancing and playing a tambourine. Jephthah was in anguish; he had made a solemn vow to the Lord, and thus he offered his only child as a sacrifice. In a male conception, the relationship of concern is that between Jephthah and the Lord, because the orientation is to abstract principles. In Kohlberg's conception, even a person operating at Stage 6, who might advise Jephthah to disregard his vow, would emphasize the *right* of human life, including the life of his daughter. But Gilligan would propose that a woman would focus on Jephthah's *responsibility* to his daughter. For women, valued moral development reflects concerns with attachment and relationships, rather than autonomy and achievement. Gilligan's (1982) biblical model is the woman who comes before Solomon and "verifies her motherhood by relinquishing truth in order to save the life of her child" (pp. 104-105). Research is beginning to appear that supports this gender-role distinction (Gilligan, Langdale, Lyons, & Murphy, 1982). For example, Ford and Lowery (1986) found that female subjects were more consistent in resolving a moral dilemma through a care orientation, and males were more consistent in the use of a justice orientation.

As psychologists have considered these contrasting conceptions of the nature of moral behavior, recent thinking has rejected a *categorical* distinction that claims that men operate out of an ethic of justice whereas women operate out of an ethic of care (Pratt &

Royer, 1982; Brabeck, 1983). Rather, these can be seen as two "conceptually distinct frameworks within which people organize their moral thinking" (Langdale, 1986, p. 16). Although each may develop in childhood as a correlate of differing sex role orientations for boys and girls, shifts in orientation may occur in mid-life, congruent with the shifting conceptions of one's sex role described in Chapter 8. To test such ideas Lyons (1982, 1983) divided 144 subjects into three age groups—childhood (ages 6 to 12), adolescence (ages 13 to 23), and adulthood (ages 24 to 60 and above)—and presented them with four contrasting ethical dilemmas (one was a real-life dilemma, generated by the subject; the other three came from the research of Kohlberg and Gilligan, reflecting justice and care orientations).

Lyons found that 85% of the responses to these ethical dilemmas could be coded into either justice or care orientations. More females than males gave responses reflecting a care orientation, regardless of the type of dilemma, whereas more males than females gave a justice orientation for each dilemma.

Lyons did not find a statistically significant relationship between the moral orientation chosen and age in any of the dilemmas; she concluded that both orientations appear systematically across the life cycle. But we should note several qualifications to this conclusion; first, the number of subjects who were older than their mid-twenties was quite limited. Second, among the females, the percentage choosing a justice orientation in Kohlberg's original ethical dilemma, the "Heinz drug" dilemma, increases from 37% to 48% with increasing ages. Another interesting result was the greater tendency of the females than the males to give several different orientations in response to a moral dilemmas; approximately one-third of the females did so (in the Heinz-drug dilemma), though only about 8% of males did.

Langdale (1986, p. 45), in reviewing these findings, reaffirms the conception "that there may be critical experiences at different points in the life cycle influencing the predominance of the justice and care orientations." It seems appropriate to think of these orientations as two paths along which moral development progresses simultaneously. In fact, a dialectical conception may be useful; at certain periods in life, development along one path may speed up, while the other slows down. Later, the pattern may reverse.

STAGES IN RELIGIOUS DEVELOPMENT

Religious faith may also be thought of as developing through a set of stages. Fowler and Lovin (1980) have proposed that religious faith possesses, for different people, different basic structures. These theorists propose that a structure of faith is a set of beliefs; but more than that, it is "a way that the mind operates in reasoning or judging about whatever content it focuses on" (p. 18).

The emerging stages of religious faith, in this conception, represent a series of tasks "in which each new life challenge arises in part from the limits of previous faith solutions" (1980, p. 23); a conception in keeping with the stage theories previously reviewed in this book.

Fowler and Lovin (1980) propose six stages, as follows:

Stage 1: Intuitive-projective faith. Children ages three to seven are oriented toward fantasy and imitation, but the content of thought patterns is rather fluid. Similar to Kohlberg's Stage 1, the child here is egocentric, but is becoming aware of strong taboos against certain actions.

Stage 2: Mythic-literal faith. In Stage 2, persons begin to internalize the stories, beliefs, and observances that characterize belonging to a particular society. Moral rules and beliefs are quite concrete and literal. Stage 2 also reflects "an increased accuracy in taking the perspective of other persons" (1980, p. 26); reciprocal fairness and imminent justice become determinant.

Stage 3: Synthetic-conventional faith. At this stage awareness of the world comes to extend beyond the family. At this point religious faith serves the function of providing a coherent orientation to the world in the midst of a more varied and complex world and synthesizing contrasting viewpoints. The authors state:

Stage 3 typically has its rise and ascendancy in adolescence, but for many adults it becomes a permanent equilibration. It structures the ultimate environment in interpersonal terms. Its images of unifying value and power derive from the extension of qualities experienced in personal relationships. It is a 'conformist' stage in the sense that it is acutely tuned to the expectations and judgments of significant others, and as yet does not have a sure enough grasp on its own identity and autonomous judgment to construct and maintain an independent perspective. While beliefs and values are deeply felt, they typically are tacitly held—the person 'dwells' in them and the meaning world they mediate, but there has not been occasion to step reflectively outside them to examine them explicitly or systematically. At Stage 3 a person has an 'ideology,' a more or less consistent clustering of values and beliefs, but he or she has not objectified it for examination, and in a sense is unaware of having it. Differences of outlook with others are experienced as differences in 'kind' of person. Authority is located in the incumbents of traditional authority-roles (if perceived as personally worthy) or in the consensus of a valued, face-to-face group. (Fowler & Lovin, 1980, p. 27)

Stage 4: Individuative-reflective faith. The transition from Stage 3 to Stage 4 is especially important because at this point the adolescent or young adult must accept responsibility for his or her own life-style, values, and commitments.

At this stage, a form of "demythologizing" may take place.

Stage 5: Paradoxical-consolidative faith. Stage 5 responds to a crisis that often happens in mid-life. Previous certainty of values is questioned by forces that in earlier years had been suppressed from consciousness or ignored. The authors of the theory speak of "opening to the voices of one's deeper self" (Fowler & Lovin, 1980, p. 29); they note "this involves a critical recognition of one's *social* unconscious—the myths, ideal images, and prejudices built deeply into the self-system by virtue of one's nurture within a particular social class, religious tradition, ethnic group, or the like" (p. 29).

Stage 6: Universalizing faith. Like the Stage 6 morality in Kohlberg's conception, the authors see this as the highest development of religious faith, but that its occurrence is quite rare. Those persons who have achieved this perspective "have generated faith compositions in which their felt sense of an ultimate environment is inclusive of all being" (Fowler & Lovin, 1980, p. 30). They facilitate and actualize the spirit of a fulfilled human community.

POLITICAL VALUES

Does development during adulthood have any impact on political attitudes? Some have even claimed that the individual differences in moral reasoning described earlier in this chapter reflect variations in political ideology rather than moral maturity (Emler, Renwick, & Malone, 1983). We assume that as people grow older in our society they become more "conservative" (Glenn, 1974). But is that assumption generally true, and if so, does it apply to political conservatism? And, given that conservatism is defined partly as the preservation of tradition, how does political conservatism jibe with the radical change shown in some people in mid-life? Even if older age is associated with right-wing attitudes, may it best be accounted for by a cohort effect, or by age differences in income or standard of living? These are challenging questions.

Statements about age and political values are also confounded by differing meanings of political values. At one level, we could focus on broad ideologies such as the previously mentioned conservatism and liberalism (Cutler, 1983). Somewhat related to these, but still distinguishable, would be an emphasis on political alienation, cynicism, and trust. A third emphasis would be on voter participation and community involvement. Confounding these is the changing level of importance of political-party identification with age and cohort, as well as the very centrality of political parties in the contemporary political process.

For example, some evidence exists that older people often adopt more conservative positions on contemporary social issues such as legalization of marijuana, abortion, or school busing (Cutler, 1974), on foreign policy (Back & Gergen, 1963) and on political party preference (Crittenden, 1962).

But Cutler (1983) in an extensive review, notes that such findings need to be qualified in several ways:

(1) Not all young people are on one side of an issue and not all older people are on the other side.
(2) Political-party identification by the respondent may modify the relationship between age and political attitudes more for some types of attitudes than others.
(3) The findings often confound age differences and cohort effects.
(4) For some issues, increased age may lead to liberal rather than conservative shifts in political attitudes, specifically those, such as medical care or social security, that are relevant personally.

11

REACTIONS TO DEATH AND DYING

Awareness of death is present in some undifferentiated way even in young children, and some psychiatrists have speculated that a child's early response to death affects the whole of personality development (Lifton & Olson, 1982). But for the most of us, death becomes a personal issue only much later in our lives except for brief periods; for example, when a classmate dies. It was only after he suffered a stroke in 1987, for example, that Mayor Edward Koch of New York City carried his musings about his own mortality to the point of preparing for his funeral and composing his own epitaph (Finder, 1987). Even for most adults, who do not dwell constantly on their own death, the issue sooner or later has an impact on their personality development. This chapter deals with various aspects of death and dying, including the role of religion and support groups, the function of bereavement, and personality factors in adaptation. Noted here—and emphasized at several points subsequently—is the observation that although the concepts of "death and dying" are often linked together in the professional literature (even here!), they are also separate issues with respect to personality development in adulthood. For example, the death of a spouse leaves adjustment challenges for the survivor, challenges that may only very slightly overlap with the survivor's own fears of death. "Dying," as a concept present within one's thought processes, may be quite different from "death." The term *death anxiety,* as it is usually referred to in the literature, may refer to a multitude of fears, some of which deal with the finality of death and some of which deal with the process of dying (Kastenbaum & Costa, 1977).

Awareness of One's Mortality

How much do children understand about death? This is a question that seemingly is best answered either by the imprecise "It depends" or by another question: "How can we know?" But psychiatrists and social scientists have sought more precise answers. Lifton and Olson (1982) report awareness of death in some form by pre-school-age children; as early as age 3, the child may be able to differentiate death from sleep. But the preschool child often conceptualizes death as possessing a property, like sleep, of being reversible or "coming back." For example, we are told that four-year-old Cecilia Cichan, the only survivor of a Northwest Airlines plane crash that took the lives of her parents and brother, reacted to being informed by "awareness, but not really comprehension." Awareness of the inevitability of death, conclude Lifton and Olson, comes only later. "The age at which children begin to understand all this varies tremendously, but in most cases it occurs between five and nine" (Lifton & Olson, 1982, p. 75).

Two aspects of awareness of death can be distinguished: universality versus irrevocability (Troll, 1982). By the age of 10, 90% of children recognized that death happens to everyone, but only one-third said that death was final (Childers & Wimmer, 1971). When children of differing ages are sensitively interviewed about their beliefs, three stages regarding irrevocability emerge (Nagy, 1948; Safier, 1964). Children around age 4 seem to interpret life and death as a constant flux; Safier (1964) observes, that for them, "Something goes, then it stops, then it goes again. There is an absence of the idea of absolutes" (p. 286). Nagy (1948) described this as a stage that lacked appreciation for death as final. Then, at an intermediate stage, children view death as final but, at the same time, not inevitable. Here, life and death are both caused by outside agents; "Something makes it go; something makes it stop." The children at the third stage (about age 9 or 10), could recognize that death was both inevitable and final; Safier's respondents also felt that an internal agent could cause changes; "something goes by itself; something stops by itself" (Safier, 1964, p. 286). However, age in itself is not the best guide; a Piagetian classification of a child's ability to handle different types of mental operations is a better predictor of his or her understanding of death (Koocher, 1973).

The fact that awareness in children develops slowly, in stages, should not, however, obscure that fact that even young children have ideas about death, often built upon realistic, concrete perceptions (Kastenbaum & Costa, 1977). In a review of the literature on psychological perspectives on death, Kastenbaum and Costa (1977) summarize this viewpoint as follows:

> While there remains room for disagreement on a variety of questions, it does appear that the child's development of death cognitions is intimately related to its total construction or appreciation of the world, rather than standing outside the main developmental stream as a secondary or exotic process. Curiosity about impermanence and destinations seem as much a part of the child's intellectual orbit as the more frequently researched questions of permanence and origins. We believe that developmental psychology has overemphasized the processes through which the child comes to appreciate and acquire stability and equilibrium. Real children seem just as interested in disappearances, inconstancies, and disequilibriums. This perhaps is another way of saying that loss, endings, and death are core concerns from childhood onward. (p. 232)

But when, if ever, do these attitudes become personalized? Do we ever really internalize the realization of our own finiteness? Kubler-Ross, Becker, and other experts doubt that we do. The suicide experts Shneidman and Faberow (1957) tell us that many people who "successfully" commit suicide do not really intend to end their lives; they are unable to imagine their own death (Troll, 1982). Again, three stages developing throughout life may be distinguished. First, after children develop some object constancy, they may be able to appreciate irrevocability as an abstract concept. Second, comes a more internalized level of awareness. The gerontologist Munnichs (1966) called this the awareness of finitude, and he viewed it as separating youth from old age, as it reflects a shift in focus and a related adjustment. Like Kohlberg's stages of moral development, it is hard for persons at less advanced stages to appreciate the more advanced ones. Yet some people can tell you the exact moment that they internalized this awareness of their personal mortality. Kastenbaum (1977) quotes the playwright Ben Hecht: "I can recall the hour in which I lost my immortality, in which I tried on my shroud for the first time and saw how it became me. . . . The knowledge of my dying came to me when my mother died" (p. 148).

Likewise, one of the most dramatic sections of Gail Sheehy's *Passages* (1976) describes her instant awareness: "Without warning in the middle of my thirties, I had a breakdown of nerve . . . I was talking to a young boy in Northern Ireland where I was on assignment for a magazine when a bullet blew his face off. That was how fast it all changed. . . . When I flew home from Ireland, I couldn't write the story, could not confront the fact of my own mortality. . . . Some intruder shook me by the psyche and shouted: *Take stock! Half your life has been spent. . . . You have been a performer, not a full participant. And now you are 35.* To be confronted for the first time with the arithmetic of life was, quite simply, terrifying" (pp. 2, 4, italics in original).

BOX 11.1
Kubler-Ross's "Stages of Dying"

In the 1960s Elizabeth Kubler-Ross, a psychiatrist at the University of Chicago, held conversations with more than 200 patients who were dying. From these interviews, she identified five stages in the process of accepting death. Even though she acknowledged that each of us is unique in our confronting of death, the stages she identified have been widely publicized.

(1) denial, including rejection of the possibility of imminent death
(2) anger, along with frustration; these may be vented toward others
(3) a bargaining stage, or an effort to negotiate a prolonging of life
(4) depression and grief, resulting from increasing acceptance of death's inevitability
(5) a state of peace and acceptance

BOX 11.2
DA Scale

Instructions: For each of the following statements, indicate whether or not it applies to you. Circle T if the statement is generally *true* of your feelings. Circle F if the statement is false or does not reflect your feelings.

T F   1. I am very much afraid to die.
T F   2. The thought of death seldom enters my mind.
T F   3. It doesn't make me nervous when people talk about death.
T F   4. I dread to think about having to have an operation.
T F   5. I am not at all afraid to die.
T F   6. I am not particularly afraid of getting cancer.
T F   7. The thought of death never bothers me.
T F   8. I am often distressed by the way time flies so very rapidly.
T F   9. I fear dying a painful death.
T F   10. The subject of life after death troubles me greatly.
T F   11. I am really scared of having a heart attack.
T F   12. I often think about how short life really is.
T F   13. I shudder when I hear people talking about a World War III.
T F   14. The sight of a dead body is horrifying to me.
T F   15. I feel that the future holds nothing for me to fear.

(Key: 1-T, 2-F, 3-F, 4-T, 5-F, 6-F, 7-F, 8-T, 9-T, 10-T, 11-T, 12-T, 13-T, 14-T, 15-F.)

SOURCE: Templer, 1970.

One manifestation of this shift at the second stage is more emphasis on "subjective life expectancy" or greater awareness of the "number of years left" (Lieberman & Caplan, 1970). Although previously, the person was aware that he or she would not live forever, still there wasn't any emphasis on thoughts like "I have 70 years left" or "I've already lived 20% of my life." At this second stage, the finite quality of life comes to the fore.

Lifton and Olson (1982) describe this stage this way:

On the life watershed of middle age, one becomes aware that life is not unbounded at the far end. The boundary of one's death is suddenly no more distant than the boundary marked on the other end by one's birth. One is in the middle. Of course, one has always 'known' that one would die, but now this knowledge becomes a compelling individual reality. One's life is suddenly felt to be limited, finite. It also becomes apparent that one cannot finish everything; there will not be time for all one's projects. (p. 78)

Here, the ages at which one's parents died, or the general longevity of one's family, intrude into one's thoughts more frequently. Marshall (1975) interviewed U.S. citizens between the ages of 64 and 96 about their expectations. He discovered that many of his interviewees used a formula to estimate their own life expectancies that was based on the relative length of life in their family members. One man said: "Up to now no men in my family have lived past 70. But a brother is going to be 72. But both parents died at 70. They say you die according to when your parents died." In Marshall's sample, only about one-third of those respondents who had already lived longer than both their parents expected to live at least five more years, whereas 92% of those younger than the age of their parents' deaths expected to live five more years.

But finitude of death sometimes may extend to another stage, at which it becomes even more personal. At the last stage the shift seems to be away from shock and rejection at the thought of one's own death, toward some dealing with the actuality. Whether such is fully contemplated is impossible to know, of course; Freud believed that none of us can image our own death, and Kubler-Ross (1969) has written that "in our unconscious, death is never possible in regard to ourselves" (p. 2). But clearly new emphases take place; for example, pondering what one's life has added up to. This process of "life review" apparently cannot fully operate before this stage.

DEATH ANXIETY

Existential theorists have proposed that the fear of death is the central human anxiety (May, 1973; Troll, 1982). At some deep unconscious level this may predominate; interestingly, when asked directly, most interviewees report they fear the deaths of others more than they fear their own (Geer, 1965; Schoenrade, 1986). As Chapter 6 reported, George Vaillant's (1977) subjects, former

Harvard students reinterviewed in their forties, feared the death of their spouses more than their own death.

The term *death anxiety* has been used to refer to this dread that supposedly underlies most of the other of life's fears. However, the term requires elaboration. When asked what they fear about death, different respondents give a variety of fears: pain, mutilation, loss of dignity, for example (Troll, 1982). Some fear abandoning their loved ones, especially their children, and others fear being abandoned by others. Those with certain kinds of religious values may fear punishment in afterlife, and others may fear the unknown. Death anxiety thus can refer to either fear of dying or fear of the event of death itself.

Age and Death Anxiety

Does the aging process increase levels of death anxiety? Troll (1982) notes that some investigators conclude that older people, presumably because they are nearer their own death or have had more experiences with the deaths of loved ones, have less fear of death than do younger adults (Kastenbaum & Aisenberg, 1972; Munnichs, 1966).

Richard Kalish, another distinguished observer of the aging process, takes a more detailed perspective. He offers three reasons for older people admitting to less fear of dying than do younger adults:

(1) Older people put less value on their own lives, because society tends to view them as "over the hill," "used up," and discarded.

(2) The internalized life expectancy, mentioned previously in this chapter, plays a role. If an older person has surpassed the age at which his or her parents died, the survivor may feel blessed, and hence less apprehensive about dying.

(3) The greater number of deaths of family and friends experienced by older people gives them an opportunity to "rehearse"—or at least to become accustomed to—the unavoidability of dying. A dissonance-reduction process also seems possible; "I'm going to die so I'll fear it less" (Schoenrade, 1987). Consider, for example, the situation of a healthy 75-year-old who lives in a retirement home of 100 or 200 residents. This person encounters the loss of acquaintances more often than even an equivalent-aged person who lives alone. Death

never becomes "routine" but it is likely that the frequent confronting of it that is forced upon some elderly people moderates their own death anxiety.

One study, done in Great Britain (Cartwright, Hockey, & Anderson, 1973) supports the latter conclusion. Persons who had recently suffered the loss of a loved one were studied; the proportion of bereaved people who needed assistance because of shock or distress or who reported trouble sleeping decreased with age. But as Troll (1982) asks, does this mean that the older people were really less bereaved? Or have they learned to suppress their anxieties as a result of their greater experience with death? For example, other researchers (Templer, Ruff, & Franks, 1971), after administering a death-anxiety scale to respondents of varying ages, found no major age differences past adolescence. Probably the safest conclusion is that reactions to death are too complex and too embedded at deeper levels of awareness ever to expect a consistent, straightforward relationship with age. Growing older may heighten fears in some, whereas others may—with age—experience reactions that reduce anxiety. It would be more profitable to explore how other determinants interact with age to affect death anxiety. Religion is one such variable, and to it we turn.

RELIGION AND DEATH ANXIETY

What role do one's religious beliefs play in determining one's feelings about death? And if they are a factor, does this relationship change with increasing age? Batson and Ventis (1982) state that religious beliefs are present in "whatever we as individuals do to come to grips personally with the questions that confront us because we are aware that we and others like us are alive and will die" (p. 7).

Methodological Issues

Unfortunately, much of the research done to answer these questions has used narrowly defined populations, thus creating doubt about the propriety of applying these findings to other populations (Lester, 1967). Among these specific groups were patients in mental hospitals (Feifel, 1959), older persons (Swenson, 1961), older persons who were also patients in mental hospitals (Christ, 1961), college undergraduates (Alexander & Adlerstein, 1959), theology students (Magni, 1970) and medical-school students (Siegman, 1961). The diverse nature of these samples accounts for some of the conflicting findings about how extensive is the fear of death. But even from samples of apparently similar nature, conflicting results can emerge. For instance, Feifel (1955) concludes, on the basis of interviewing a mentally ill population, that old age is the time of life when people most fear death, and childhood the period when they are least afraid. But Swenson (1961) found that death attitudes of a fearful or negative nature were not acknowledged by his elderly sample, and Christ (1961), interviewing older psychiatric patients, found that 87% of them said that they never had talked about death or dying before. Such conflicting findings can partially be clarified by the use of common measures, whether they be interviews, or questionnaires, or depth measures.

But at present the measurement techniques are another problem in drawing answers to these questions. Direct questioning, which has been used in most of the studies, may be inappropriate for reaching the real feeling of respondents, even though good rapport has been established (Kastenbaum & Costa, 1977). As Munnichs (1961) notes, it is difficult to give a real answer to the sudden question: "Are you afraid to die?" Since many people have given little or no previous reflection on a conscious level to the thought of death, their replies are likely to be negative as defenses against a direct question. Also possible is their assumption that they are not afraid because they don't think about it much (Schoenrade, 1987).

Instead of using direct questions, Jeffers, Nichols, and Eisdorfer (1961) suggest that projective techniques and depth methods may be more fruitful. The latter types, although often subjective in their scoring and interpretation, may be more valid because they probe into feelings that are much deeper than the superficial responses elicited by direct questions and true/false attitude statements. Another type of fruitful method, pioneered by Alexander, Colley, and Adlerstein (1957) is the use of the galvanic skin response and other physiological arousal measures to show that death-related words elicit more autonomic arousal than do neutral words

(Templer, 1971). This is a particularly relevant, though problematic method, because on direct measures, there are "relatively rare expressions of high manifest death concern despite widespread acceptance among researchers of the belief that death anxiety is universal" (Kastenbaum & Costa, 1977, p. 234).

The supposed validity of the measurement techniques in this area is often pragmatically determined; if a measure "works" (i.e., if its findings are in line with theoretical predictions), it is valid. Using this criterion, some direct methods appear to be more useful than others. For example, Sarnoff and Corwin (1959) constructed a Fear of Death Scale, responses to which show relatively good differentiation between greater and lesser fear of death. From a larger pool of items, five items were selected by the use of item analysis. (A sample item is "I tend to worry about the death toll when I travel on the highways.") In a test of predictions from psychoanalytic theory, Sarnoff and Corwin found that scores on the scale were related to the extent of castration anxiety reported by the subjects. But other simple, direct measures have not been as productive in confirming theory-driven hypotheses.

Another factor that needs to be given more consideration in research studies is the amount of contact with death that the respondent has experienced. It seems quite plausible that the person who has recently encountered the loss of a loved one will have thought about death much more than the person whose environment has not been so affected. This is an example of a factor that could interact with the person's age in determining death-anxiety levels.

A third type of limitation in at least the early studies was that religion was treated too broadly. Religion is now seen as a multi-dimensional construct (Batson & Ventis, 1982; Schoenrade, 1986), with many measurable components. One recent strategy—to be discussed in detail subsequently—is to relate specific death-related religious beliefs, such as a belief in an afterlife, to death anxiety (Schoenrade, 1986).

The Role of One's Philosophy of Religion

In relating extent of fears of death to religious attitudes, we need to give attention to the role of death in different religious philosophies. As Schoenrade (1986) notes, the issue of death is often a basic focus of major religious teachings. In Buddhism, "salvation ultimately means transcending death in a very radical way, by being taken out of the stream of existence into a transcendent realm" (Smart, 1968, p. 115). In Christianity, "the resurrection of the dead" may be more literal in the beliefs of some denominations than others, but it always has relevance for the individual believer (Schoenrade, 1986). In the fundamentalist denominations of Protestantism, death is seen as a doorway to either a better or a worse condition. The religion the person follows often guarantees the person the reward of eternal life as a result of faith or works. Sometimes one's trust in an afterlife with God reaches the extent that, like the apostle Paul, the person might prefer to leave this life to enter that land beyond. Whether or not one's confidence reaches this peak, it does seem that the person who believes in an afterlife has less reason to fear death than one who does not. Furthermore, it would seem that the more religious a person is and the greater claim the person has to "eternal life," the less he or she should feel anxiety concerning impending death. So at least goes the reasoning of many philosophers and social scientists (Becker, 1973; James, 1902; Kubler-Ross, 1969; Lifton, 1979; Schoenrade, 1986).

But Feifel (1959) has reasoned differently. He argued that certain people who fear death strongly may resort to a religious outlook in order to cope with their fears concerning death. He further concluded that the religious person, when compared to the less religious individual, is personally more afraid of death. For the nonreligious person, the emphasis is a philosophical one—on fear of discontinuance of life on earth rather than what will happen after death. The stress on the religious person is seen as coming from two sources: essentially religious concerns with afterlife matters such as "I may go to Hell," or "I have sins to expiate yet," as well as the philosophical concern with the cessation of present earthly experiences. Feifel's data indicated that even the belief that one is going to Heaven is not sufficient to do away with the personal fear of death in some religious persons.

Apparently the only other study to support this conclusion is that of Faunce and Fulton (1958), who reported that "emotional responses suggesting either fear of death or of the dead were more frequent among spiritually oriented than among temporally oriented individuals" (p. 208). But in both these studies absolutely no statistical techniques were employed. Feifel based his conclusions on his observations of questions asked in an interview, whereas Faunce and Fulton reached their interpretation by examination of responses to a sentence-completion task.

A few studies have found that religious feeling makes no difference in the way one views death (Feifel, 1974; Kalish, 1963; Templer & Dotson, 1970). Even when death anxiety is compared with the specific variable of nature of beliefs about an afterlife, sometimes no relationship emerges (Aday, 1984).

But a greater number of studies have shown that religious belief serves as a means of reducing anxiety about death. Jeffers, Nichols, and Eisdorfer (1961) state: "No fear of death includes a tendency to read the Bible oftener, more belief in a future life, and reference to death with more religious connotation" (p. 43). Alexander and Adlerstein (1959), on the basis of several empirical measures, reached a similar conclusion, as did studies by Lester (1970), Magni (1970), Templer (1972), and Swenson (1961), who used a sample of older persons.

Schoenrade (1986) observed that the studies described previously did not *activate* a concern with death, other than to ask the respondents for their reactions to it. What if an individual were confronted *directly* with the prospect of his or her death; then the role of religious beliefs might be more apparent. For example, Berman (1974) interviewed a small number of persons who shared the experience of having almost died. Those who strongly believed in an afterlife didn't remember any less fear at the time, but those who were active religiously were more likely to report having prayed at the time of the near-death experience.

Osarchuk and Tatz (1973) tested these ideas in a laboratory setting; they confronted undergraduates with the (artificially inflated) probability that people of the subjects' ages would die in automobile accidents. The results suggest that the death confrontation increased their belief in afterlife in those subjects who were already so predisposed, that this is one means of dealing with death (Schoenrade, 1986).

Schoenrade's (1986) careful study of undergraduates found a similar result: among those subjects who already possessed relatively strong beliefs about afterlife, forcing them to confront their deaths through a laboratory manipulation enabled them to embrace a positive view of death and to accept its negative implications. For those subjects who lacked strong beliefs in afterlife, the confrontation did not affect their attitudes toward death.

In an effort to deal with methodological limitations of some earlier studies, Martin and Wrightsman (1965) administered a variety of instruments to 58 members of three churches. Ages of the subjects ranged from 18 to 75; the mean age was 44. Two different measures of religious values were given, one assessing extent of participation in religious activities (church services, Sunday school, personal prayer, and reading of religious materials) and the other measuring two factors of religious attitude, a "nearness to God" dimension and a "fundamentalism-humanism" dimension (Broen, 1957). Three measures of fear of death were included; two of these were traditional Likert-type attitude scales, including Sarnoff and Corwin's Fear of Death Scale, but the third was a sentence-completion measure of concern over death constructed for that study. In all, 13 incomplete sentences were constructed by the authors to tap death concern or death involvement. Each statement included some word or phrase that served as a death cue, such as "cemetery," "ambulance siren," or "airplane crash." Additionally, a measure of nearness of death in the respondent's family was collected. In general, religious participation was negatively correlated with concern over death; in one of the churches two of these correlations were −.73 and −.70. That is, the more religious activity a person reported, the less he or she feared death. But the responses to Broen's Religious Attitude Inventory did not significantly correlate with measure of death anxiety. Religious participation, but not religious attitude, seemed to serve as a means of comfort.

There was no clear cut relationship between age of the respondents and the extent of their fear or involvement over death. More of the correlations were negative than positive; thus the trend in the results went against Feifel's (1944) claim that "Old age is the time when people most fear death" (p. 375). In two of the three congregations, older church goers reported less concern over death.

Since this study was done, the thinking about attitudes toward death has become more sophisticated. Reactions to one's own eventual death are now considered to be more complex than a simple fear/no fear dimension; that is, it is now possible to hold several different—even seemingly contradictory—perspectives on death (Schoenrade, 1986, p. 12). Kastenbaum and Costa (1977) suggest that "it is possible that the focus on 'fear' or 'anxiety' has led to the neglect of other orientations toward death. The total human interpretation of death is too complex to be subsumed under concepts most favored by research. Sorrow, curiosity, and even a sense of joyous expectation are among the orientations that have been observed in non-research contexts" (p. 236). In a study that rectifies this lack, Spilka and his colleagues (Minton & Spilka, 1976; Spilka, Stout, Minton, & Sizemore, 1977) constructed a death perspective questionnaire, which includes eight subscales: Death as Pain and Loneliness, Failure, Forsaking Dependents plus Guilt, Unknown, Natural End, Courage, Afterlife of Reward, and Indifference. Each of the subscales contains four to six statements. In contrast to the earlier assessment of a single dimension, Spilka's scale allows for positive, negative, and neutral views of death within the same individual. As Schoenrade (1986) observes, "If religious beliefs do function to highlight the positive implications of death, it is not a logical necessity that they also diminish the negative implications. Indeed, when death is confronted, awareness of both positive and negative implications might increase, the former helping the individual to accept the latter" (p. 13). A study that looks at age differences in the relationship of religion to these different reactions to death apparently has not yet been done, but is a likely next step.

REACTIONS TO THE DEATH OF A LOVED ONE

Previous references to reactions to the death of one's spouse highlight its importance to a chapter on developmental factors in reactions to death and dying. Researchers and health-service delivery workers agree that the experience of losing one's spouse or significant other person is related to increases in the occurrence of depression and physical illness, and even a greater vulnerability to death in the survivor (Stroebe & Stroebe, 1983).

A comprehensive review of the rapidly accumulating psychological literature on this topic has centered on sex differences rather than age differences in bereavement, but we may draw conclusions about the effects of age on loss of partner from this review, given that a significant number of the studies reviewed are longitudinal in nature (Stroebe & Stroebe, 1983).

Distress and Depression

Integral to the feeling of grief are responses reflecting distress and depression; thus such responses are considered normal and should be distinguished from the depression that is a part of chronic psychological disorder (Averill, 1968). One study (Bornstein, Clayton, Halikas, Maurice, & Robbins, 1973) interviewed 65 women and 27 men shortly after the death of their spouses and again between one year and 20 months later. At one month, 35% were depressed; a year later 17% were depressed.

Another longitudinal study (Parkes & Brown, 1972; also described in Glick, Weiss, & Parkes, 1974) has two distinctive qualities; it compared the widowed spouses with matched controls of married persons, and more relevant for our purposes, all the widowed subjects were under the age of 45 (49 widows and 19 widowers). A summary of this important study is as follows:

The women showed more overt distress than the men after bereavement, and a year later their social and psychological adjustment was poorer than that of the widowers. However, the same adjustment measures also revealed large differences between married men and women in the matched control group, and 'when this was taken into account it seems that the widowed women showed no greater *decline* in adjustment than the widowed men: moreover, at a follow-up two to four years after bereavement, it was the men who were found to have taken longer to recover than the women' (Parkes, 1972, p. 149). After 14 months the control women scored almost as high on the depression score as the bereaved men and much higher than the control men. . . . The longer term follow-up showed a steady decline in depression, and by the third year the difference between the bereaved and the controls was slight. Pertinent here is the fact that, though the widows had higher depression scores than widowers 1 year after bereavement, at the later follow-up the widows were no more depressed than married women. Widowers, on the other hand, remained significantly more depressed than married men. (Stroebe & Stroebe, 1983, pp. 285-286)

Although studies with large samples, of varying ages, and with appropriate control groups are limited in number, the pattern of results indicates that adjustment to the loss of a partner requires several years, and that men may remain more depressed for longer times than women.

The findings for other psychiatric reactions, especially those requiring hospitalization, are generally similar to those for depression. Of 17 cross-sectional studies reviewed by Gove (1972), all find higher rates of mental illness for the widowed, both males and females, than for their married counterparts (Stroebe & Stroebe, 1983). However, most of these cross-sectional studies found that the difference between being married and being widowed is greater for the men than for the women. Widowed men had higher rates of mental illness than had widowed women. But the pattern of results from longitudinal studies is less consistent.

Physical Health and Illness

Bereavement has long been associated with a marked deterioration not only in mental health but in physical health. Those who have lost their partners consult physicians more often, consume more drugs, and have higher incidence of symptoms and illness rates than do controls (Stroebe & Stroebe, 1983).

Here, the evidence from longitudinal studies is consistent with the findings on previous aspects: "if there is any sex difference at all, bereavement affects the physical health of men more severely than of women" (Stroebe & Stroebe, 1983, p. 290).

Of more relevance to our developmental focus is the conclusion that the effects of loss are greatest in the younger widows and widowers, and physical health effects are less pronounced among those who are older when they lose their spouses. An important study here is that by Heyman and Gianturco (1973), whose subjects were 41 elderly persons (14 men and 27 women), all over age 60, who were participants in a longitudinal aging project at Duke University. They were examined both before and after the death of their spouses. In this older sample, there was no general health deterioration as a result of bereavement, a finding in contrast to studies of younger widowed. Heyman and Gianturco (1973) concluded that the elderly are better prepared psychologically to expect and accept the death of a spouse.

Mortality

Mortality rates are higher for widowed than for still married people of the same age, but the excess risk is much greater for men than for women. Consistent with the earlier findings, loss of spouse has more dire effects on men than on women.

Causes of widowers' deaths with excessively high rates include homicide, cirrhosis of the liver, and suicide (Stroebe & Stroebe, 1983, p. 291). Also, for widowers, there is an excessively high death rate, especially from heart disease, during the first six months after the spouse's death. Causes of widows' deaths with excessively high rates are accidents (other than automobile accidents), suicide, and arteriosclerotic heart and coronary disease. In contrast to men, the period of highest risk of death for widows seems to be in the second year of bereavement rather than in the first six months or year.

Suicide

Ever since the publication of Durkheim's ground breaking work in 1897, social scientists have known that the rate of suicide is higher among the widowed than among the married. Men commit more "successful" suicides than do women, but the ratio is even greater for those who have lost a spouse. The widowed-to-married suicide ratio for men is more than twice that for women.

Suicide rate is especially high in the first year or two after the spouse's death (MacMahon & Pugh, 1965; Bojanovsky & Bojanovsky, 1975, cited by Stroebe & Stroebe, 1983).

Interestingly, like the earlier mortality-rate difference, for males suicide rate was highest in the first six months of bereavement, whereas for females, the peak suicide rate came in the second year (Bojanovsky & Bojanovsky, 1975, cited by Stroebe & Stroebe, 1983).

Explanations for Reactions to Bereavement

In summary, there are consistent sex differences in the effects of loss of a spouse. Less clear but a general trend is the indication that loss of a spouse has more devastating effects on relatively younger adults than on the elderly. A number of explanations have been offered for these differences. Although these concepts are primarily oriented to explaining the sex differences, they also provide insight into the developmental changes.

Stress theory, one of these, assumes that stressful life events play an important role in the causes of various somatic and psychiatric disorders. Clearly bereavement is stressful. But why do men seem to suffer more from bereavement than do women? Why younger adults more than older adults? There are no clear-cut answers. Some physiologists (e.g., Ramey, 1987) argue that the male of every species is more fragile than the female, and there is evidence that the human male is considerably more vulnerable to a variety of diseases than the female (Gove & Hughes, 1979; Hamburg & Lunde, 1966). But these would not seem to account for all the differences (Stroebe & Stroebe, 1983).

Role theory, in contrast, assumes that the roles played by persons in different marital statuses may differentially expose them to risk. Gove (1972, 1973) attributes the better health of married people than single people to the fact that "single men and women tend to lack close interpersonal ties and are relatively isolated" (p. 35). Therefore, greater strain is present in the single role. But, Gove proposes, being married is less advantageous to a woman than to a man. Gove's argument centers around the "captive state" of the woman as a housewife/homemaker—in some cases, her only role—whereas the man can enjoy gratification from two roles, that of household head and breadwinner. With the changing role of women in the work force, this explanation appears less applicable. But the flip side still seems valid; when a two-career married couple splits up, the man must adjust more to two roles (launderer, house cleaner, cook, and so on.) than the woman because even among two-career couples the woman continues to do the majority of maintenance tasks in the home.

A third explanation, *interpersonal protection theory*, extends one of Gove's role-theory ideas. It proposes that close interpersonal relationships buffer individuals against the negative impact of stressful life events. Three types of social support have been identified (by Stroebe, Stroebe, Gergen, & Gergen, 1982):

(1) material and task support, or the provision of material aid by the partner; examples would be doing the laundry, yard work, generating income;

(2) validational support, or playing a role as a reference person in helping the partner to evaluate and structure his or her social

environment; examples would be acting as a critic, a "sounding board," or best friend;

(3) emotional support; that is, contributing to the partner's feeling of self-worth and positive self-regard.

It has been found that if a person experiences many stressful life events but has a high level of social support, the usual physical effects are less likely to occur. The death of a spouse not only removes this protective screen of social support that was provided by the partner but it may also leave the surviving partner worse off than if she or he had never married. The person, in a good marriage, has lost a major source of emotional and validational support and is likely also to have lost material support. Women are more able than men to obtain alternative or substitute sources of social support. They can also admit to feelings of loneliness and needs for companionship (Stroebe & Stroebe, 1983). Also, men are more isolated from social contacts outside their work environment, and husbands often leave it to their wives to establish contacts with the neighborhood and maintain contacts with friends and relatives (Bock & Webber, 1972). Further, they seem more likely to rely exclusively on their spouses as confidants (Fischer & Phillips, 1982). Partly for such reasons, and partly because there are fewer widowers than widows, surviving husbands have fewer community-based support groups available than do widows (Silverman & Cooperband, 1975).

All of this makes sense. Stroebe and Stroebe (1983), after reviewing evidence for the three approaches, conclude:

Interpersonal protection theory offers a reasonable account for the pattern of health findings reported in this paper. Furthermore, there is empirical evidence to support the protection theory assumptions about the processes which mediate the relationship between marital status and health. There is evidence that social support buffers individuals against deleterious effects of life stress (e.g., Berkman & Syme, 1979; Brown & Harris, 1978; Eaton, 1978; Surtees, 1980) and that widows can draw on more extensive social support. There can be no doubt, therefore, that at present there is more empirical support for an interpretation of marital health differentials in terms of protection rather than role theory. (p. 299)

12

THE USE OF PERSONAL DOCUMENTS IN UNDERSTANDING ADULT PERSONALITY DEVELOPMENT

This book began by describing, analyzing, and contrasting three different ways of conceptualizing personality development during the adult years. Then separate chapters were directed to the application of these theoretical constructs to different aspects of adult development. The purpose of this final chapter is to describe the use of personal documents in furthering our understanding of the concepts and processes presented in the earlier chapters.

TYPES OF PERSONAL DOCUMENTS

Gordon Allport (1942) defined personal documents as "any self-revealing record that intentionally or unintentionally yields information regarding the structure, dynamics, and functioning of the author's mental life" (p. xii). He limited the term to first-person documents; the restriction has continued. Generally, the term *personal documents* refers to autobiographies, memoirs, oral histories, diaries, collections of letters, and similar materials. Note that all of these "intentionally" (to rely on Allport's definition) tell the reader about the author. But given that Allport includes "unintentional" revelations of personal information, the term *personal documents* could be broadened to include the products of novelists, painters, poets, song writers, and even architects and clothes designers. It could be argued that the clothes we wear, the kinds of cars we drive, and the places we live unintentionally—if not intentionally—reveal information about our mental lives. However, most analyses of personal documents have restricted their sources to the narrower conception—autobiographies, diaries, letters—and that is the focus of this chapter.

Just as the topic of personality development in adulthood was neglected by psychologists for many years, so too has the method-ology of the analysis of personal documents. It is not much of an exaggeration to claim that the "state of the art" regarding the use of personal documents in psychology has not—until the last decade—advanced beyond that summarized in Allport's (1942) monograph review published more than 45 years ago.

It is especially regrettable that personal documents were for so long overlooked as sources of data, because each type of personal document is congenial with a contrasting theory of adult personality development. For example, diaries, daily personal records, and collections of letters are more relevant to a dialectical theory, because they represent an ongoing, but continuously changing, production of raw material. Chapter 6, in describing the collection of letters by Jenny Masterson (Allport, 1965), demonstrated the utility of dialectical theory in understanding this long-running expression of personal information. What you write in your diary today may reflect concern with a different problem from your diary entry of three months before or three months in the future. Diary entries and letters to friends may also be useful in identifying how one works through a critical period or crisis in adulthood, as emphasized in stage theories. In contrast, autobiographies are retrospective; we describe what has happened to us in the past. I would argue that analysis of an autobiography, as a personal document, is most congenial with life script theory, because it is usually the case that in writing our autobiography we succumb to strong pressures to fit everything within a certain theme. As George Kelly would remind us, we cannot even view our own lives completely and objectively. An autobiography is not just a random collection of memories. We pick and choose what to remember, and what is chosen is partly determined by the constructs we apply to ourselves and our own lives.

Much more methodological work has been devoted to an analysis of autobiographies than to letters and diaries; therefore the focus of this chapter will be on that type of personal document.

THE HISTORY OF AUTOBIOGRAPHY

Have people always written autobiographies? No; generally it is a relatively recent phenomenon. With a few exceptions (including St. Augustine's "confessions" in 400 A.D.) writing one's own life story is a phenomenon of the nineteenth and twentieth centuries.

The first book with the actual word "autobiography" in its title was published in 1834, *The Autobiography of a Dissenting Minister* by W. P. Scargill. Earlier books, now thought of as autobiographies, such as those by Rousseau or Benjamin Franklin or St. Augustine, were originally titled "confessions" or "memoirs" (Olney, 1980).

A listing of 7,000 British autobiographies indicated that 90% of them were written in the nineteenth or twentieth centuries. Only 200 had been written in the seventeenth century and 400 in the eighteenth century. Why this rapidly accelerating trend over the last 400 years? In earlier times the concept of "the self" was unknown or little acknowledged; neither individuality nor introspection was valued. Weintraub (1978) writes: "During the millennium from 800 B.C. to 200 A.D., the conditions of ancient life neither stimulated nor promoted the growth of autobiography. The ancients did not put a premium on the life devoted to settling the quandary: Who am I? How did I become what I am? In what sense am I a distinctive personality? And what complex interplay of external forces and internal characteristics accounts for my specific configuration? There was no need to use autobiography as a basic quest for the self, or as a tool for self-clarification" (p. 13).

Thus, during the Middle Ages and up through the fifteenth or sixteenth century, it was not considered appropriate to introspect about oneself or consider oneself to be unique. Individual differences were apparent but the causes for them were seen to be external.

The autobiographical movement got its second wind in the seventeenth century (Olney, 1980). This was a period that experienced a transformation—actually a breakdown—in traditional social customs. When this outer framework, or social structure, falls apart, people turn inward for understanding of what is happening. Protestant England in the seventeenth century was an especially fertile ground. Religious groups shared their testimony through some of their members writing their memoirs, capitalizing on the adventurous exploratory spirit. The journal of George Fox, the founder of the Religious Society of Friends (Quakers), was published about this time.

Individual Reasons for Writing an Autobiography

Why write your autobiography? It is easy to do. There are no rules, no structure that is uniform. Furthermore, it is an ego trip. Hence many people have.

But certainly members of some occupational groups do so more than others. Among American autobiographers, ministers traditionally have been most prolific. Also, many journalists, writers, doctors, scientists, entertainers, and politicians have prepared their memoirs. In contrast, there are relatively few from business people or farmers.

The above distinctions imply that some personal characteristics seem necessary or relevant to the decision to report one's life story. For example, an autobiography is more likely to emerge if the person is introspective or self-reflective. Also, if the person is self-confident and has positive self-regard, such will be the result. That is, the person says, "I am important in my own right." In ancient Greece and Rome, the gods determined one's fate. In the early Middle Ages, self-expression was little done because people's lives derived from kinship relations; that is, "I am X, son of Y, grandson of Z." Autobiographers are more likely to have some belief in their own uniqueness, or at least being different and seeing oneself as different. Furthermore, a sense of internal locus of control leads to autobiographical writing; some degree of belief that one is the cause of one's own outcomes in life would seem to be a requirement.

Motives for Writing One's Autobiography

Several analysts have categorized the motivations for writing one's autobiography. Krueger and Reckless (1931) claimed that all personal documents were either *confessional* or *detached*. Clark (1935) offered a four-fold typology:

(1) appeal for sympathy
(2) need for self-justification
(3) desire for appreciation and praise
(4) need for artistic communication

Gordon Allport's early but still influential monograph provides a more detailed and comprehensive listing. Allport (1942) first makes the basic distinction between authors who spontaneously create their products and those who provide a product at the instigation of some outsider. But he notes that "valuable documents have been secured under both types of instigation" (p. 69). Combining several of these and other earlier classifications, Allport distinguished about a dozen different motives.

Special Pleading

The motivation of the autobiographer here is to prove that he or she is more sinned against than sinning. Such autobiographers may blame others for failure to understand them. Politicians want vindication; much of the thrust of President Lyndon Johnson's memoirs reflects this motivation. Several years ago Mary Cunningham, who rapidly moved up the managerial ranks at the Bendix Corporation, was accused in the media of using an alleged personal relationship with her boss to achieve these promotions. Her autobiography was an attempt literally to prove that she had been more sinned against than sinning.

One special aspect of this motivation is to counter interpretations by biographers and others who have written about the person's life. Henry Adams stated in his autobiography that setting the record straight was "a shield of protection in the grave."

Furthermore, as Barrett Mandel (1980) notes:

Writing an autobiography ratifies the form one has given to one's life. The ongoing activity of writing discloses the being's ratification of the ego's illusion of the past, thereby solidifying it. The acceptance of the illusion, occurring in the present where meaning is possible, is what makes an autobiography capable of telling the truth. . . . Autobiography is a passage to truth because, like all genuine experience, it rises from the ground of being that transcends one's memories, petty lies, grand deceptions, and even one's desire to be honest. (p. 64)

Exhibitionism

Some autobiographers seek always to display themselves in as vivid a light as possible (Allport, 1942). "Sins as well as virtues may be exposed with such relish and satisfaction that we are likely to dismiss the author as hopelessly narcissistic" (Allport, 1942, p. 70). The autobiographies of some movie stars seem to reflect this motivation; Shelly Winters's (1980) book, for example, seems to take pleasure in revealing her intimate relationships with other named celebrities. For example, she wrote: "I told Marlon [Brando] to hurry and get all his clothes together and go up on the roof because I didn't know whether Burt [Lancaster] would come back up the elevator or run up the stairs (p. 287). Likewise, in *Bittersweet*, actress Susan Strasberg (1980) tattles about her adolescent affair with Richard Burton; and Margaret Trudeau, then the wife of the Canadian prime minister, wrote in *Beyond Reason* (1979) about her nervous breakdown and her fights with her husband.

Perhaps their model was Mae West, whose 1959 autobiography, *Goodness Had Nothing to Do with It*, reflected not only one of her most famous lines in the movies but also her personal philosophy. This book almost reads like a telephone book, listing man after man she was involved with during her long life. (Mae West was born in 1893 and died in 1980.)

But such exhibitionism is nothing new. Rousseau's *Confessions* begins with the following:

I have entered upon a performance which is without example, whose accomplishment will have no imitator. I mean to present my fellow mortals with a man in all the integrity of nature; and this man shall be myself. (quoted by Allport, 1942, p. 70)

Literary critics have been less than kind to exhibitionistically motivated autobiographies. W. H. Auden (1962) has written that "literary confessors are contemptible, like beggars who exhibit their sores for money, but not so contemptible as the public that buys their books" (p. 99). But they remain a frequent type.

Desire for Order

There are people who are desirous of keeping their lives as tidy as their rooms. In an effort to do so, they record their daily experiences and keep meticulous records. Such may be grist for the mill of an autobiography. B. F. Skinner, the leading contemporary behavioral psychologist, has now completed three volumes of his auto-biography (Skinner, 1976, 1979, 1983). The first volume, *Particulars of My Life*, is aptly named, for it is an incredibly specific compendium of the daily life and development of the author from his birth up to the age of 24. Skinner is able to recall details of such matters as how horse whips were made, how coal stoves were fired, how certain boyhood games were played. And he tells the reader all, without evaluation or interpretation. The book is not a diary; it is an autobiography, although an extreme case in its absence of self-aggrandizement, justification, or virtually any emotion. Even when recalling the death of his only sibling, a brother, Skinner reports that he was "far from unmoved." Skinner's goal, in keeping with his psychological theory, is description without subjective distortion. Reviewers have taken note of its unusual flavor; Paul Zimmerman (1976) wrote:

> Rarely has an autobiography seemed less motivated by self-justifica-tion or rancor, less clouded by sentiment or illusions of what might have been, more ruthlessly matter-of-fact about personal limitations. But Skinner's objectivity—a constant fix upon externals that is consistent with his general theory of conditional behavior—also deprives his narrative of a crucial emotional dimension. (p. 83)

Allport (1942), in describing this type of reason for writing an autobiography, concludes that it often leads to a product that "is dull and uneventful, but much of it, because of its very lack of dramatic accentuation, is true to life" (p. 71). Skinner's books reflect both aspects of this observation.

Literary Delight

Writing is an aesthetic art, at least to some of those proficient and experienced at it. For a writer of fiction, the challenge of writing about one's own life may be met through an expression of the writer's characteristic motivations. Allport (1942) notes: "The narrowly aesthetic motive can be traced in innumerable literary biographies wherein personal experience is revealed in a delicate and pleasuring way. Symmetry, perfection of expression, artistic form, are obviously intended by the author" (p. 71).

But the aesthetic motive may extend beyond professional writers. Bette Midler's autobiography, titled *A View from a Broad* (1980), seems to be motivated by a combination of aesthetic and exhibitionistic needs; she writes, "I never know how much of what I say is true. If I did, I'd bore myself to death."

Securing a Personal Perspective

As Erikson has told us, a manifestation of the later years is a need to take stock of one's life. H. G. Wells gave this as the driving force for the writing of his *Experiment in Autobiography* (1934). Stern (1925), in his writings on life history, poses an interesting research hypothesis: That periods of change and transition are the periods when personal documents are more likely to be produced. Stern does not believe that an autobiography can be produced at any arbitrary point in a person's life; rather, the stress of change brings forth a desire for stock taking and planning new ways to respond.

Certainly some autobiographies are generated by the desire to answer one's own question: "How do I know what I feel until I hear what I say?" And by taking Allport's label, "securing personal perspective," we can see the breadth of this motive. For example, Mandel (1980), commenting on Rousseau's *Confessions*, writes: "We see Rousseau, struggling to believe the very words he writes, but find them pulling him toward conflicting interpretations of his own past experiences. Rousseau's *Confessions* is a masterpiece of the genre because it allows these conflicting truths to manifest themselves, creating a complex unity" (p. 71).

Relief from Tension

Sometimes autobiographies are written for others; sometimes, as the preceding Desire for Order and Securing a Personal Reflection reflect, for oneself. Perhaps the ultimate in this type is the autobiography written in order to gain relief from mental tension. Krueger (cited by Allport, 1942, p. 71) claims that catharsis is the underlying motivation when a person writes a confessional document. Certainly John Stuart Mill's autobiography reflects this goal;

he shed tears, discovered new possibilities for himself, and emerged from a period of depression.

Redemption and Social Reincorporation

Following from the previous motivation, the autobiography may reflect a plea for forgiveness and social reacceptance. Confession is, after all, a precondition for absolution or forgiveness. Alfred Kazin (1979) observes, "For the nonfiction writer, as I can testify, personal history is directly an effort to find salvation, to make one's own experience come out right" (p. 79).

Many of the memoirs and autobiographies by President Nixon's associates who were involved in the Watergate burglary cover-up reflect this motivation, but none is more pervasive in its emphasis on redemption than Charles W. Colson's *Born Again* (1976). Colson, formerly Nixon's White House "hatchet man," became a born-again Christian in the midst of the Watergate investigations. He served a prison term and decided to devote the rest of his life to prison reform. *Born Again* may be read as an entirely credible account of a man who came to realize that he was experiencing a spiritual crisis (translation: nervous breakdown) while at the pinnacle of success, achievement, and influence.

Monetary Gain

Autobiographies have become popular reading material. "Instant celebrities," especially, are tempted to write their autobiographies, or assist someone else who "ghostwrites" it, in order to capitalize on their newfound fame. Although this is probably not the only motivation for most of the rash of "kiss-and-tell" autobiographies recently, it certainly contributes to their profusion.

Assignment

Allport (1942) notes that autobiographies are sometimes written as a requirement, either for a class in school or as a part of an application for admission to graduate school or a professional school.

Assisting in Therapy

Similar to the above type in its original instigation being outside the author is the example of an autobiography written by a patient or client in psychotherapy, as a part of diagnosis or treatment.

Scientific Interest

Allport (1942) uses this category, "scientific interest," to refer to persons who "will frequently offer their diaries or their candid autobiographies to psychologists interested in problems of personality" (p. 73). Each is sure that his or her life experiences are unique, that he or she "has suffered what others have not suffered, that scientists may find his [or her] story novel and significant" (p. 73). Allport may be uncharacteristically condescending here; psychologists' understanding has benefited from the availability of such personal documents.

Allport does not mention a resource that has provided a valuable collection of brief autobiographies for scientific analysis. In the 1920s psychologist Carl Murchison began to compile the autobiographies of prominent psychologists. Six volumes of these have now been published (Murchison, 1930, 1932, 1936; Boring, Langfeld, Werner, & Yerkes, 1952; Boring & Lindzey, 1967; Lindzey, 1974). The series contains autobiographies of 86 psychologists, mostly North American and mostly men. The autobiographies average about 25-30 pages in print (although Carl Seashore found it necessary to spend 75 pages on his!). Although the emphasis is on professional development and contributions, some of the accounts (especially those by Henry Murray, Sidney Pressey, and Karl Dallenbach) reveal intimate personal matters. Another psychologist, T. S. Krawiec (1972, 1974) has compiled 23 psychologists' autobiographies in two volumes. Like the Murchison-initiated series, the contributors here were selected on the basis of their distinguished achievements in the field of psychology. Between the two series, after removing duplications, there are autobiographies of 105 psychologists, written at the height of their careers. I know of no other discipline that contains as extensive a repository of autobiographical information about its makers and shapers.

Public Service and Example

Allport observes that there are autobiographies written for the express purpose of achieving a reform, or offering a model to help others through their difficulties. Clifford Beers (1928) wrote about his experiences as a mental patient in order to improve the lot of the insane. Likewise, Booker T. Washington wished to assist black people, and Jane Addams the slum dweller.

Desire for Immortality

Allport's last motive is perhaps the most elusive and maybe the most general. Marie Bonaparte (1939), a psychoanalyst, wrote that personal documents were a part of humankind's "battle against oblivion" because "to be forgotten is to die a second and more complete death." But rarely do the authors of autobiographies express the desire for immortality as their motive.

Ways of Classifying Autobiographies

The rather extended classification of motives in the previous section is not the only way to subdivide autobiographies.

James Olney (1972), a professor of English, classifies writers of autobiographies into two types: Those whom he called "auto-biographers of the single metaphor" (p. 39) include Charles Darwin, George Fox, and John Stuart Mill. In contrast, the auto-biographers Carl Jung, T. S. Eliot, and Michel de Montaigne (author of *The Essays*), among others, are "autobiographers of the double metaphor." The essential distinction seems to be a certain kind of single-mindedness present in the single-metaphor group. Olney (1972) calls it a "daimon," or "a personal genius and guardian spirit, a dominant faculty or function or tendency that formed a part of his whole self and from which there was no escape, even had he wished it" (p. 39). As I try to translate this into psychological language, it seems to me that Olney is proposing that single-metaphor auto-biographers fixate upon an idea at a relatively early age and henceforth fail to grow. For example, Olney claims that George Fox's development ceased at about the age of 11. Olney bases this conclusion on the Quaker religion founder's *Journal* and other evidence from his life; Olney (1972) writes, "Once the single light of the Lord had shown in and onto him, Fox was set for life, and though he performed many actions and provoked many reactions, these were all repetitions, more or less, of his first witness to the light; they were not done from any essentially new basis in personality" (pp. 40-41). Likewise, Charles Darwin reached a clearly defined, self-labeled end point in development—what Olney says is a specific date beyond which there was no change, but only more of the same. This occurred well before the completion of his autobiography; there Darwin wrote: "I have now mentioned all the books which I have published, and these have been the milestones in my life, so that little remains to be said. I am not conscious of any change in my mind during the last thirty years, excepting in one point presently to be mentioned (the curious and lamentable loss of the higher aesthetic tastes); nor indeed could any change have been expected unless one of general deterioration" (Darwin, 1958, p. 136).

The idea that some people "rigidify" in development at a relatively early age, even despite their influential contribution to society, is a provocative one, and clearly of relevance to various theories of adult development. It may have merit, but relying on only the autobiography (as opposed to further information from work products, letters, observations of contemporaries, and so on) as evidence for the distinction is not sufficient. Some autobiographers—perhaps including George Fox and Charles Darwin—can be too harsh on themselves.

ARE AUTOBIOGRAPHIES FACT OR FICTION?

That autobiographers are too harsh upon themselves is seldom considered, but the general accuracy of autobiographies is a matter of great concern. Is an autobiography, "a biography of oneself," even possible? Dostoevsky wrote in *Notes from the Underground* that "Every man has reminiscences which he would not tell to everyone, but only to his friends. He has other matters in his mind which he would not reveal even to his friends, but only to himself and that are secret. But there are other things which a man is afraid to tell even to himself, and every decent man has a number of such things stored away in his mind. . . . A true autobiography is almost an impossibility. . . Man is bound to lie about himself."

Literary critics struggle a great deal over the distinctions, if any, between autobiography and fiction. Mandel (1980) writes: "After all, as James Joyce knew so well, any human verbalizing is a process that by its very nature fictionalizes the experience. . . . [Both fiction and autobiography are] a pretense, a construction, an illusion" (p. 53).

And if autobiography truly is so unrepresentative of reality, of what use is it in understanding human development in adulthood?

Allport's (1942) classic monograph dealt with some of these troubling issues. He noted the following limitations of autobiographies, in particular, and personal documents, in general, as sources of data for psychological theorizing and research:

(1) the unrepresentativeness of the sample

(2) the writer's possible fascination with style rather than sincerity and fact

(3) nonobjectivity

Allport (1942) notes here that "by definition personal documents are subjective data" (p. 126), and hence are not in keeping with the prevailing American scientific emphasis on objectivity. (Taking a long view over the last 100 years, one might say a dialectic has been present in psychological science, shifting from the subjectivity of introspection to the objectivity of laboratory manipulation but then a modest shift back toward the richness of personal experience.)

(4) deception (intended by author)

Self-Deception, or Unintentional Self-Justification

Box 12-1 reflects one view of the frequency of deception and self-deception.

Blindness to Motives

"A person of fifty in writing of himself at nineteen may ascribe motives to his conduct that are, in reality, only appropriate to him at the time of the writing" (Allport, 1942, p. 133).

Oversimplification

Allport (1942) observes that "in response to his (or her) drive for consistency the writer may soften the contradictions, join together the incompatible features of his (or her) life, and produce a shipshape structure in which all parts fit" (p. 134). As noted earlier, this tendency is more likely in an autobiography than in a diary or set of letters.

Effects of Mood (Generally, of Unreliability)

The parenthetical *unreliability* in the label reflects Allport's concern with inconsistency in content or revelations over time. We may add another aspect—the general rule that autobiographical

---

BOX 12.1
Can an Autobiographer Acknowledge Distortion
even if He or She Doesn't Recognize It?

In a review of Patrick White's (1982) autobiography, *Flaws in the glass: A self-portrait,* reviewer Humphrey Carpenter wrote:

> Autobiography is probably the most respectable form of lying. No one expects the whole truth; in any case how could it be revealed, since the person we know least is likely to be ourself? The worst autobiographies are those that exploit it. This one, by Patrick White, the Nobel laureate, is in the second group. This title, "Flaws in the Glass," is a declaration at the onset that the mirror by means of which the self-portrait is drawn is at least a faulty device. In one of the many houses where the Whites lived during the author's childhood, there was a "Long Room" with at one end a "great gilded mirror, all blotches and dimples and ripples." A lesser writer might have labored this image again and again throughout the book; Mr. White allows the single use of it to suffice. (p. 9)

---

writing seems to be preoccupied with conflict and turmoil, whereas happy peaceful periods in the person's life are passed over in silence or with little comment.

Also success seems less interesting and worthy of comment than failure. Critic Joseph Epstein (1981) wrote:

> Certainly, the confession of imperfections makes for interesting reading: and it is undeniably true that autobiography generally becomes dull exactly at that point when the author arrives at success, where only acquaintance with the famous or a taste for vengeance through paying off old scores seems to enliven an autobiographical work. No, the trick in much modern autobiography is somehow to display oneself as a failure or a swine, but emerge at the end an attractive failure or charming swine. (p. 7)

The above quotation meshes with my impression (not empirically verified) that the last halves of autobiographies are not as interesting as the first halves are; they are not on the cutting edge.

Errors of Memory

At a party honoring Leonard Bernstein's sixty-second birthday, the composer Aaron Copeland was telling listeners the problems in writing his autobiography. "I have no trouble remembering everything that happened 40 or 50 years ago—dates, places, faces, music. But I'm going to be 90 my next birthday, November 14, and I find I can't remember what happened yesterday or last month." Then one listener politely pointed out, "Mr. Copeland, you're going to be 80 this year" (quoted by Wallis, 1980, p. 57).

Implicit Conceptualization

This is Allport's term for what George Kelly would call the individual's construing of his or her world. Selection of materials requires implicit interpretation. The selection may take place on the basis of the writer's own conceptual or diagnostic biases. Although the autobiographer's use of an implicit conceptualization can be seen as a limitation, it validates George Kelly's claim that personal constructs are inevitable. Even before Kelly developed his theory, Allport recounted an experience that shows the dangers of forcing people into a conceptual framework foreign to their own:

> In one study the investigator secured fifty topical autobiographies, forcing all writers to tell about radicalism and conservatism in their lives. Having forced his cases into this mold, the investigator was tempted to 'discover' that each case could be rated on the radical-conservative continuum according to his self-revealed nature; this suggested to him further that radicalism-conservatism constitutes one of those first-order variables of which all personalities are compounded. But the circularity of this reasoning became evident in time to save him. A closer reading of the fifty documents convinced him that in most lives the concept of radicalism-conservatism was wholly irrelevant. The lives were organized according to *other* principles, and the foci or centers of organization were different in each life. (Allport, 1942, pp. 137-138, italics in original)

Arbitrariness of Conceptualization

Though seeming to overlap with other criticisms, "arbitrariness of conceptualization" is Allport's (1942) label for the situation when "personal documents . . . take their meaning from the author's conceptual framework rather than supply its basis" (p. 138). This is analogous to the psychological researcher's rejecting those data that don't fit the theory.

Scarcity and Expense

Allport regretted that no systematic collection of personal documents, intelligently indexed, had been achieved at the time of his monograph. We still lack such archives, but the availability of individual autobiographies, diaries, and collections of letters is certainly not lacking.

Many of these limitations are justified when we choose to analyze specific personal documents. But not always. Mandel (1980), a literary critic, observes: "In my experience most autobiographies are honest (that's the whole point of the genre) with occasional distortions, honest evasions, and discrete pockets of noncommunication. An honest autobiography puts its illusion of the past forward in good faith, not suspecting that it is but one angle of perception" (p. 66).

In truth, every source of information on adult development has its limitations. If it is the case that many autobiographers are self-deceptive, the task of writing about someone else's life has perils of its own. For example, it is exceedingly difficult for biographers to remain open-minded about their subjects. William Zinsser (1986) asks "Can the biographer trust his (or her) objectivity after years of round-the-clock living with a saint who turns out to be only human?" (p. 18). Biographer Jean Strouse (1986) recalls that at one point she got terribly mad at her subject, Alice James, the sister of novelist Henry James and psychologist William James. When asked by an interviewer if she *liked* her subject, Strouse (1986) replied:

Sometimes yes and sometimes no. My reactions to her were extremely complex and interesting, and at one point during the writing I got so mad at her that I just got completely stuck. Alice was in her late twenties and early thirties, and she was systematically closing down every option that might have led her away from a life of invalidism. She wasn't doing any intellectual work, although she had some that she could have been doing. She was being awful to every man who approached her and wasn't even very nice to her female friends. She was turning into a tyrannical invalid who collapsed in order to get people to take care of her. And I hated it. I really got so mad that I couldn't continue writing. It was amazing, because I had known all along that that's how the story was going to come out. That's why I hesitated at the beginning—because the story seemed too depressing. But I had decided to go ahead, and thought I'd dealt with the problem—until, at this point in the process of writing, I just got too furious at her to go on. What I did was take a month off. And I remembered that Erik Erikson had had a similar problem when he was writing his biography of Gandhi. He had been writing about this saintly man and then he found out how awful Gandhi was to his family, and he was horrified. I think he actually sat down and wrote out all his objections in a letter to Gandhi—who wasn't around anymore to receive it, of course—but that was Erickson's way of working out the problem. In my case, I didn't write it out, but I had long conversations with Alice and Henry in my head. (p. 192)

An even greater threat to a biographer's objectivity is his or her discovery that the subject of the biography has been duplicitous. Robert Caro (1986) began his biography of President Lyndon Johnson with admiration and respect for Johnson's efforts to benefit the blacks and the poor. But gradually he uncovered Johnson's lifelong habit of lying and betrayal. He recalls: "I still can remember my feeling, which was: 'God, I hope this doesn't mean what I think it does'" (Caro, 1986, p. 217). But it did, and Caro was forced to tell a story as sordid as he had feared it to be.

These are not the only psychological research methods free of limitations. Consider the methods used to develop the knowledge reported in the earlier chapters of this book. Interviews and questionnaires are subject to response biases such as acquiescence response set and the desire to look good. Clinical judgments are subjective and often are limited in their predictive accuracy. Laboratory experimentation may deal with responses far removed from the real world.

Personal Documents and Adult Personality Development

Within the decade of Allport's 1942 monograph, there had been a fertile development of the personal documents approach. Charlotte Buehler (1935), Else Frenkel-Brunswik (Frenkel, 1936; Frenkel-Brunswik, 1939), John Dollard (1935), Henry A. Murray (1938), Jerome Bruner (Allport, Bruner, & Jandorf, 1941), Alfred Baldwin (1940, 1942), and other prominent psychologists used diaries, life histories, and other autobiographical material to understand responses to catastrophe, mechanisms of self-deception, and

---

BOX 12.2
Allport's List of Purposes for Psychologists'
Use of Personal Documents

---

(1) Phenomenological investigations

Definition: "interest in complex phenomenal states" (p. 37).

(Allport's famous quotation, from page 37: "If we want to know how people feel: what they experience and what they remember, what their emotions and motives are like, and the reasons for acting as they do—why not ask them?"

Example: Galton's accounts of the imagery of his correspondents.

(2) The study of religious experience

Example: Several investigators—Hoffding, Clark, and so on—have analyzed diaries and autobiographies from the point of view of religious experience.

(3) Study of the psychological effects of unemployment

Example: Zawadski and Lazarsfeld analyzed autobiographies of unemployed writers in Poland, leading to a grouping into four types.

(4) Mental life of adolescents

Rationale: G. Stanley Hall (1942) and others have argued that personal documents are the *best* means of studying adolescence because the "experiences peculiar to adolescence are inaccessible to adults whose later encounters with love and life have the effects of recasting to tally the nascent and turbulent groping of adolescents in their struggle to come to terms with physical reality and social responsibility" (p. 39).

Example: Normal Kiell, in 1964, collected a set of autobiographical materials prepared by adolescents in an effort to demonstrate that the internal and external agitations of the adolescent are present in every part of the world and hence only partly determined by culture.

(5) Didactic uses

Rationale: It has been claimed that practice in writing self-reports increases insight, powers of observation, and self-control in adolescents.

(6) Practical use of experience records

Rationale: Social progress may result from the analysis of vivid stories about one's personal experiences.

Example: Clifford Beers's *A Mind that Found Itself.*

(7) Autoanalysis

> Purpose: Autobiographical outpourings that aim at catharsis may be useful as teaching devices, or as an aid in evolving a theory of personality.
>
> Example: W.E. Leonard's *Locomotive God.*

(8) Historical diagnoses

> Purpose: To shed light upon the personalities of writers, artists, and other gifted people.
>
> Examples: Bragman's studies of Rossetti, Squires's study of Dostoevsky.

(9) Supplement to psychiatric examination

> Purposes: Besides providing new leads for diagnosis, there may be a therapeutic value, "initiating and helping to guide the course of treatment" (p. 44).

(10) The subject's verification and validation

> Purpose: A "rebuttal" by a subject to another's analysis of him or her.
>
> Example: John Dewey responded to his expositors and critics in a series titled *The Library of Living Philosophy.*

(11) Mental effects of special physical conditions

> Purpose: Autobiographical materials may help "to keep the influence of physical factors in perspective" (p. 45).

(12) Light on creative processes and the nature of genius

> Purpose: To study creativity.
>
> Example: Willa Cather's account of her conception and writing of *Death Comes For the Archbishop.*

(13) The psychologizing of the social sciences

> Purpose: The application of "psychohistory" and "psycho-biography" to historical or cultural phenomena. (These terms were generated later than Allport's 1942 monograph.)

(14) The psychologizing of literature

> Purpose: The probing of motivation by literary critics and biographers.
>
> Example: Robert Sears's (1979) comparison of Mark Twain's letters and his novels, to identify periods of depression in his life.

(15) Illustration

> Purpose: "Perhaps the commonest use of documents is to provide illustrative material for authors who wish to exemplify some generalization already in mind" (p. 48).

(16) Induction

    Purpose: To derive general principles from raw material, or particulars.

    Example: Charlotte Buehler's *Lebenspsychologie,* based on 200 life histories.

(17) Occupational and other types

    Purpose: The derivation of types, or clustering cases according to similarities.

    Example: Donley and Winter's (1970) scoring of U.S. presidential inaugural addresses in order to classify them on strength of achievement, affiliative, and power motives.

(18) Interpersonal relations

    Purpose: "The possibility of using exchanges of letters between two persons as a means of studying the dyadic relations of friendship, of marriage, of the parent-child bond seems almost overlooked by social psychologists" (p. 50).

(19) First step in the construction of tests and questionnaires

    Purpose: To provide insights for generating items in standardized tests and questionnaires.

(20) Reinforcement and supplementation

    Purpose: "Often the personal document merely falls into place as one of several methods in a battery. It serves no other purpose than adding credibility to the total picture developed through interviews, tests, ratings, institutional reports, or other methods" (p. 51).

(21) Methodological objectives

    Purpose: Social scientists may use personal documents "simply in order to find out how they may be used to the best advantage" (p. 51). There is an allusion here to theory development; focus is not so much on the individual or on general laws of behavior, as it is on "the *process* by which the significance of behavior becomes known and evaluated" (p. 51).

    Example: Allport's derivation of an empirical-intuitive theory of understanding from the reactions of students in reading Leonard's *Locomotive God.*

---

changes over the life cycle, among other matters. After World War II, interest dwindled. There were exceptions of course: Robert White's (1975) continuing interest in the growth of personality; the intensive case analyses of a small number of adult males by Smith, Bruner, and White (1956), done in an attempt to understand how opinions are developed and maintained; and the analysis of Theodore Drieser's writings by Seymour Rosenberg and Russell Jones (1972) in order to understand Drieser's implicit personality theory.

It has been only in the last decade that a resurgence of interest in these materials has occurred.

Chapter 3 of Allport's 1942 monograph listed and annotated 21 different purposes for the use of personal documents. Box 12.2 reprints these, using Allport's labels and providing his definitions and examples, plus some more recent examples that I've added.

Several of these purposes are relevant to adult personality development. Chapter 5 described how the analyses of autobiographies of psychologists could be used to understand the prevalence of the mentoring process. As mentioned earlier, Chapter 6 illustrated the use of *Letters from Jenny* (Allport, 1965) to illustrate dialectical changes in major issues during adulthood.

An ingenious demonstration that uses the approach of psychobiography plus several types of personal documents is that of Robert Sears (1979a), which attempts to illustrate the effects of an early experience of loss of love in the letters and novels of Mark Twain. Sears was aware of many facts in Samuel Clemens's (Mark Twain's) boyhood that could lead to the development of separation anxiety; among these were the presence of a mother who mixed love and rejection, the death of a brother and a sister before he was 10 years old, his father's death when the novelist was 12, and later the death of his first-born child at 18 months of age. Sears has content analyzed letters written by Mark Twain between 1868 and 1904, as well as novels composed over that period. Thus he was able "to match the peaks and valleys of [Twain's] suppressed feelings with the events of his adult life" (Sears, 1979a, p. 100). Sears concludes that the analysis of letters, in combination with fiction writings, provides additional understanding of a long-standing fear, "because fictional expression is under less conscious control than are direct communications such as letters" (Sears, 1979a, pp. 102, 104).

As we search for an understanding of the process of personality development during our adult lives, we should not ignore these materials, as they not only provide illustrations of how other people have changed, but they urge us to explore our own lives.

References

Abrahamsen, D. (1977). *Nixon vs. Nixon: An emotional tragedy.* New York: Farrar, Straus & Giroux.

Adams, B. (1979). Mate selection in the United States: A theoretical summarization. In W. Burr, R. Hill, I. Nye, & R. Reiss (Eds.), *Contemporary theories about the family: Research-based theories* (Vol. 1). New York: Free Press.

Aday, R. H. (1984). Belief in afterlife and death anxiety: Correlates and comparisons. *Omega: Journal of Death and Dying, 15,* 67-75.

Adler, M. J. (1927). *Dialectic.* New York: Harcourt, Brace.

Adler, M. J. (Ed.). (1952). *The great ideas: A syntopicon of great books in the western world.* Chicago: Encyclopedia Britannica.

Adorno, T., Frenkel-Brunswick, E., Levinson, D. J., & Sanford, N. (1950). *The authoritarian personality.* New York: Harper & Row.

Alexander, I. E., & Adlerstein, A. M. (1959). Death and religion. In H. Feifel (Ed.), *The meaning of death.* New York: McGraw-Hill.

Alexander, I. E., Colley, R. S., & Adlerstein, A. M. (1957). Is death a matter of indifference? *Journal of Psychology, 43,* 277-283.

Allport, G. W. (1937). *Pattern and growth in personality.* New York: Holt, Rinehart & Winston.

Allport, G. W. (1942). *The use of personal documents in psychological science.* New York: Social Science Research Council.

Allport, G. W. (1965). *Letters from Jenny.* New York: Harcourt, Brace.

Allport, G. W. (1967). Autobiography. In E. G. Boring & G. Lindzey (Eds.), *A history of psychology in autobiography* (Vol. 5, pp. 1-26). New York: Appleton-Century-Crofts.

Allport, G. W., & Vernon, P. E. (1931). *A study of values.* Boston: Houghton-Mifflin. (Revised in 1951 in collaboration with G. Lindzey)

Allport, G. W., Bruner, J. S., & Jandorf, E. M. (1941). Personality under social catastrophe: An analysis of German refugees' life histories. *Character and Personality, 10,* 1-22.

Altman, I., Vinsel, A., & Brown, B. B. (1981). Social penetration and privacy regulation. In L. Berkowitz (Ed.), *Advances in experimental social psychology* (Vol. 14). New York: Academic Press.

Anderson, J. W. (1981). Psychobiographical methodology: The case of William James. In L. Wheeler (Ed.), *Review of personality and social psychology* (Vol. 2, pp. 245-272). Beverly Hills, CA: Sage.

Anderson, P. (1977, March 27). Review of *Nixon vs. Nixon. New York Times Book Review*, p. 5.

Andrews, F. M. (1988). Measures of subjective well-being. In J. P. Robinson, P. Shaver, & L. S. Wrightsman (Eds.), *Measures of social psychological attitudes* (2nd ed.). New York: Academic Press.

Associated Press. (1987, March 21). Growing number of older men shift direction, enter seminaries. *Lawrence Journal-World*, p. 8A.

Associated Press. (1987, June 29). Pollster says divorce rate is 13 percent. *Lawrence Journal-World*, p. 10B.

Auden, W. H. (1962). *The dyer's hand and other essays.* New York: Random House.

Averill, J. (1968). Grief: Its nature and significance. *Psychological Bulletin, 70,* 721-728.

Babchuk, N., & Bates, A. P. (1963). The primary relations of middle-class couples: A study in male dominance. *American Sociological Review, 8,* 377-384.

Bachman, J. G., O'Malley, P. M., & Johnston, L. (1978). *Adolescence to adulthood: Change and stability in the lives of young men.* Ann Arbor, MI: Institute for Social Research.

Back, K. W., & Gergen, K. G. (1963). Apocalyptic and serial time orientations and the structure of opinions. *Public Opinion Quarterly, 27,* 427-442.

Bakan, D. (1966). *The duality of human existence: Isolation and communion in Western man.* Boston: Beacon.

Baldwin, A. L. (1940). The statistical analysis of the structure of a single personality. *Psychological Bulletin, 37,* 518-519.

Baldwin, A. L. (1942). Personal structure analysis: A statistical method for investigating the single personality. *Journal of Abnormal and Social Psychology, 37,* 163-183.

Baltes, P. B., & Schaie, K. W. (1976). On the plasticity of intelligence in adulthood and old age: Where Horn and Donaldson fail. *American Psychologist, 31,* 720-725.

Barber, J. D. (1972). *The presidential character.* Englewood Cliffs, NJ: Prentice-Hall.

Bardwick, J. M. (1980). The seasons of a woman's life. In D. G. McGuigan (Ed.), *Women's lives: New theory, research and policy.* Ann Arbor: University of Michigan Center for Continuing Education of Women.

Barnett, R. C., & Baruch, G. K. (1980). Toward economic independence: Women's involvement in multiple roles. In D. G. McGuigan (Ed.),

Women's lives: New theory, research and policy. Ann Arbor: University of Michigan Center for Continuing Education of Women.

Basow, S. A. (1986). *Gender stereotypes: Traditions and alternatives* (2nd ed.). Pacific Grove, CA: Brooks/Cole.

Batson, C. D., & Ventis, L. W. (1982). *The religious experience.* New York: Oxford University Press.

Baucom, D. H. (1987). Attributions in distressed relations: How can we explain them? In D. Perlman & S. Duck (Eds.), *Intimate relationships: Development, dynamics, and deterioration* (pp. 177-206). Newbury Park, CA: Sage.

Baumeister, R. F. (1986). *Identity.* New York: Oxford University Press.

Beard, G. M. (1874). *Legal responsibility in old age.* New York: Russell.

Becker, E. (1973). *The denial of death.* New York: Free Press.

Beers, C. W. (1928). *A mind that found itself: An autobiography* (5th ed.). New York: Doubleday, Doran.

Bell, A. P., & Weinberg, M. S. (1978). *Homosexualities: A study of diversity among men and women.* New York: Simon & Schuster.

Bem, S. L. (1974). The measurement of psychological androgyny. *Journal of Consulting and Clinical Psychology, 42,* 155-162.

Bem, S. L. (1981). Gender schema theory: A cognitive account of sex typing. *Psychological Review, 88,* 354-364.

Bem, S. L. (1982). Gender schema theory and self-schema compared: A comment on Markus, Crane, Bernstein, and Siladi's "Self schemas and gender." *Journal of Personality and Social Psychology, 43,* 1192-1194.

Bem, S. L. (1983). Gender schema theory and its implications for child development: Raising gender-aschematic children in a gender-schematic society. *Signs, 8,* 598-616.

Bem, S. L. (1984). Androgyny and gender schema theory: A conceptual and empirical integration. In T. B. Sonderegger (Ed.), *Nebraska Symposium on Motivation.* Lincoln: University of Nebraska Press.

Bergen, C. (1984). *Knock wood.* New York: Simon & Schuster.

Berkman, L. F., & Syme, L. S. (1979). Social networks, host resistance, and mortality: A nine-year follow-up study of Alameda county residents. *American Journal of Epidemiology, 109,* 186-204.

Berman, A. L. (1974). Belief in afterlife, religion, religiosity, and life-threatening experiences. *Omega: Journal of Death and Dying, 5,* 127-135.

Bernard, J. (1973). *The future of marriage.* New York: Bantam.

Berne, E. (1961). *Transactional analysis in psychotherapy.* New York: Grove.

Berne, E. (1964). *Games people play.* New York: Grove.

Berne, E. (1972). *What do you say after you say hello?* New York: Grove.

Berzins, J. I., Welling, M. A., & Wetter, R. E. (1975). *The PRF ANDRO scale user's manual.* Unpublished manual, University of Kentucky.

Binion, R. (1978). Doing psychohistory. *Journal of Psychohistory, 5,* 313-323.

Block, J. (1971). *Lives through time*. Berkeley, CA: Bancroft.

Block, J. H. (1973). Conceptions of sex roles: Some cross-cultural and longitudinal perspectives. *American Psychologist, 28,* 512-526.

Blumstein, P., & Schwartz, P. (1983). *American couples: Money/work/sex.* New York: William Morrow.

Bock, E. E., & Webber, I. L. (1972). Suicide among the elderly: Isolating widowhood and mitigating alternatives. *Journal of Marriage and the Family, 34,* 24-31.

Bojanovsky, J., & Bojanovsky, A. (1975). Zur Risikozeit des Selbstmordes bei Geschiedenen und Verwitweten. *Nervenarzt, 47,* 307-309.

Bonaparte, M. (1939). A defense of biography. *International Journal of Psycho-Analysis, 20,* 231-240.

Boring, E. G., & Lindzey, G. (Eds.). (1967). *A history of psychology in autobiography* (Vol. 5). New York: Appleton-Century-Crofts.

Boring, E. G., Langfeld, H. S., Werner, H., & Yerkes, R. M. (Eds.). (1952). *A history of psychology in autobiography* (Vol. 4). Worcester, MA: Clark University Press.

Bornstein, P. E., Clayton, P. J., Halikas, J. A., Maurice, W. L., & Robbins, E. (1973). The depression of widowhood after thirteen months. *British Journal of Psychiatry, 122,* 561-566.

Botwinick, J. (1967). *Cognitive processes in maturity and old age.* New York: Springer.

Botwinick, J. (1978). *Aging and behavior* (2nd ed.). New York: Springer.

Bourne, E. (1978). The state of research on ego identity: A review and appraisal: Part II. *Journal of Youth and Adolescence, 7,* 371-392.

Bourque, L. B., & Back, K. W. (1977). Life graphs and life events. *Journal of Gerontology, 32,* 669-674.

Brabeck, M. (1983). Moral judgment: Theory and research on differences between males and females. *Developmental Review, 3,* 274-291.

Brandes, S. (1985). *Forty: the age and the symbol.* Knoxville: University of Tennessee Press.

Brim, O. G., Jr. (1977). Theories of the male mid-life crisis. In N. K. Schlossberg & A. D. Entine (Eds.), *Counseling Adults* (pp. 1-18). Pacific Grove, CA: Brooks/Cole.

Broderick, C. B. (1982). Adult sexual development. In B. B. Wolman & G. Stricker (Eds.), *Handbook of developmental psychology* (pp. 726-733). Englewood Cliffs, NJ: Prentice-Hall.

Brodie, F. M. (1974). *Thomas Jefferson: An intimate history.* New York: Norton.

Brodie, F. M. (1981). *Richard M. Nixon: The shaping of his character.* New York: Norton.

Broen, W. E. (1957). A factor-analytic study of religious attitudes. *Journal of Abnormal and Social Psychology, 54,* 176-179.

Brown, G. W., & Harris, T. (1978). *Social origins of depression: A study of psychiatric disorders in women.* London: Tavistock.

Brown, L. F. (1967, January). Book review of *Thomas Woodrow Wilson. Book of the Month Club News,* p. 8.

Buehler, C. (1935). The curve of life as studied in biographies. *Journal of Applied Psychology, 19,* 405-409.

Bush, G., with Gold, V. (1987). *Looking forward.* New York: Doubleday.

Bushman, R. L. (1966). On the uses of psychology: Conflict and conciliation in Benjamin Franklin. *History and Theory, 5,* 225-240.

Butler, R. N. (1967). Creativity in later life. In S. Levin & R. J. Kahana (Eds.), *Psychodynamic studies on aging: Creativity, reminiscing, and dying.* New York: International Universities Press.

Cairns, R. B. (1983). The emergence of developmental psychology. In P. M. Mussen (Ed.), *Handbook of child psychology: Vol. I, History, theory, and methods* (4th Ed., pp. 41-101). New York: John Wiley.

Candee, D. (1980). The moral psychology of Watergate and its aftermath. In R. W. Wilson & G. J. Schochet (Eds.), *Moral development and politics* (pp. 172-189). New York: Praeger.

Candy, S. (1977). A comparative analysis of friendship functions in six age groups of men and women. Unpublished doctoral dissertation, Wayne State University.

Carlson, R. (1971). Sex differences in ego functioning. *Journal of Consulting and Clinical Psychology, 37,* 267-277.

Caro, R. A. (1986). Lyndon Johnson and the roots of power. In W. Zinsser (Ed.), *Extraordinary lives: The art and craft of American biography* (pp. 197-231). New York: Book of the Month Club.

Carpenter, H. (1982, February 7). Patrick White explains himself. *New York Times Book Review,* pp. 9, 41.

Cartwright, A., Hockey, L., & Anderson, J. S. (1973). *Life before death.* London: Routledge and Kegan Paul.

Casady, M. (1975, November). If you're active and savvy at 30, you'll be warm and witty at 70. *Psychology Today,* p. 138.

Cherlin, A. (1979, October). Cohabitation: How the French and Swedes do it. *Psychology Today,* pp. 18-24.

Chesen, E. (1973). *President Nixon's psychiatric profile.* New York: Peter Weyden.

Childers, P., & Wimmer, M. (1971). The concept of death in early childhood. *Child Development, 42,* 705-715.

Christ, A. E. (1961). Attitudes toward death among a group of acute geriatric psychiatric patients. *Journal of Gerontology, 16,* 44-55.

Clark, A. M. (1935). *Autobiography: Its genesis and phases.* Edinburgh: Oliver & Boyd.

Clayton, V. P., & Birren, J. E. (1980). The development of wisdom across the life span: A re-examination of an ancient topic. In P. B. Baltes & O. G.

Brim (Eds.), *Life-span development and behavior* (Vol. 3, pp. 103-135). New York: Academic.

Cocks, G., & Crosby, T. L. (Eds.). (1987). *Psycho/history: Readings in the method of psychology, psychoanalysis, and history.* New Haven, CT: Yale University Press.

Cohen, A. M. (1980). Stages and stability: The moral development approach to political power. In R. W. Wilson & G. J. Schochet (Eds.), *Moral development and politics* (pp. 69-84). New York: Praeger.

Cohen, R. (1987, October 5). Why Elizabeth Dole should not have resigned. *Washington Post National Weekly Edition*, p. 29.

Coleman, J. (1974). *Blue-collar journal: A college president's sabbatical.* Philadelphia: Lippincott.

Coles, R. (1987). On psychohistory. In G. Cocks & T. L. Crosby (Eds.), *Psycho/history: Readings in the method of psychology, psychoanalysis, and history* (pp. 83-108). New Haven, CT: Yale University Press.

Colson, C. W. (1976). *Born again.* New York: Bantam.

Constantinople, A. (1973). Masculinity-femininity: An exception to a famous dictum? *Psychological Bulletin, 80,* 389-407.

Cooper, M. W. (1977). An empirical investigation of the male midlife period: A descriptive cohort analysis. Unpublished undergraduate honors thesis, University of Massachusetts at Boston.

Costa, P. T., Jr., & McCrae, R. R. (1976). Age differences in personality structure: A cluster analytic approach. *Journal of Gerontology, 31,* 564-570.

Costa, P. T., Jr., & McCrae, R. R. (1977). Age differences in personality structure revisited: Studies in validity, stability, and change. *Aging and Human Development, 8,* 261-275.

Costa, P. T., Jr., & McCrae, R. R. (1978). Objective personality assessment. In M. Storandt, I. D. Siegler, & M. F. Elias (Eds.), *The clinical psychology of aging* (pp. 119-143). New York: Plenum.

Costa, P. T., Jr., & McCrae, R. R. (1980). Still stable after all these years: Personality as a key to some issues in childhood and old age. In P. B. Baltes & O. G. Brim, Jr. (Eds.), *Life span development and behavior* (Vol. 3, pp. 65-102). New York: Academic Press.

Costa, P. T., Jr., & McCrae, R. R. (1985). Concurrent validation after 20 years: Implications of personality stability for its assessment. In J. N. Butcher & C. D. Spielberger (Eds.), *Advances in personality assessment* (Vol. 4, pp. 31-54). Hillsdale, NJ: Lawrence Erlbaum.

Costa, P. T., Jr., McCrae, R. R., & Arenberg, D. (1980). Enduring dispositions in adult males. *Journal of Personality and Social Psychology, 38,* 783-800.

Craik, K. H. (1976). The personality research paradigm in environmental psychology. In S. Wapner, S. B. Cohen, & B. Kaplan (Eds.), *Experiencing the environment* (pp. 55-79). New York: Plenum.

Crapanzano, V., Ergas, Y., & Modell, J. (1986, June). Personal testimony: Narratives of the self in the social sciences and the humanities. *Items, 40*(2), 25-30.

Crittenden, J. A. (1962). Aging and party affiliation. *Public Opinion Quarterly, 26,* 648-657.

Crosby, F., & Crosby, T. L. (1981). Psychobiography and psychohistory. In S. L. Long (Ed.), *The handbook of political behavior* (pp. 195-254). New York: Plenum.

Cruver, D. (1986, July 14). Most husbands say "I'd marry her again." *USA Today,* p. 1D.

Cuber, J. F., & Harroff, P. B. (1965). *The significant Americans: A study of sexual behavior among the affluent.* New York: Appleton-Century-Crofts.

Cutler, N. E. (1974). The impact of subjective age identification on social and political attitudes. Paper presented at the meetings of the Gerontological Society, Portland, Oregon.

Cutler, N. E. (1983). Age and political behavior. In D. S. Woodruff & J. E. Birren (Eds.), *Aging: Scientific perspectives and social issues* (2nd ed., pp. 409-442). Pacific Grove, CA: Brooks/Cole.

Dacey, J. (1982). *Adult development.* Glenview, IL: Scott Foresman.

Darwin, C. (1958). *Autobiography* (Edited by N. Barlow). London: Collins.

Denney, N. W. (1982). Aging and cognitive changes. In B. Wolman & G. Stricker (Eds.), *Handbook of developmental psychology* (pp. 807-827). Englewood Cliffs, NJ: Prentice-Hall.

Dennis, W. (1958). The age decrement in outstanding scientific contributions: Fact or artifact? *American Psychologist, 13,* 457-460.

Dennis, W. (1966). Creative productivity between the ages of 20 and 80 years. *Journal of Gerontology, 21,* 1-8.

Dennis, W. (1968). Creative productivity between the ages of 20 and 80 years. In B. L. Neugarten (Ed.), *Middle age and aging.* Chicago: University of Chicago Press.

Desjardins, C. (1978). Self perceptions of women across the adult lifespan. Unpublished Ph.D. dissertation, Arizona State University.

Dollard, J. (1935). *Criteria for a life history.* New Haven, CT: Yale University Press.

Donovan, J. M. (1975). Identity status and interpersonal style. *Journal of Youth and Adolescence, 4,* 37-55.

Douvan, E. (1979). Differing views of marriage 1957 to 1976. *Newsletter, Center for Continuing Education of Women* (University of Michigan). *12*(1), 1-12.

Durkheim, E. (1951). *Suicide: A study of sociology.* Glencoe, IL: Free Press. (Originally published in 1897.)

Eaton, W. W. (1978). Life events, social supports, and psychiatric symptoms: A re-analysis of the New Haven data. *Journal of Health and Social Behavior, 19,* 230-234.

Elias, M. (1984, October 19). What keeps couples together? *USA Today*, pp. 1D, 2D.

Elias, M., Elias, P., & Elias, J. (1977). *Basic processes in adult developmental psychology*. St. Louis: Mosby.

Elkind, D. (1982). Erik Erikson's eight stages of man. In L. R. Allman & D. T. Jaffe (Eds.), *Readings in adult psychology: Contemporary perspectives* (2nd ed., pp. 13-22). New York: Harper & Row.

Ellett, S. O. (1986). Identity formation and family functioning. Unpublished Ph.D. dissertation proposal, University of Kansas.

Elms, A. (1976). *Personality and politics*. New York: Harcourt Brace Jovanovich.

Elo, A. F. (1965). Age changes in master chess performance. *Journal of Gerontology, 20*, 289-299.

Emler, N., Renwick, S., & Malone, B. (1983). The relationship between moral reasoning and political orientation. *Journal of Personality and Social Psychology, 45*, 1073-1080.

Epstein, C. F. (1970). Encountering the male establishment: Sex-status limits on women's careers in the professions. *American Journal of Sociology, 75*, 965-982.

Epstein, J. (1981, February 15). Confessions of an Australian charmer. *New York Times Book Review*, pp. 7, 30.

Erikson, E. H. (1958). *Young man Luther*. New York: Norton.

Erikson, E. H. (1959). Identity and the life cycle: Selected papers. *Psychological Issues, 1*(1), 5-165.

Erikson, E. H. (1963). *Childhood and society*. New York: Norton. (2nd ed., originally published, 1950).

Erikson, E. H. (1968, Summer). On the nature of psycho-historical evidence: In search of Gandhi. *Daedalus, 97*, No. 3.

Erikson, E. H. (1969). *Gandhi's truth: On the origins of militant nonviolence*. New York: Norton.

Erikson, E. H. (1974). *Dimensions of a new identity*. New York: Norton.

Erikson, E. H. (1975). *Life history and the historical moment*. New York: Norton.

Evans, R. I. (1967). *Dialogue with Erik Erikson*. New York: Harper.

Eysenck, H. J., & Wilson, G. D. (Eds.). (1973). *The experimental study of Freudian theories*. London: Methuen.

Farmer, P. (1979). An exploratory investigation into the nature of the mid-life transition of a group of selected women. Unpublished Ed. D. dissertation, Temple University.

Faunce, W. A., & Fulton, R. L. (1958). The sociology of death: A neglected area of research. *Social Forces, 3*, 205-209.

Feifel, H. (1955). Attitudes of mentally ill patients toward death. *Journal of Nervous and Mental Diseases, 122*, 375-380.

Feifel, H. (1959). Attitudes toward death in some normal and mentally ill persons. In H. Feifel (Ed.), *The meaning of death*. New York: McGraw-Hill.

Feifel, H. (1974). Religious conviction and the fear of death among the healthy and the terminally ill. *Journal for the Scientific Study of Religion, 13*, 353-360.

Finder, A. (1987, September 15). Koch writes an epitaph in musing on mortality. *New York Times*, p. 21.

Fine, R. (1973). *The development of Freud's thought*. New York: Jason Aronson.

Fischer, C. S., & Phillips, S. L. (1982). Who is alone? Social characteristics of people with small networks. In L. A. Peplau & D. Perlman (Eds.), *Loneliness: A sourcebook of current theory, research, and therapy*. New York: John Wiley.

Fisher, S., & Greenberg, R. P. (1977). *The scientific credibility of Freud's theories and therapy*. New York: Basic Books.

Fisher, S., & Greenberg, R. P. (Eds.). (1978). *The scientific evaluation of Freud's theories and therapy*. New York: Basic Books.

Ford, M. R., & Lowery, C. R. (1986). Gender differences in moral reasoning: A comparison of the use of justice and care orientations. *Journal of Personality and Social Psychology, 50*, 777-783.

Foreman, J. (1986, December 16). 'Rage' brings wrath from Goetz worshipers. *Kansas City Star*, p. 3C.

Fowler, J. W., & Lovin, R. W. (1980). *Trajectories in faith*. Nashville, Abingdon.

Franklin, B. (1961). *The autobiography and other writings*. New York: New American Library.

Frenkel, E. (1936). Studies in biographical psychology. *Character and Personality, 5*, 1-35.

Frenkel-Brunswik, E. (1939). Mechanisms of self-deception. *Journal of Social Psychology, 10*, 409-420.

Freud, S. (1933). *New introductory lectures in psychoanalysis* (Translated by J. H. Sprott). New York: Norton.

Freud, S. (1952). *Collected works* (Vol. IV). London: Hogarth.

Freud, S. (1963). Introductory lectures on psychoanalysis. In J. Strachey (Ed.), *The standard edition of the complete psychological works of Sigmund Freud* (Vols. 15 and 16). London: Hogarth. (Originally published in 1917.)

Freud, S. (1966). *Introductory lectures on psychoanalysis*. (Translated by J. Strachey). New York: Norton. (Originally published in 1916.)

Freud, S., & Bullitt, W. C. (1967). *Thomas Woodrow Wilson*. Boston: Houghton-Mifflin.

Fromm, E. (1959). *Sigmund Freud's mission*. New York: Harper & Row.

Garnets, L., & Pleck, J. H. (1979). Sex role identity, androgyny, and sex role transcendence: A sex role strain analysis. *Psychology of Women Quarterly, 3,* 270-283.

Garrow, D. J. (1986). *Bearing the cross: Martin Luther King, Jr., and the Southern Leadership Conference.* New York: William Morrow.

Geer, J. (1965). The development of a scale to measure fear. *Behavior Research and Therapy, 3,* 45-53.

George, A. L., & George, J. L. (1956). *Woodrow Wilson and Colonel House.* New York: John Day.

Gilligan, C. (1977). In a different voice: Women's conceptions of self and morality. *Harvard Educational Review, 47,* 481-517.

Gilligan, C. (1980). Woman's place in man's life cycle. *Harvard Educational Review, 49,* 431-446.

Gilligan, C. (1982). *In a different voice: Psychological theory and women's development.* Cambridge MA: Harvard University Press.

Gilligan, C., Langdale, S., Lyons, N., & Murphy, M. (1982). The contribution of women's thought to developmental theory: The elimination of sex bias in moral development research and education. Final report, National Institute of Education.

Gindick, T. (1985, October 8). Romance is back, love experts say. *Kansas City Times,* p. B-5.

Glenn, N. D. (1974). Aging and conservatism. *Annals of the American Academy of Political and Social Science, 415,* 176-186.

Glick, I., Weiss, R. S., & Parkes, C. M. (1974). *The first year of bereavement.* New York: John Wiley.

Goldman-Eisler, F. (1951). The problem of "orality" and of its origin in early childhood. *Journal of Mental Science, 97,* 765-782.

Goleman, D. (1984, December 6). Perspectives on love. *Kansas City Times,* pp. C-1, C-2.

Goleman, D. (1985, September 12). Affairs of the heart: Changes occur as relationships bloom. *Kansas City Times,* pp. B-5, B-7.

Goleman, D. (1986, July 22). Psychologists pursue the irrational aspects of love. *New York Times,* pp. 17, 20.

Goleman, D. (1987, June 23). In memory, people re-create their lives to suit their images of the present. *New York Times,* pp. 17, 20.

Goodman, S. F. (1980). Women in their later years: A study of the psychosocial development of women between 45-60. Unpublished doctoral dissertation, School of Education, Boston University.

Gould, R. (1975, January). Adult life stages: Growth toward self-tolerance. *Psychology Today,* pp. 74-78.

Gould, R. (1978). *Transformations: Growth and change in adult life.* New York: Simon & Schuster.

Gould, R. L. (1972). The phases of adult life: A study in developmental psychology. *American Journal of Psychiatry, 129,* 521-531.

Gove, W. R. (1972). The relationship between sex roles, marital roles, and mental illness. *Social Forces, 51,* 34-44.

Gove, W. R. (1973). Sex, marital status and mortality. *American Journal of Sociology, 79,* 45-67.

Gove, W. R., & Hughes, M. (1979). Possible causes of apparent sex differences in physical health: An empirical investigation. *American Sociological Review, 44,* 126-146.

Green, M. (1983). *Tolstoy and Gandhi: Men of peace.* New York: Basic Books.

Greenacre, P. (1955). *Swift and Carroll: A psychoanalytic study of two lives.* New York: International Universities Press.

Gunderson, E. (1987, May 19). Fears and facts often don't match. *USA Today,* p. 6D.

Hall, C. S., & Lindzey, G. (1970). *Theories of personality* (2nd ed.). New York: John Wiley. (3rd ed., 1978)

Hall, D. T. (1986). Breaking career routines: Midcareer choice and identity development. In D. T. Hall and associates (Eds.), *Career development in organizations* (pp. 120-159). San Francisco: Jossey-Bass.

Hall, D. T., & Richter, J. (1985). The baby boom and management: Is there room in the middle? Unpublished paper, School of Management, Boston University.

Hamburg, D. A., & Lunde, D. R. (1966). Sex hormones in the development of sex differences in human behavior. In E. E. Maccoby (Ed.), *The development of sex differences.* Stanford, CA: Stanford University Press.

Hargrove, E. C. (1966). *Presidential leadership: Personality and political style.* New York: Macmillan.

Harris, R. L., Ellicott, A. M., & Holmes, D. S. (1986). The timing of psychosocial transitions and changes in women's lives: An examination of women aged 45 to 60. *Journal of Personality and Social Psychology, 51,* 409-416.

Hartshorne, H., & May, M. A. (1928). *Studies in the nature of character: Vol. I, Studies in deceit.* New York: Macmillan.

Havighurst, R. J. (1972). *Developmental tasks and education.* (3rd ed.). New York: David McKay.

Hazan, C., & Shaver, P. (1987). Romantic love conceptualized as an attachment process. *Journal of Personality and Social Psychology, 52,* 511-524.

Hebb, D. O. (1978). On watching myself grow old. *Psychology Today, 15*(12), 20-23.

Heilbrun, A. B., Jr. (1976). Measurement of masculine and feminine sex role identities as independent dimensions. *Journal of Consulting and Clinical Psychology, 44,* 183-190.

Herbert, W. (1985, December). The turning point. *Psychology Today*, p. 77.

Herbert, W. (1987, January). A national morality play. *Psychology Today*, p. 80.

Hess, B. (1972). Friendship. In M. W. Riley, M. Johnson, & A. Foner (Eds.), *Aging and society: Vol. 3, A sociology of age stratification.* New York: Russell Sage.

Heyman, D. K., & Gianturco, D. T. (1973). Long-term adaptation by the elderly to bereavement. *Journal of Gerontology, 28,* 359-362.

Hite, S. (1987). *Women and love: A cultural revolution in progress.* New York: Knopf.

Holland, J. L. (1963). Explorations of a theory of vocational choice and achievement. *Psychological Reports, 12,* 547-594.

Holland, J. L. (1973). *Making vocational choices.* Englewood Cliffs, NJ: Prentice-Hall.

Holmes, D. S. (1972). Repression and interference: A further investigation. *Journal of Personality and Social Psychology, 22,* 163-170.

Holmes, D. S. (1974). Investigations of repression: Differential recall of material experimentally or naturally associated with ego threat. *Psychological Bulletin, 81,* 632-653.

Holtzworth-Munroe, A., & Jacobson, N. S. (1985). Causal attributions of married couples: When do they search for causes? What do they conclude when they do? *Journal of Personality and Social Psychology, 48,* 1398-1412.

Horn, J. L., & Cattell, R. B. (1967). Age differences in fluid and crystallized intelligence. *Acta Psychologica, 26,* 107-129.

Horn, J. L., & Donaldson, G. (1976). On the myth of intellectual decline in adulthood. *American Psychologist, 31,* 701-709.

Horn, J. L., & Donaldson, G. (1977). Faith is not enough: A response to the Baltes-Schaie claim that intelligence does not wane. *American Psychologist, 32,* 369-373.

Horn, J. L., Donaldson, G., & Engstrom, R. (1981). Apprehension, memory, and fluid intelligence decline in adulthood. *Research on Aging, 3,* 33-84.

Horney, K. (1950). *Neurosis and human growth.* New York: Norton.

Howell, D. (1987, Spring). Clause and effect. *Teacher to Teacher,* p. 2.

Hultsch, D. (1969). Adult age differences in the organization of free recall. *Developmental Psychology, 1,* 673-678.

Hultsch, D. (1971). Adult age differences in free classification and free recall. *Developmental Psychology, 4,* 338-342.

Hultsch, D. (1974). Learning to learn in adulthood. *Journal of Gerontology, 29,* 302-308.

Huston, T. L., Robins, E., Atkinson, J., & McHale, S. M. (1987). Surveying the landscape of marital behavior: A behavioral self-report to studying marriage. In S. Oskamp (Ed.), *Family processes and problems: Social psychological aspects* (pp. 45-72). Newbury Park, CA: Sage.

Huyck, M. H., & Hoyer, W. J. (1982). *Adult development and aging.* Belmont, CA: Wadsworth.

Ickes, W. (1981). Sex-role influences in dyadic interaction: A theoretical model. In C. Mayo & N. Henley (Eds.), *Gender and non-verbal behavior.* New York: Springer-Verlag.

Ickes, W., & Barnes, R. D. (1977). The role of sex and self-monitoring in unstructured dyadic interactions. *Journal of Personality and Social Psychology, 35,* 315-330.

Ickes, W., & Barnes, R. D. (1978). Boys and girls together—and alienated: On enacting stereotyped sex-roles in mixed-sex dyads. *Journal of Personality and Social Psychology, 36,* 669-683.

Jackson, P. F. (1975). Disruption and change in mid-life: An exploratory study of women in their fifth decade. *Dissertation Abstracts, 35* (12-B), 6074. (University Microfilms No. 75-13, 194).

Jacob, B. (1986, July 18). Modern love: Share pad, tie knot. *USA Today,* p. 1D.

Jaffe, D. T., & Allman, L. R. (1982). Adaptation and development. In L. R. Allman & D. T. Jaffe (Eds.), *Readings in adult psychology: Contemporary perspectives* (2nd ed.) (pp. 3-12). New York: Harper & Row.

James, W. (1902). *Varieties of religious experience.* New York: New American Library.

Jaques, E. (1965). Death and the mid-life crisis; *International Journal of Psychoanalysis, 46,* 502-514.

Jaquish, G., & Ripple, R. (1980). Divergent thinking and self-esteem in pre-adolescents and adolescents. *Journal of Youth and Adolescence, 9*(2), 143-152.

Jeffers, F., Nichols, C., & Eisdorfer, C. (1961). Attitudes of older persons toward death: A preliminary study. *Journal of Gerontology, 16,* 34-43.

Johnson, K. (1986, October 19). Review of *Quiet Rage. New York Times Book Review,* p. 31.

Jung, C. G. (1961). *Memories, dreams, reflections.* New York: Vintage.

Kalish, R. A. (1963). An approach to the study of death attitudes. *American Behavioral Scientist, 6*(9), 68-71.

Kalish, R. A. (1976). Death and dying in a social context. In R. Binstock & E. Shanas (Eds.), *Handbook of aging and the social sciences.* New York: Van Nostrand Reinhold.

Kangas, J., & Bradway, K. (1971). Intelligence at middle-age: A thirty-eight year follow-up. *Developmental Psychology, 5,* 333-337.

Kantrowitz, B. (1987, August 24). How to stay married. *Newsweek,* pp. 52-57.

Kastenbaum, R. (1977). *Death, society, and human experience.* St. Louis: C. V. Mosby.

Kastenbaum, R., & Alsenberg, R. (1972). *The psychology of death.* New York: Springer.

Kastenbaum, R., & Costa, P. T., Jr. (1977). Psychological perspectives on death. *Annual Review of Psychology, 28,* 225-249.

Kausler, D. H. (1982). *Experimental psychology and human aging.* New York: John Wiley.

Kazin, A. (1979). The self as history: Reflections on autobiography. In M. Pachter (Ed.), *Telling lives: The biographer's art* (pp. 74-89). Washington, DC: New Republic.

Kelley, J. (1985, November 20). Live-ins drops out of style; marriage in. *USA Today,* p. 1D.

Kelly, G. A. (1955). *The psychology of personal constructs.* New York: Norton.

Kelly, G. A. (1963). *A theory of personality.* New York: Norton.

Kemper, S. (1987). Life-span changes in syntactic complexity. *Journal of Gerontology, 42,* 323-328.

Kimmel, D. C. (1980). *Adulthood and aging: An interdisciplinary developmental view.* (2nd ed.). New York: John Wiley.

Kinsey, A., Pomeroy, W., Martin, C., & Gebhard, P. (1953). *Sexual behavior in the human female.* Philadelphia: Saunders.

Kohlberg, L. (1958). The development of modes of thinking and choices in years 10 to 16. Unpublished doctoral dissertation, University of Chicago.

Kohlberg, L. (1963). The development of children's orientations toward a moral order: Vol. I, Sequence in the development of moral thought. *Vita Humana, 6,* 11-33.

Kohlberg, L. (1971). From is to ought: How to commit the naturalistic fallacy and get away with it in the study of moral development. In T. Mischel (Ed.), *Cognitive development and epistemology* (pp. 151-235). New York: Academic Press.

Kohlberg, L. (1973). Continuities in childhood and adult moral development revisited. In P. Baltes & K. W. Schaie (Eds.), *Lifespan developmental psychology* (pp. 179-204). New York: Academic Press.

Kohlberg, L. (1980). The future of liberalism as the dominant ideology of the west. In R. W. Wilson & G. J. Schochet (Eds.), *Moral development and politics* (pp. 55-68). New York: Praeger.

Kohlberg, L. (1981). *Essays on moral development* (Vol. 1). San Francisco: Harper & Row.

Koocher, G. (1973). Childhood, death, and cognitive development. *Developmental Psychology, 9,* 369-375.

Krantz, D. L. (1977). The Santa Fe experience. In S. B. Sarason, *Work, aging, and social change: Professionals and the one-life, one-career imperative* (pp. 165-188). New York: Free Press.

Krawiec, T. S. (Ed.). (1972). *The psychologists* (Vol. 1). New York: Oxford University Press. (Vol. 2, 1974)

Krueger, E. T., & Reckless, W. C. (1931). *Social psychology.* New York: Longmans.

Kubler-Ross, E. (1969). *On death and dying.* New York: Macmillan.

Kuhn, D., Langer, J., Kohlberg, L., & Haan, N. (1977). The development of formal operations in logical and moral judgment. *Genetic Psychology Monographs, 95,* 97-188.

Landers, A. (1985, January 15). Verdict: Tender words, caresses. *Lawrence Journal-World,* p. 5.

Langdale, C. J. (1986). A re-vision of structural-developmental theory. In G. L. Sapp (Ed.), *Handbook of moral development* (pp. 15-54). Birmingham, AL: Religious Education Press.

Lasswell, H. D. (1930). *Psychopathology and politics.* Chicago: University of Chicago Press.

Lawrence, B. S. (1980, Summer). The myth of the midlife crisis. *Sloan Management Review, 21*(4), 35-49.

Lehman, H. C (1962). The creative production rates of present versus past generations of scientists. *Journal of Gerontology, 17,* 409-417.

Lehman, H. C. (1953). *Age and achievement.* Princeton, NJ: Princeton University Press.

Leichtman, M. (1987, December). *Developmental psychology and psychoanalysis: Vol. I, The context for a contemporary revolution in psychoanalysis.* Paper presented at the meetings of the American Psychoanalytic Association, New York City.

Leon, G. R., Gillum, B., Gillum, R., & Gouze, M. (in press). Personality stability and change over a 30-year period—middle age to old age. *Journal of Clinical and Consulting Psychology,* in press.

Lester, D. (1967). Experimental and correlational studies of the fear of death. *Psychological Bulletin, 67,* 27-36.

Lester, D. (1970). The fear of death. *Omega: Journal of Death and Dying, 1,* 181-188.

Levinger, G. (1979). A social psychological perspective on marriage dissolution. In G. Levinger & O. C. Moles (Eds.), *Divorce and separation.* New York: Basic Books.

Levinson, D. J. (1979). Adult development—or what? *Contemporary Psychology, 24,* 727.

Levinson, D. J. (1980). Toward a conception of the adult life course. In N. J. Smelser & E. H. Erikson (Eds.), *Themes of work and love in adulthood* (pp. 265-290). Cambridge, MA: Harvard University Press.

Levinson, D. J. (1985, July 8). Personal communication.

Levinson, D. J., Darrow, C. N., Klein, E. B., Levinson, M. H., & McKee, B. (1977). Periods in the adult development of men: Ages 18 to 45. In N. K. Schlossberg & A. D. Entine (Eds.), *Counseling adults* (pp. 47-59). Pacific Grove, CA: Brooks/Cole.

Levinson, D. J., in collaboration with Darrow, C. N., Klein, E. B., Levinson, M. H., & McKee, B. (1978). *The seasons of a man's life.* New York: Knopf.

Lieberman, M. A., & Caplan, A. S. (1970). Distance from death as a variable in the study of aging. *Developmental Psychology, 2,* 71-84.

Lief, H. (1978). Unpublished research cited in C. B. Broderick (1982).

Lifton, P. D. (1986). Personological and psychodynamic explanations of moral development. In G. L. Sapp (Ed.), *Handbook of moral development* (pp. 55-73). Birmingham, AL: Religious Education Press.

Lifton, R. J. (1979). *The broken connection.* New York: Simon & Schuster.

Lifton, R. J., & Olson, E. (1982). Death and the life cycle. In L. R. Allman & D. T. Jaffe (Eds.), *Readings in adult psychology: Contemporary perspectives* (2nd ed.). (pp. 73-79). New York: Harper & Row.

Lindzey, G. (Ed.). (1974). *A history of psychology in autobiography* (Vol. 6). Englewood Cliffs, NJ: Prentice-Hall.

Loevinger, J. (1976). *Ego development: Conceptions and theories.* San Francisco: Jossey-Bass.

Loewenberg, P. (1987). Why psychoanalysis needs the social scientist and the historian. In G. Cocks & T. L. Crosby (Eds.), *Psycho/history: Readings in the method of psychology, psychoanalysis, and history* (pp. 30-44). New Haven, CT: Yale University Press.

Lowenthal, M. F., Thurnher, M., Chiriboga, D., & Associates. (1975). *Four stages of life: A comparative study of women and men facing transitions.* San Francisco: Jossey-Bass.

Lyons, N. (1982). Conceptions of self and morality and modes of moral choice: Identifying justice and care in judgments of actual dilemmas. Unpublished doctoral dissertation, Harvard University.

Lyons, N. (1983). Two perspectives: On self, relationship, and morality. *Harvard University Review, 53*(1), 125-145.

Maas, H., & Kuypers, J. (1974). *From thirty to seventy.* San Francisco: Jossey-Bass.

MacKinnon, D. W., & Dukes, W. F. (1963). Repression. In L. Postman (Ed.), *Psychology in the making* (pp. 662-744). New York: Knopf.

MacMahon, B., & Pugh, T. F. (1965). Suicide in the widowed. *American Journal of Epidemiology, 81,* 23-31.

Magni, K. (1970). Reactions to death stimuli among theology students. *Journal for the Scientific Study of Religion, 9,* 247-248.

Mandel, B. J. (1980). Full of life now. In J. Olney (Ed.), *Autobiography: Essays theoretical and critical* (pp. 49-72). Princeton, NJ: Princeton University Press.

Manniche, E., & Falk, G. (1957). Age and the Nobel prize. *Behavioral Science, 2,* 301-307.

Marcia, J. E. (1966). Development and validation of ego-identity status. *Journal of Personality and Social Psychology, 3,* 551-558.

Marcia, J. E. (1967). Ego-identity status: Relationship to change in self-esteem, "general maladjustment," and authoritarianism. *Journal of Personality, 35,* 118-133.

Marcia, J. E. (1980). Identity in adolescence. In J. Abelson (Ed.), *Handbook of adolescent psychology.* New York: John Wiley.

Marcia, J. E., & Friedman, M. L. (1970). Ego identity status in college women. *Journal of Personality, 38,* 249-263.

Marshall, V. (1975). Age and awareness of finitude in developmental gerontology. *Omega, 6*(2), 113-127.

Martin, D., & Wrightsman, L. S. (1965). The relationship between religious behavior and concern about death. *Journal of Social Psychology, 65,* 317-323.

Masson, J. (1984). *The assault on truth: Freud's suppression of the seduction theory.* New York: Farrar, Straus & Giroux.

Masters, W., & Johnson, V. (1966). *Human sexual response.* Boston: Little Brown.

May, W. (1973). Attitudes toward the newly dead. *Hastings Center Studies, 1*(1), 3-13.

Mazlish, B. (1973). *In search of Nixon.* Baltimore: Penguin.

McAdams, D. P. (1985). *Power, intimacy, and the life story: Personological inquiries into identity.* Homewood, IL: Dow Jones-Irwin.

McAdams, D. P. (1987). A life-story model of identity. In R. Hogan & W. H. Jones (Eds.), *Perspectives on personality* (Vol. 2, pp. 15-50). Greenwich, CT: JAI.

McAdams, D. P., & Bryant, F. B. (1985). Intimacy motivation and subjective mental health in a nationwide sample. Paper presented at the meetings of the American Psychological Association, Los Angeles, August 1985.

McAdams, D. P., Ruetzel, K., & Foley, J. M. (1986). Complexity and generativity at mid-life: Relations among social motives, ego development, and adults' plans for the future. *Journal of Personality and Social Psychology, 50,* 800-807.

McFarlane, J. (1987, August 17). The meaning of marriage. *Newsweek,* p. 8.

Mednick, S. (1963). Research creativity in psychology graduate students. *Journal of Consulting Psychology, 27,* 265-266.

Meyerhoff, H. (1987). On psychoanalysis as history. In G. Cocks & T. L. Crosby (Eds.), *Psycho/history: Readings in the method of psychology, psychoanalysis, and history* (pp. 17-29). New Haven, CT: Yale University Press.

Midler, B. (1980). *A view from a broad.* New York: Simon & Schuster.

Mill, J. S. (1874). *Autobiography of John Stuart Mill.* New York: Henry Holt.

Miller, J. (1984, February 6). An attack on Father Freud. *Time,* pp. 86-87.

Minton, B., & Spilka, B. (1976). Perspectives on death in relation to powerlessness and form of personal religion. *Omega: Journal of Death and Dying, 7,* 261-267.

Mischel, W. (1968). *Personality and assessment.* New York: John Wiley.

Moffitt, P. (1986, December). Cooling out. *Esquire,* pp. 47-48.

Mulvey, M. (1963). Psychological and sociological factors in prediction of career patterns for women. *Genetic Psychology Monographs, 68,* 313-386.

Munnichs, J. M. (1961). Comments. In R. Havighurst (Ed.), Attitudes toward death in older persons: A symposium. *Journal of Gerontology, 16,* 44-66.

Munnichs, J. M. (1966). *Old age and finitude.* New York: Karger.

Murchison, C. (Ed.). (1930). *A history of psychology in autobiography* (Vol. 1). Worcester, MA: Clark University Press. (Vol. 2, 1932; Vol. 3, 1936).

Murray, H. A. (1938). *Explorations in personality.* New York: Oxford University Press.

Nagy, M. H. (1948). The child's theories concerning death. *Journal of Genetic Psychology, 73,* 3-27.

Neuber, K. A., & Genthner, R. W. (1977). The relationship between ego identity, personal responsibility, and facilitative communication. *Journal of Psychology, 95,* 45-49.

Neugarten, B. L. (1968). The awareness of middle age. In B. L. Neugarten (Ed.), *Middle age and aging.* Chicago: University of Chicago Press.

Neugarten, B. L. (1979). Time, age, and the life cycle. *American Journal of Psychiatry, 136,* 887-894.

Neugarten, B. L., & Neugarten, D. A. (1987, May). The changing meanings of age. *Psychology Today,* pp. 29-33.

Neugarten, B. L., & Peterson, W. A. (1957). A study in the American age-grade system. *Proceedings of the Fourth Congress of the International Association of Gerontology, 3,* 497-502.

Neugarten, B. L., Moore, J. W., & Lowe, J. C. (1965). Age norms, age constraints, and adult socialization. *American Journal of Sociology, 70,* 6.

Olney, J. (1972). *Metaphors of self: The meaning of autobiography.* Princeton, NJ: Princeton University Press.

Olney, J. (1980). Autobiography and the cultural moment: A thematic, historical, and bibliographical introduction. In J. Olney (Ed.), *Autobiography: Essays theoretical and critical* (pp. 3-27). Princeton, NJ: Princeton University Press.

O'Neil, J. M. (1981). Male sex role conflicts, sexism, and masculinity: Psychological implications for men, women, and the counseling psychologist. *Counseling Psychologist, 9,* 61-80.

O'Neil, J. M. (1982). Gender-role conflict and strain in men's lives: Implications for psychiatrists, psychologists, and other human-service providers. In K. Solomon & N. Levy (Eds.), *Men in transition: Changing male roles, theory, and therapy* (pp. 5-43). New York: Plenum.

O'Neil, J. M., & Fishman, D. M. (1986). Adult men's career transitions and gender-role themes. In R. Leibowitz & D. Lea (Eds.) *Adult career development.* Alexandria, VA: AACD.

O'Neil, J. M., Helms, B. J., Gable, R. K., David, L., & Wrightsman, L. S. (1986). Gender-role conflict scale: College men's fear of femininity. *Sex Roles, 14,* 335-350.

Orlansky, H. (1949). Infant care and personality. *Psychological Bulletin, 40,* 1-48.

Orlofsky, J. L., Marcia, J. E., & Lesser, I. M. (1973). Ego identity status and the intimacy versus isolation crisis of young adulthood. *Journal of Personality and Social Psychology, 27,* 211-219.

Osarchuk, M., & Tatz, S. J. (1973). Effect of induced fear of death on belief in afterlife. *Journal of Personality and Social Psychology, 27,* 256-260.

Osherson, S. D. (1980). *Holding on or letting go: Men and career change at midlife.* New York: Free Press.

Ostling, R. N. (1983, October 31). Giant of his time and ours. *Time,* pp. 100-103.

Owens, W. (1953). Age and mental abilities: A longitudinal study. *Genetic Psychology Monographs, 48,* 3-54.

Owens, W. (1959). Is age kinder to the initially more able? *Journal of Gerontology, 14,* 334-337.

Parkes, C. M. (1971). Psycho-social transitions: A field for study. In C. M. Parkes (Ed.), *Social science and medicine* (Vol. 5). London: Pergamon.

Parkes, C. M. (1972). *Bereavement: Studies of grief in adult life.* London: Tavistock.

Parkes, C. M., & Brown, R. (1972). Health after bereavement: A controlled study of young Boston widows and widowers. *Psychosomatic Medicine, 34,* 449-461.

Parron, E. (1979). Relationship of Black and White golden wedding couples. Unpublished doctoral dissertation, Rutgers—The State University.

Pearlman, C. (1972, November). Frequency of intercourse in males at different ages. *Medical Aspects of Human Sexuality,* 92-113.

Peck, R. (1968). Psychological developments in the second half of life. In B. L. Neugarten (Ed.), *Middle age and aging.* Chicago: University of Chicago Press.

Perun, P. J., & Bielby, D. D. (1981). Toward a model of female occupational behavior: A human development approach. *Psychology of Women Quarterly, 6,* 234-250.

Peters, R. G. (1971). Moral development: A plea for pluralism. In T. Mischel (Ed.), *Cognitive development and epistemology.* New York: Academic Press.

Piaget, J. (1932). *The moral judgment of the child.* New York: Free Press. (Republished in 1965).

Pietropinto, A., & Simenauer, J. (1979). *Husbands and wives.* New York: Times Books.

Pineo, P. (1961). Disenchantment in the later years of marriage. *Marriage and Family Living, 23,* 1-12.

Pleck, J. H. (1981, September). Prisoners of manliness. *Psychology Today,* pp. 69-83.

Pleck, J. H. (1982). The male sex role: Definitions, problems, and sources of change. In L. R. Allman & D. T. Jaffe (Eds.), *Readings in adult psychology: Contemporary perspectives* (2nd ed., pp. 153-159). New York: Harper & Row.

Pocs, O., & Godow, A. G. (1977). Can students view parents as sexual beings? In D. Byrne & L. Byrne (Eds.), *Exploring human sexuality.* New York: Crowell.

Poitier, S. (1980). *This life.* New York: Knopf.

Pratt, M. W., & Royer, J. M. (1982). When rights and responsibilities don't mix: Sex and sex-role patterns in moral judgment orientation. *Canadian Journal of Behavioral Science, 14,* 190-214.

Pruyser, P. W. (1987). Creativity without noted talent in aging persons. Unpublished paper, Menninger Foundation, Topeka, Kansas.

Radloff, L. S. (1975). Sex differences in depression: The effects of occupation and marital status. *Sex Roles, 1,* 249-265.

Raines, H. (1986, November 30). Driven to martyrdom. *New York Times Book Review,* pp. 1, 33-34.

Ramey, E. (1987, June). Hormones, stress, and aging. Address to the National Press Club, Washington, D. C.

Raskin, P. M. (1984). Procedures in research on identity status: Some notes on method. *Psychological Reports, 54,* 719-730.

Rawls, J. (1971). *Theory of justice.* Cambridge, MA: Harvard University Press.

Rebecca, M., & Hefner, R. (1982). The future of sex roles. In L. R. Allman & D. T. Jaffe (Eds.), *Readings in adult psychology: Contemporary perspectives* (2nd ed., pp. 160-170). New York: Harper & Row.

Reichard, S., Livson, F., & Peterson, P. G. (1962). *Aging and personality.* New York: John Wiley.

Reid, H. G., & Yanarella, E. J. (1980). The tyranny of the categorical: On Kohlberg and the politics of moral judgment. In R. W. Wilson & G. J. Schochet (Eds.), *Moral development and politics* (pp. 107-132). New York: Praeger.

Reinke, B. (1982). Psychosocial change among women from early adulthood to middle age as a function of chronological age and family cycle phase. Unpublished doctoral dissertation, University of Kansas.

Reinke, B. J. (1981, August 1). Personal communication.

Reinke, B. J., Holmes, D. S., & Harris, R. L. (1985). The timing of psychosocial changes in women's lives: The years 25 to 45. *Journal of Personality and Social Psychology, 48,* 1353-1364.

Renner, V. J., Alpaugh, P. K., & Birren, J. E. (1978, November). Divergent thinking over the life span. Paper presented at the annual meetings of the Gerontological Society, Dallas, Texas.

Riegel, K. F. (1976). The dialectics of human development. *American Psychologist, 31,* 689-700.

Roazen, P. (1976). *Erik H. Erikson: The power and limits of a vision*. New York: Free Press.

Roberts, R. E. (1971). *The new communes: Coming together in America*. Englewood Cliffs, NJ: Prentice-Hall.

Robinson, J. P., & Shaver, P. R. (1969). *Measures of social psychological attitudes*. Ann Arbor, MI: Institute for Social Research, University of Michigan.

Rogers, C. R. (1967). Autobiography. In E. G. Boring & G. Lindzey (Eds.), *A history of psychology in autobiography* (Vol. 5, pp. 343-384). New York: Appleton-Century-Crofts.

Rokeach, M. (1968). *Beliefs, attitudes and values*. San Francisco: Jossey-Bass.

Rosenberg, S., & Jones, R. A. (1972). A method for investigating and representing a person's implicit theory of personality: Theodore Drieser's view of people. *Journal of Personality and Social Psychology, 22*, 372-386.

Rosenfeld, A., & Stark, E. (1987, May). The prime of our lives. *Psychology Today*, pp. 62-72.

Rossi, A. (1965). Barriers to the career choice of engineering, medicine, or science among American women. In J. A. Mattfield & C. Van Aken (Eds.), *Women and the scientific professions*. Cambridge: MIT Press.

Rubin, D. C. (Ed.). (1986). *Autobiographical memory*. Cambridge: Cambridge University Press.

Rubin, I. (1965). Transition in sex values: Implications for the evaluation of adolescents. *Journal of Marriage and the Family, 27*, 185-189.

Rubin, L. B. (1979). *Women of a certain age: The midlife search for self*. New York: Harper & Row.

Rubin, L. B. (1986). *Quiet rage: Bernie Goetz in a time of madness*. New York: Farrar, Straus & Giroux.

Rubin, Z. (1981, May). Does personality really change after 20? *Psychology Today, 15*, 18-27.

Runyan, W. M. (1982). *Life histories and psychobiography: Explorations in theory and method*. New York: Oxford University Press.

Ryff, C. D., & Heincke, S. G. (1983). Subjective organization of personality in adulthood and aging. *Journal of Personality and Social Psychology, 44*, 807-816.

Safier, G. (1964). A study of relationships between the life and death concepts of children. *Journal of Genetic Psychology, 105*, 283-294.

Sales, E. (1978). Women's adult development. In I. Frieze et al. (Eds.), *Women and sex roles*. New York: Norton.

Sampson, E. E. (1977). Psychology and the American ideal. *Journal of Personality and Social Psychology, 35*, 767-782.

Sanford, N. (1980). *Learning after college*. Orinda, CA: Montaigne.

Sarason, S. B. (1977). *Work, aging, and social change: Professionals and the one life-one career imperative*. New York: Free Press.

Sarnoff, I., & Corwin, S. (1959). Castration anxiety and the fear of death. *Journal of Personality, 27,* 374-385.

Schaeffer, D. L. (Ed.). (1971). *Sex differences in personality: Readings.* Pacific Grove, CA: Brooks/Cole.

Schaie, K. W. (1983). Age differences in adult intelligence. In D. S. Woodruff & J. E. Birren (Eds.), *Aging: Scientific perspectives and social issues* (2nd ed., pp. 137-148). Pacific Grove, CA: Brooks/Cole.

Schaie, K. W., & Baltes, P. B. (1977). Some faith helps to see the forest: A final comment on the Horn and Donaldson myth of the Baltes-Schaie position on adult intelligence. *American Psychologist, 32,* 1118-1120.

Schlein, S. (Ed.). (1987). *A way of looking at things: Selected papers of E. H. Erikson from 1930 to 1980.* New York: Norton.

Schmid, R. E. (1985, November 20). Census says fewer unmarried couples living together. *Lawrence Journal-World,* p. 34.

Schmid, R. E. (1987, June 12). America's marriages setting records high and low. *Lawrence Journal-World,* p. 8D.

Schochet, G. J. (1980). From household to polity. In R. W. Wilson & G. J. Schochet (Eds.), *Moral development and politics* (pp. 206-215). New York: Praeger.

Schoenrade, P. A. (1986). Belief in afterlife as a response to awareness of individual mortality. Unpublished doctoral dissertation, University of Kansas.

Schoenrade, P. A. (1987, October 7). Personal communication.

Sears, R. R. (1943). *Survey of objective studies of psychoanalytic concepts.* New York: Social Science Research Council.

Sears, R. R. (1979a, June). Mark Twain's separation anxiety. *Psychology Today,* pp. 100-104.

Sears, R. R. (1979b). Mid-life development. *Contemporary Psychology, 24,* 97-98.

Sheehy, G. (1976). *Passages: Predictable crises of adult life.* New York: Dutton.

Shneidman, E., & Faberow, N. (1957). *Clues to suicide.* New York: McGraw-Hill.

Siegman, A. W. (1961). The relationship between religion, personality variables, and attitudes and feelings about death. Paper presented at the meetings of the Society for the Scientific Study of Religion, New York City.

Silverman, P. R., & Cooperband, A. (1975). On widowhood: Mutual help and the elderly widow. *Journal of Geriatric Psychiatry, 8,* 9-27.

Simmel, G. (1950). *The sociology of Georg Simmel* (K. H. Wolff, translator). New York: Free Press.

Simonton, D. K. (1985). Quality, quantity, and age: The career of ten distinguished psychologists. *International Journal of Aging and Human Development, 21,* 241-254.

Skinner, B. F. (1976). *Particulars of my life.* New York: Knopf.

Skinner, B. F. (1979). *The shaping of a behaviorist.* New York: Knopf.

Skinner, B. F. (1983). *A matter of consequences.* New York: Knopf.

Smart, N. (1968). Attitudes toward death in eastern religions. In A. Toynbee, A. K. Mant, N. Smart, J. Hinton, C. Yudkin, E. Rhode, R. Heywood, & H. H. Price (Eds.), *Man's concern with death* (pp. 95-115). London: Hodder & Stroughton.

Smelser, N. J. (1980). Issues in the study of work and love in adulthood. In N. J. Smelser & E. H. Erikson (Eds.), *Themes of work and love in adulthood* (pp. 1-26). Cambridge, MA: Harvard University Press.

Smetana, J. G. (1981). Reasoning in the personal and moral domains: Adolescent and young adult women's decision-making regarding abortion. *Journal of Applied Developmental Psychology, 2,* 211-226.

Smith, M. B. (1977). A dialectical social psychology? Comments on a symposium. *Personality and Social Psychology Bulletin, 3,* 719-724.

Smith, M. B., Bruner, J. S., & White, R. W. (1956). *Opinions and personality.* New York: John Wiley.

Snyder, C. R., & Fromkin, H. L. (1980). *Uniqueness: The human pursuit of difference.* New York: Plenum.

Sommers, D., & Eck, A. (1977). Occupational mobility in the American labor force. *Monthly Labor Review, 100*(1), 3-19.

Spence, J. T., & Helmreich, R. (1978). *Masculinity and femininity: Their psychological dimensions, correlates, and antecedents.* Austin: University of Texas Press.

Spence, J. T., Helmreich, R., & Stapp, J. (1974). The Personal Attributes Questionnaire: A measure of sex-role stereotypes and masculinity-femininity. *JSAS Catalog of Selected Documents in Psychology, 4,* 127.

Spilka, B., Stout, L., Minton, B., & Sizemore, D. (1977). Death and personal faith: A psychometric investigation. *Journal for the Scientific Study of Religion, 16,* 169-178.

Spitz, L. W. (1973). Psychohistory and history: The case of *Young Man Luther. Soundings, 56*(2), 181-209.

Spranger, E. (1928). *Types of men* (translated by P. J. Pigors). New York: Stechert-Hafner.

St. Clair, M. (1986). *Object relations and self psychology: An introduction.* Pacific Grove, CA: Brooks/Cole.

Stannard, D. E. (1980). *Shrinking history: On Freud and the failure of psychohistory.* New York: Oxford University Press.

Staude, J. R. (1981). *The adult development of C. G. Jung.* Boston: Routledge & Kegan Paul.

Steiner, C. M. (1974). *Scripts people live: Transactional analysis of life scripts.* New York: Grove.

Stern, D. (1985). *The interpersonal world of the infant.* New York: Basic Books.

Stern, W. (1925). *Anfange der Reifezeit.* Leipzig: Quelle & Meyer.

Sternberg, R. J. (1986). A triangular story of love. *Psychological Review, 93,* 119-135.

Stewart, S. A. (1985, August 27). Affairs in our 30s: Both sexes sneak. *USA Today,* p. 1D.

Stewart, W. A. (1977). A psychosocial study of the formation of early adult life structures in women. Unpublished doctoral dissertation, Columbia University.

Stolorow, R. D., & Atwood, G. E. (1979). *Faces in a cloud: Subjectivity in personality theory.* New York: Jason Aronson.

Strasberg, S. (1980). *Bittersweet.* New York: Putnam.

Stroebe, M. S., & Stroebe, W. (1983). Who suffers more? Sex differences in health risks of the widowed. *Psychological Bulletin, 93,* 279-301.

Stroebe, W., Stroebe, M. S., & Gergen, K. J., & Gergen, M. (1982). The effects of bereavement on mortality: A social psychological analysis. In J. R. Eiser (Ed.), *Social psychology and behavioral medicine.* Chichester, England: John Wiley.

Stroud, J. (1981). Women's careers: Work, family, and personality, In D. Eichorn, J. Clausen, N. Haan, M. Honzik, & P. Mussen (Eds.), *Present and past in middle life* (pp. 353-390). New York: Academic Press.

Strouse, J. (1986). The real reasons. In W. Zinsser (Ed.), *Extraordinary lives: The art and craft of American biography.* (pp. 161-195). New York: Book of the Month Club.

Strozier, C. B. (1976). Disciplined subjectivity and the psychohistorian: A critical look at the work of Erik H. Erikson. *Psychohistory Review, 53,* 28-31.

Super, D. E. (1957). *The psychology of careers.* New York: Harper & Row.

Super, D. E. (1966). A theory of vocational development. In H. J. Peters & J. C. Hansen (Eds.), *Vocational guidance and career development* (2nd ed). New York: Macmillan.

Super, D. E. (1986). Life career roles: Self-realization in work and leisure. In D. T. Hall and associates (Eds.), *Career development in organizations* (pp. 95-119). San Francisco: Jossey-Bass.

Surtees, P. G. (1980). Social support, residual adversity, and depressive outcome. *Social Psychiatry, 15,* 71-80.

Swenson, W. (1961). Attitudes toward death in an aged population. *Journal of Gerontology, 16,* 56-66.

Tamir, L. M. (1980). Men at middle age. In D. G. McGuigan (Ed.), *Women's lives: New theory, research, and policy.* Ann Arbor, MI: University of Michigan Center for Continuing Education of Women.

Taylor, M. C., & Hall, J. A. (1982). Psychological androgyny: Theories, methods, and conclusions. *Psychological Bulletin, 92,* 347-366.

Templer, D. I. (1970). The construction and validation of death anxiety scale. *Journal of General Psychology, 82,* 165-177.

Templer, D. I. (1971). The relationship between verbalized and nonverbal-

Templer, D. I. (1971). The relationship between verbalized and nonverbalized death anxiety. *Journal of Genetic Psychology, 119,* 211-214.

Templer, D. I. (1972). Death anxiety in religiously very involved persons. *Psychological Reports, 31,* 361-362.

Templer, D. I., & Dotson, E. (1970). Religious correlates of death anxiety. *Psychological Reports, 26,* 895-897.

Templer, D. I., Ruff, C., & Franks, C. (1971). Death anxiety: Age, sex, and parental resemblance in diverse populations. *Developmental Psychology, 4,* 108.

Tomkins, S. S. (1979). Script theory: Differential magnification of affects. In H. E. Howe, Jr., & R. A. Dienstbier (Eds.), *Nebraska Symposium on Motivation, 1978* (Vol. 26). Lincoln: University of Nebraska Press.

TRB. (1985, October 14). Dohrn again. *New Republic,* pp. 4, 41.

Troll, L. E. (1982). *Continuations: Adult development and aging.* Pacific Grove, CA: Brooks/Cole.

Trudeau, M. (1979). *Beyond reason.* New York: Beekman.

Tyler, L. (1977). The encounter with poverty—its effects on vocational psychology. In H. J. Peters & J. C. Hansen (Eds.), *Vocational guidance and career development* (3rd ed.). New York: Macmillan.

Uhlenhuth, K. (1987, September 5). A matter of conscience. *Kansas City Times,* pp. E-1, E-2.

Vaillant, G. E. (1977). *Adaptation to life.* Boston: Little, Brown.

Veroff, J., & Feld, S. (1971). *Marriage and work in America: A study of motives and roles.* New York: Van Nostrand.

Vondracek, F. W., Lerner, R. M., & Schulenberg, J. E. (1986). *Career development: A life-span developmental approach.* Hillsdale, NJ: Lawrence Erlbaum.

Waite, R.G.L. (1977). *The psychopathic god: Adolf Hitler.* New York: Basic Books.

Walker, C. (1974, June 2). The cycle of life. *Parade,* p. 20.

Walker, L. J. (1986). Cognitive processes in moral development. In G. L. Sapp (Ed.), *Handbook of moral development* (pp. 109-145). Birmingham, AL: Religious Education Press.

Wallis, C. (1980, September 8). People and things. *Time,* p. 57.

Walsh, D. A. (1983). Age differences in learning and memory. In D. S. Woodruff & J. E. Birren (Eds.), *Aging: Scientific perspectives and social issues* (2nd ed., pp. 149-177). Pacific Grove, CA: Brooks/Cole.

Waterman, C. K., & Waterman, A. S. (1974). Ego identity status and decision styles. *Journal of Youth and Adolescence, 3,* 1-6.

Watson, R. (1982, December 13). The Mahatma's legacy. *Newsweek,* pp. 67-68.

Wechsler, D. (1958). *The measurement and appraisal of adult intelligence* (4th ed.). Baltimore: Williams & Wilkins.

Weinraub, B. (1987, September 30). Are female tears saltier than male tears? *New York Times*, p. 12.

Weintraub, K. J. (1978). *The value of the individual*. Chicago: University of Chicago Press.

Wells, H. G. (1934). *Experiment in autobiography*. New York: Macmillan.

West, M. (1959). *Goodness had nothing to do with it*. New York: Woodhill. (Republished in 1976)

Whitbourne, S. K., & Weinstock, C. S. (1979). *Adult development: The differentiation of experience*. New York: Holt, Rinehart & Winston.

White, P. (1982). *Flaws in the glass: A self-portrait*. New York: Viking.

White, R. W. (1975). *Lives in progress: A study of the natural growth of personality* (3rd ed.). New York: Holt, Rinehart & Winston.

Winters, S. (1980). *Shelly, also known as Shirley*. New York: William Morrow.

Wolff, G. (1978, January 9). Vaillant effort falls short. *New Times*, pp. 96-97.

Zimmerman, P. D. (1976, April 5). Writer into scientist. *Newsweek*, pp. 83-84.

Zinsser, W. (Ed.). (1986). *Extraordinary lives: The art and craft of American biography*. New York: Book of the Month Club.

Name Index

Subject Index

About the Author

Lawrence S. Wrightsman is Professor of Psychology at the University of Kansas, where he served as department chair from 1976 to 1981. For the academic year 1981-1982 he was Intra-University Visiting Professor at the University of Kansas School of Law. He received a B.A. and an M.A. from Southern Methodist University and Ph.D. in social psychology from the University of Minnesota. The author or editor of 10 books (including *On the Witness Stand* and *In the Jury Box,* Sage) and numerous journal articles, he has also served as President of the Society for the Psychological Study of Social Issues (SPSSI) and the Society for Personality and Social Psychology (Division 8 of the American Psychological Association). He currently directs the Kansas Jury Research Project and teaches a course on jury decision making to law students there.